CONGREGATION

CONGREGATION

THE POPULATION OF MY LIFE: VOLUME I

RONALD E. MARKSITY

Deeds Publishing | Athens

Published by Deeds Publishing in Athens, GA
www.deedspublishing.com

Printed in The United States of America

Cover design by Mark Babcock.

ISBN 978-1-950794-48-5

Books are available in quantity for promotional or premium use. For information, email info@deedspublishing.com.

First Edition, 2021

10 9 8 7 6 5 4 3 2 1

To Olga and George

CONTENTS

INTRODUCTION

The desire to share my life originated the first time I was asked, "Ron, who's the most unforgettable person you ever met?"

I smiled as a face immediately came to mind. But before I could give his name, another face popped into my head. Then another and another and another until there was a crowd from which to choose. I paused. My mind was grid locked. I couldn't decide who was the most unforgettable person I ever met?

Was it the single mother who escaped Serbia with her four small children by killing a farm animal?

Was it the boy who shot me in the heart?

Was it the Dutch Jew who spent two years living in a wall during the occupation of Amsterdam?

Was it the Chemist who was also a Physicist but wanted to be an opera singer and ordered six drinks at once?

Was it the spy who ran a ring of operatives from Cincinnati?

Was it the Reverend who touched the goiter and the goiter disappeared?

Was it the Colonel who threatened to shoot the medics unless they put his insides back inside?

Was it the Frenchman whose sister married coincidence?

Was it the woman who was so beautiful waves of sound and bobbing heads acknowledged her passage through public places?

Was it the boy who was recruited from Montenegro to be a tailor for the House of Dior in Paris?

Was it the Serbian POW who fell in love with a German girl and got both of them to America?

The options continued but I couldn't decide. The fact that I couldn't identify the most unforgettable person I ever met nagged at me, annoyed me, frustrated me. I determined to come to an answer just for my personal satisfaction.

I sincerely tried, but no individual of the multitude — that's not even enough, there had been so many unforgettable people in my life they could be a population. And then it hit me, they were a population. The population of my life.

The intent of this writing is to welcome you to my life, share its population from 1943 to 1955, and let you decide who was the most unforgettable person I ever met.

These stories are presented from several different perspectives. When my recall is perfect, we listen to a boy reliving his life. When I have to plumb my memory, we listen to the detailed reporting of a sincere observer. When I am affected by my emotions, we listen to a man looking at his past.

Like every story there has to be a starting point. I thought these stories could begin with our family tree to provide points of reference along the way. But that's not how my life happened. As a youngster, I asked questions about our family and our history. No matter who or when I asked the questions the answers were the same, vague, disconnected, and more often than not, contradictory. None of my relatives found this strange. None felt any obligation to help me see the truth. Finally I accepted I was going to have to identify our family tree myself.

Over time what seemed to be our family tree came into focus. However, as soon as that happened, the tree changed. I adjusted and focused on the new version and then it changed too. Then it happened again. In fact, this cycle of identification and change was continuous. At times, branches that had been there, disappeared. At other times, branches that had not been there, appeared. Three times the roots changed. My life uncovered and exposed so many configurations of our family tree that if each configuration were shown, ours would be a family forest.

So I'll begin with the first family tree I could physically see. A tree with one root and two branches. My Baba, Maria Vukich and my parents, Olga Lubica Vukich and Svetozar Musco Mrksic. Their stories begin before I was born.

THE MATRIARCH

Maria Vukich was born in Kikinda, Serbia, Yugoslavia, April 18, 1883. She was not a Vukich when she was born but she was a Serbian and the defining characteristic of Serbs is that we never forget. Whatever it was she refused to forget, caused her to never mention her maiden name.

She was a typical Serb with dark complexion, full lips, high cheek bones, significant nose, wide set large eyes, and silky dark hair. Not unattractive, she was average height, coordinated, extremely strong, and blessed with uncommon stamina.

In a mountainous rural setting, she and her family lived off their land. She was careful not to describe them as farmers. Rather, they were a family that pooled its resources and talents to make a life.

What education she had was extremely limited. However, she could read and write Serbian, wrote letters periodically, and read her bible daily.

There is nothing of her mother.

As for her father, only the following was passed on. He was strong and renown for the stamina she inherited. On this day, she took his midday meal out to the field where he was working.

1

They sat down where she had laid the meat, bread, fruit, salt, water, bowl, knife, and wooden spoon. He cut the meat, bread, and fruit into the bowl, sprinkled it all with salt and ate using the spoon. This was his habit, regardless it be spring pig roasts, summer feasts, breakfast, lunch, supper, soup, bread, meat, fish, fowl, vegetables, fruit, cheese, dessert, Christmas dinner, no matter. Her father ate every meal with a spoon, after putting everything served into one large bowl.

That these are the only facts Baba told me about her parents suggests Maria Vukich had no history. That is not the case. Like most things in her life, she controlled her history. Her four children were part of her history but they had nothing to say. They knew she didn't want them to pass on anything. They knew who was in control. They kept their mouths shut.

As it had to be, in the right season Maria married Ponta Vukich. Powerfully structured, he was larger than most of his contemporaries and his coordination and strength were proportionate. He was a tireless worker who understood how to take advantage of his physical prowess. On this occasion there was an errant ram causing nuisance in one of the fields. This had been going on for some time and nothing seemed to settle the animal. Ponta announced he would look into the matter the next day. Maria decided to follow and see what he would do. The next day when he entered the field the ram took a territorial stance of defiance. Ponta decided to go about his work and see what developed. As he turned to work, the ram moved closer. Time passed and as Ponta continued to work, the ram continued edging closer. Suddenly, the ram charged. Maria yelled. Ponta Vukich turned and as the ram attacked, hit it in the head with his fist, splitting its skull. The ram was dead before its body hit the ground.

Together, Ponta and Maria had four children, Rose, Viola,

Olga, and Botta. It was Maria's plan to have them all born as American citizens. To make this happen she made several trips between Yugoslavia and America. She was not totally successful. Rose the oldest and Botta the youngest were born in Kikinda while her second daughter Viola and third daughter Olga, were born in America.

Maria's foresight and pragmatism were wonderfully displayed in her plan for her children's citizenship. However, her thinking can only be accurately valued when considered in the context of the historical events that followed. Her thinking was more global than rural.

Ponta died before Maria's last trip to America. That was all she ever told me.

That voyage with all four children was prompted when she felt an unnatural spirit in the air. It was not that the crops were bad or anyone was sick. It was more that the place where she was born, the land, the village and the surroundings no longer comforted her. She felt as if she didn't belong there anymore.

It was 1913. There were rumors of war. There were always rumors but it was her habit not to listen to them. She preferred to listen to what was in the air. The air told her the situation was changing, things were going to get worse and there would be war. The air warned her it was not going to be easy to get to America.

She began preparing to leave as she had for her other trips. This time, however, she was told by people that helped her before, people she trusted, that it was impossible for her to leave. She ignored their advice and continued her preparations. Nothing was impossible. She'd work at it.

Her contacts held firm. They insisted it had nothing to do with her, it wasn't personal, it was the situation, the times. She had to realize what was going on. They tried to make her understand.

Now there were new regulations, paperwork, roadblocks. She was shown a new special visa that was required regardless passports, papers, previous trips, contacts, influence, anything. This new visa even required a special seal to be authenticated and it was impossible for anyone except the authorities to get the seal.

In time she relented. Her contacts felt satisfied they had prevented her from making a mistake. But, in fact she was still working at it. She had decided to take matters into her own hands.

On the day the ship began loading, Maria Vukich packed her four children and as much of her belongings as she could and marched down to the docks. She headed to the ship and the administrative personnel responsible for granting travel to America. It was not just her appearance, with her brood and meager belongings that confronted the bureaucracy. In addition to the normal paperwork, passports, and the proofs of her previous passages, she had five copies of the new special visa required for emigration. Upon inspection some questions were raised because each of the seals was somewhat smudged and no two were the same size. After some bureaucratic posturing, the burdened mother and her foursome were motioned on the ship.

The Matriarch had found someone who could provide the blank forms but not the special seal. She had the forms filled out for her and her children. Two days before the scheduled loading, she killed a chicken. While the chicken bled, she broke a few dry corncobs in half. Dipping the broken ends of the corncobs into the blood, she tried various methods of making marks. When she was satisfied with the results, she used a cob in the blood to make the seals and brought her children to America.

OLGA LUBICA VUKICH

She was born August 4, 1911 in Cincinnati, Ohio.

The pictures of her childhood include her mother, sisters, and brother, all dressed in their best. Not Sunday best, only best. She has dark curly hair, large dark eyes, a prominent nose and full, bow shaped lips. All of these pictures are formal and staged. None record spontaneity, frivolity, or even one smile. They are testaments that life was hard.

All the pictures of her as a young lady show a well-proportioned female, five feet tall with slightly curly dark hair. She has the same large dark eyes and full bow shaped lips but her cheek bones have asserted themselves and her nose has taken a minor role. She is altogether a lovely woman. None of these pictures are staged, all depict a candid relaxed atmosphere and she is smiling in every one. The pretty young lady has a charismatic look with a tangible portion of mystery and just a dash of imp.

The pictures of her late twenties and early thirties show her matured. The eyes are still large and dark but now are knowing and have seen more than enough human suffering. Her face reflects the weight of trying to help anyone and everyone. The smiles are not from an inner imp but of appreciation for a moment without demands.

Her mother and siblings provide a crisp and detailed portrait of Olga. To them she lacked the pragmatism, objectivity, discipline, and seriousness of their lives. She was a romantic whose imagination was her defining characteristic. She probably single handedly caused The Family Words To Live By to include, "You should be back from the errand before I remember I sent you."

Olga completed the eighth grade and went to work full time. She had a quick mind. In those lessons that were compatible with her makeup, history and reading, she excelled. But in general she was not a good student.

She was a loyal and sincere employee but was taken to daydreaming. She worked the longest in a tailor shop and for a time in a candy factory. In the factory the employees where permitted to eat as much as they wanted. Olga set a new standard for eating the most chocolates for the longest period of time before getting her fill.

Olga was curious and adventuresome. An example was asking her sister Rose's husband, Lou, to teach her to box. She wanted to put the gloves on during the first lesson. Lou said no. Every time they got together Olga insisted to put the gloves on and he said no. One day, while alone, she found the gloves and put them on. With the gloves on she was ready to box. She jumped about and mimicked Lou. She took a terrific swing which turned her around so that she hit her jaw and knocked herself out.

She was in love or wanted to be in love with a local shoemaker. Olga saw him as full of potential that only a romantic could nurture. The family however was not pleased because the man was thought to be an alcoholic. Olga never abandoned this fixation. Her stamina for optimism equaled the physical stamina of her mother and grandfather.

On the spiritual side, the Serbian Orthodox Church was not enough for her. She investigated other churches. She got interested in The Assembly Of God and was saved. The Pastor encouraged her and she joined, was baptized, entered school, was ordained, and became an assistant pastor on the Church staff.

Olga was not interested in George Marksity, the tailor, but he was head over heels in love with her. The family didn't know how she felt about him but they felt he was much better than that drunk shoemaker. George had a real trade and would always be able to provide. When George and Olga were married it was bliss for George and a relief for the family. What it was for Olga was undetermined. She was a dreamer, flitting from notion to notion and frequently deciding not to distinguish fairyland from the world around her.

No question, Olga was different from her mother, sisters, and brother. They felt the differences were not good. She was playing at life, while they had to work hard to live. She refused to see reality and tended to stir things up. But they couldn't help but like her. And if one looked carefully at their portrait, it was clear she was her mother's favorite and the envy of her siblings.

By the time she was ordained as a Pastor, she had demonstrated she could communicate and cause understanding. She was naturally charismatic, dominant, credible, overwhelming, perceptive, and personal in her communications with crowds of thousands or one-on-one. Plus, she had a gift.

If asked to talk about herself, she was quick to answer. She loved The Lord. He was first in her life. She consecrated herself to Him. Serving Him was her life's ambition. Being useful to Him was her purest dream.

In her mind she had no background before being saved. In her daily life, she had no time to discuss the irrelevant.

SVETOZAR MUSCO MRKSIC

He was born in 1905 in Yugoslavia. He had no recollection of his father and was reared by his mother.

The only pictures of his youth were taken when he was in his late twenties and present a small, good looking man, in perfectly tailored clothes of the finest material in the latest fashion. He is dressed as a gentleman of the times dressed and looks to be successful and in perfect health. Five foot two with a lean frame, his hands were a clue to his wiry musculature as they were sinewy and amazingly strong. His gait and the fluidity of his movement reflected coordination. There was an energy about him and he always seemed occupied. He had coal black hair and dark eyes. The small mole on the right side of his face seemed necessary to keep him from looking pretty because his Slavic features were neither sharp nor harsh, but sculpted and softened so that he can only be described as handsome.

During his childhood and adolescence, Svetozar was sickly. People told him he had tuberculosis but he was not certain that was correct. He went to school where he was a good pupil but due to his health had a difficult time finding work. When the First World War broke out, he tried to join the military in any capacity but was rejected because of his age and physical history. He felt even the Army wouldn't take him.

One of the very few job opportunities presented to him was as an apprentice in a tailor shop where his physical limitations were irrelevant. In quick time it became clear Svetozar was a natural with fabric, tape measure, chalk, scissors, needle and thread. He distinguished himself by his work and his reputation spread. People came from beyond his home town to see the prodigy and commission his efforts. Among them were some visitors from France.

A few months after the French visitors left, he was invited to Paris. To say the trip was successful is an understatement. He was offered a position as a tailor with the prestigious House of Dior. This was an unimaginable opportunity and he made the decision to take advantage of it even though it meant moving to Paris and leaving his mother and home.

Not too long after he was settled in Paris, his mother died. At this point he began referring to himself as an orphan and it was as an orphan that he saw himself thereafter.

During his years in Paris, his health steadily improved and he eventually completely recovered.

His career with The House of Dior was bountiful and provided him the means to realize his dream of moving to America. Before departing he began referring to himself differently and Svetozar Musco Mrksic became Svetozar George Marksity. Once in the United States, he headed for Cincinnati where he had a distant relative. In Cincinnati, his credentials from Christian Dior opened the doors to all the local tailoring operations and he immediately found employment.

Svetozar also found true love. From the beginning, he was smitten with the young Olga Vukich. No matter she did not return the sentiments, he knew she was for him. The courtship was long and difficult, but finally his persistence paid off and they were married.

Settled and successful in his profession and marriage, he focused on becoming a citizen. Svetozar Musco Mrksic, by order of the court on April 28, 1941, officially became Svetozar George Marksity who preferred to be called George and was a Naturalized Citizen of The United States Of America.

In addition to finding employment, his true love and citizenship in Cincinnati, George also found God. While courting Olga he was saved. During the early years of their marriage he studied and satisfied the requirements so that he too was ordained and joined the Assembly Of God system as The Reverend S. G. Marksity.

ME

In 1943, the family tree of Baba, Olga, and George, sprouted a new branch.

My first memories have stayed with me because I have always reflected on them.

The very first was when suddenly I knew I was. Perhaps that was consciousness or awakening.

I didn't know where I had been, I just knew I was.

I knew I was surrounded by Peace. I knew the Peace was engulfed by Protection. I knew the Protection was ensconced in the security of Ultimate Strength. I came to know that the Peace, Protection, and Strength were God.

The sense of Something Bigger, that would remain beyond my comprehension, was not frightening. It was pacifying, nurturing, guiding, and made me feel secure. It was wonderful to become aware under the overwhelming auspices of God. He seemed to be there just for me.

For the record, I was born Ronald Earl Marksity, 1:55 AM May 3, 1943 in Cincinnati to Svetozar George Marksity, age 38, and Olga Lubica Vukich Marksity, age 31. I weighed eight pounds six ounces and had no congenital malformation. There were things off the record.

The record does not show that my middle name came from my early time of birth. The record does not show that my Serbian name was Zoran Mrksic. It did not appear on the birth certificate but Zoran Mrksic was the name people would use more than Ronald Earl Marksity. Zoran, when pronounced correctly ends in 'ron' and is derived from the Serbian word for sunrise, zora. All in all I think 1:55 AM is a little early for sunrise and a lot odd for naming babies, but I didn't have much say in the matter.

The record does not show that I was a Serbian Prave. "Sir-bean pRav-v" translates literally to real Serb. From the beginning I was told I was a real Serb, the authentic one hundred percent full blooded version from pure Serb stock. This was instilled in such a way that it became a responsibility.

It made sense that since I had two names and two nation-alities, I should have two languages. I learned both Serbian and American naturally, just like children all over the world who grow up in homes where multiple languages are spoken. I learned to think and speak in Serbian first. This was not a positive hap-penstance because the Serbian we spoke was unsophisticated and limited in scope. I am unaware when I began to think and speak in American. But, from the beginning, Serbians called me Zoran and Americans called me Ronnie.

The record does not show that I knew who George and Olga were but wasn't sure what to call them. Based on what I saw them do and how I felt, Mom and Dad was simply not enough. They were much more than my parents. But what should I call them? Reverend George and Reverend Olga? Tailor? House-wife? Brother Marksity and Sister Marksity? Olga? George? Minister Marksity? Pastor Marksity? Svetozar? Should I call him Missionary Marksity and refer to her as The-One-With-The-Gift? What should I call them?

The answer was provided by the unsophisticated and limited Serbian we spoke. It was rural and basic. People addressed each other as "you". There were two versions of "you". One, pronounced "tee", was informal, casual, and appropriate for associates. The other, pronounced "vee", was formal and the mandatory way to show respect. "Vee" was expected from a child when addressing adults. I was reprimanded whenever I used the wrong "you". I grew up in an environment with adults who accepted and expected to be called "vee".

The record does not show that eventually I would learn Olga and George were very comfortable with me not calling them Mom and Dad. They had no feelings about how I referred to them because they had their own version of who was my parents.

64 EAST MCMICKEN: HOME

Olga and George said we lived in two other places before we moved here, but my first memories of home are of 64 East Mc-Micken Avenue. The building was built as a retail store. The front half was one big room, with twenty foot ceilings, a glass front door and two glass display windows. The back half was divided into two equal sized rooms. The back half was our home. I lived there until I started going to school.

To get home we took the narrow covered alleyway on the right side of the building as you faced it, which separated home from the building next door. After forty feet, the alleyway opened to a forty by ten foot courtyard. The walls of the courtyard were brick and stone. The floor was concrete except for two small patches of dirt, our yard. Two thirds of the way to the rear of the courtyard was the door to home.

Crossing that threshold, we entered the room farthest from the street. In the middle of this square room, on a round metal sheet that it thought was its throne, was a black iron stove, dominating the scene and demanding to be looked at first. To the right and left of the door, various chests, boxes, and racks served as furniture and closets. On the far wall were two beds, separated by a large chiffonnier which faced the bed on the right. The left bed was for me and Baba. The right bed was for Olga and George. This was the furnace room, living room, and bedrooms of home.

In the center of the wall on the left was the doorway to the next room which, since it was closest to the street, was the front room. As you entered, a table and chairs where to the right. To the left was a cabinet which supported a thinner tall cabinet with a built in flour sifter. There was a box for keeping food cool, an overhead light fixture and, facing you from left to right, a cabinet with metal counter-top, a large double sink, a stove, and the door leading to the front half of the building. There was a wash tub, bucket, and various implements in the corners. The front room was the kitchen, dining, and other room, depending on the situation.

Going through the door to the front of the building, you entered a short hallway that ended with a step down at another door. At that point, to the left was the rest of home — another narrow hallway that led to the bathroom. The bathroom had a toilet and small hand sink and was one of the reasons our front room served other purposes. For a bath, the front room was closed off and became the bathroom. The large galvanized tub was placed on the floor, the sink taps provided the water, and a bath was enjoyed like certain theaters, in the round.

There were no windows at home. There was still a lot to see.

THE MATRIARCH

Maria Vukich may have been The Matriarch, but I had no concept what that meant. To me she was Baba, my grandmother. Baba Maria may have been the most powerful presence of my infancy and early childhood but I was unaware of that as well. To me she was who I spent the most time with. Baba Maria may have been the reason I learned to think and speak in Serbian first, but I couldn't make that connection either. The only thing I knew for sure was that from my earliest memories, Baba was the one who loved me.

Baba felt our family tree was of little importance. What was important was where the tree was planted. Our tree was planted in the hard mountain country of Serbia. We were Serbians. She made it very clear we were not Yugoslavians. She admitted Serbia was one of the seven Slavic nationalities united under Tito to form Yugoslavia but in the context of history that was a minor incident. The overall history of Serbia was the more important matter and the backdrop for everything past and future. I must never forget this point, we were Serbs.

I learned I was a Serbian Prave. I also learned that was not enough. I had the right blood but had to master the mentality and behavior. Baba made it very clear I had one option. If I wanted to live as a Serbian Prave and be one of them, I would have to adopt the Serbian perspective of life. She would help me. She would teach me who Serbians were and how to become one. I couldn't wait and so the lessons started.

Never forget. That was our defining characteristic. Once that was understood, 'never forget' maintained itself, not like a thread through our evolution, but as a mandate for our beliefs and behaviors. 'Never forget' was the way of life. She taught me what this meant in day-to-day living. Positive treatment was to be remembered. The smallest hint of a perceived slight, was never to be forgotten. 'Never forget' was The Serb's coat of arms.

Around this core, in such a way as to become armor, was the chain mail of Serbian characteristics. Stubborn. Social. Menacing. Loyal. Hateful. Honorable. The ability to instill fear. Emotional. Proud. Planting, cultivating, growing, harvesting. Cruel. Patriotic. A potential explosiveness. Suspicious. Secretive. Fearless. Protective of family members and the family as a whole. Passionate. Ruthless. Subjective.

As the knights of Medieval times were shown in lore and legend, Baba demonstrated and practiced the rituals and traditions of her native land. In so doing, she taught me the definition of each Serbian characteristic and let me learn, uncensored, the positive and negative aspects of each. However, the most formidable lesson was to never waver from adherence to the coat of arms. Serbians never forget.

This was not all she was to teach me.

64 EAST MCMICKEN: CHURCH

Our church was the front half of the building. As you stood on the front sidewalk there was glass everywhere and it was clear this had been a store. The one step up from the sidewalk put you on a four by five foot stoop, under cover, and in front of the glass entrance door. To either side were equal-sized, glass-enclosed display windows. Both windows carried the same three line announcement.

PENIEL MISSIONARY ASSEMBLY
A Nondenominational Church
Everyone Welcome

The times of the Sunday morning and evening services, and the Wednesday evening prayer meetings, were inked on the glass entrance door with the disclaimer, "All Welcome Anytime."

Once through the front door, the large rectangular room was surprisingly bright due to the all-glass front and overhead lighting. The storage cabinets below the display windows were easily recognized but the first impression was not of retail sales. The first impression was simple, safe, and friendly.

Rows of neatly aligned wooden folding chairs, every other one holding a song book, formed the pews and were separated by a generous center aisle which pulled the eye to the raised altar.

The altar extended about ten feet from the back wall. It was a little over two feet high and ended about six feet from either side wall. There was a podium and a semicircle of wooden folding chairs. On the wall to the right and behind the altar, was a wooden display board which could be changed to show attendance and other related facts.

To the right of the altar, on the floor, was an upright piano, a moveable blackboard, and a cabinet for song books, bibles, and materials for administering communion.

To the left of the altar an aisle led to a door. Passing through this door you were facing a single step and a short hallway to another door which led to home. To the right was a hallway leading to the bathroom for church—a small room with a toilet and hand sink.

The chair pews filled the floor except for the area halfway up the room against the left wall where the large pot-bellied stove stood. In the winter, this section of the chair pews filled up first.

In the summer there was no way to get cool. The large expanses of glass promoted oven-like temperatures. There were two huge movable electric fans twisting from side to side but moving hot air is still hot air. There were silly little fans of bible shaped paper glued on a stick, but no matter how hard you waved them at yourself you only got hotter from the exertion. We didn't know the temperature but knew how hot it was by keeping track of the 'stick-um ratio'. This was the ratio of how much of your skin that was touching the chair you were sitting on stuck to the chair when you tried to get up. When it was oppressively hot, we employed the 'deposit ratio'. This calculated how much of your clothing stuck to the chair after you left. I never got used to my shirts leaving a thin layer of material stuck to the backs of the wooden chairs. It was as if the chairs had grown peach fuzz.

When it was empty, the church was still friendly but it never gave the impression it was a place to play. When it was full, it became any number of wonderful things, depending on the congregation and spirit. What I saw from the last row of wooden folding chairs, between my first memory and my thirteenth year, stays with me as cameos of the congregations and my life.

CONGREGATION

To me he was not Claude Benton. Claude was his given name but he was never referred to as Claude, or even Mister Benton. As a member of our congregation he was, Brother Benton.

Brother Benton. Just the sound of his name goes a long way toward describing the man. Balanced. Starts and ends equally strong. Complete. Stable and solid but not harsh or rough. American.

He was tall with long arms, legs, and fingers, and a frame upon which gaunt could have hung. But he was somehow round rather than angular and smooth rather than sharp. His face was long and topped by an almost bushy head of brown hair. His eyes were keen, nose pronounced, cheeks recessed and chin pointed. His smile was what affected me. When I saw that large imposing Lincoln like face sitting atop his shirt and tie, the last thing I expected was to see it creep into the widest most genuine smile imaginable.

Brother Benton was a painter, a "sign painter." Many people have never seen a "sign painter" use paint and brush on a white billboard and actually create the picture. The art is gone, replaced by workmen who paste printed panels. Brother Benton specialized in those projects that required him to climb anything and create from scratch. His works were paint and inspiration, not paper hangings. He was an artist who included proof of his gift in everything he did.

It was a thrill when riding in the car to look up and see a billboard and hear Olga or George say, "That's Brother Benton's." I was in awe standing on a street, head flung back as far as it would go, staring up at the giant picture painted on the building because I knew the artist. His portfolio covered the commercial gamut and his signs and posters were envied and collected. The Peniel Missionary Assembly announced it was non-denominational and welcomed all by the signs he painted on the windows and door.

He was married but all I remember of his wife was one Sunday School Class. As usual the front room of home was used as the classroom and the lesson was going on when Sister Benton came in with her baby and sat on the side of the room. Soon after getting settled she began unbuttoning her shirt. I didn't know what to do and more particularly where to look. As the lesson continued I couldn't stop looking. Sister Benton systematically opened her shirt and that thing that was under it and casually, as if it were the natural thing to do, fed her baby. I don't remember the subject of the lesson.

However it wasn't his wife or his work by which he painted his memory on my life, it was his worship. Every once in a while he would join us in Sunday School. Whoever was the teacher was glad to have him there. As the teacher presented the lesson, all were listening but none were looking. Eyes were riveted on Brother Benton. Using the most amazing collection of chalks and a blackboard, or an easel with a pad of delicate paper, he would create a picture that highlighted the point of the lesson.

Similarly, he would sometimes, not often, get up before the sermon and place his blackboard or easel to the right of the altar. As the sermon was given, Brother Benton would turn it into a visual masterpiece. These lessons and sermons were never forgotten.

I loved his creations. But this was real life and there was a down side. The chalk on blackboard could not remain forever. I lamented the fact that there was no way to save those bits of genius. Olga and George knew my feelings for his creations and unlike any other work done on the blackboards, never made me erase his drawings. As for the creations on paper he would normally tear them off at the end of Sunday School or Church and give them away without any thought to who or why. As the pastor's son, it was not seemly for me to get such a gift. I surely sinned by coveting each. Over time I did manage to collect several chalk on paper Benton's. I kept them like the treasures they were, but to no avail as they deteriorated and eventually disappeared.

Sometime later Sister Benton accused him of bad things. I'm not sure I knew what the bad things were. I certainly don't remember them. I do remember there was not much disturbance in the Church. The congregation of The Peniel Missionary Assembly was a family that anticipated and accepted its members were human and cared for them accordingly.

I don't know what happened to the Bentons but I can still see his calm and humble face as he celebrated and shared his gift. He turned lessons and sermons into brilliant images that filled me with wonder. His gift ignited in me an appreciation and awe of art that continues to this day. A respect for all art that magnified the beauty in my life.

64 EAST MCMICKEN:
THE HALLWAY

It would be reasonable to assume that of our home, church, and the hallway between them, the hallway had the least impact on my life. Reasonable, but wrong. Over time I came to realize my fundamental characteristics and behaviors were formed and matured in the hallway.

I learned early that my life included contrary elements. I was born an American yet I was a Serbian. I was to speak only Serbian. I was to speak only American. I was to speak both. I was an only child yet I had countless Brothers and Sisters. Even more demanding were the contradictions between home and church.

Not just anyone was welcome at home. Who was welcome depended on who they were, what they did, and when they came. How long they stayed depended on what happened while they were there. At church, anyone and everyone was always welcome for any length of time.

People who came home were categorized: male, female, a certain nationality, lady, gentlemen, married, single, child, parent, grandparent, laborer, artist, non-believer, saved, Catholic,

Protestant, Jew, Greek Orthodox, young, old, poor, wealthy and more. People who came to church were never categorized, they were all Brothers and Sisters.

I could decide how I felt about people who came home. I "would" love and respect anyone who came to church.

It was not easy living with such contrary elements. At times they would merely be opposite each other but sometimes they would be in real conflict. I was supposed to tell them apart and then figure out how to act toward each. It was in the hallway that I learned to do this and thereby developed my fundamental characteristics and behaviors.

The hallway taught me to differentiate. I lived in two very different environments, at the same time. The hallway provided a physical distinction between church and home and made it easier for me to know which was which. I lived with The Matriarch and The Reverend, two women many considered larger than life. Of no little consequence was the fact they were mother and daughter. Olga took care of the church, Baba took care of the home. The hallway made it easier for me to know who was who and which was which. In church, life was spiritual. I was expected to practice what I was, a Christian. At home, life was secular. I was allowed to be what I was, a boy. The hallway made it easier for me to know which me to be.

The hallway taught me the value of flexibility. In church I was the respectful well mannered son of the Reverends Olga and George, the Christian who was courteous and sincere, and the mature- for-his-age-helper who was always busy doing anything asked of him. At home I was Ronnie, Zoran and Baba's buddy, the curious kid who loved to read and was alone a lot. It was easier to be the right me in the right place if I remained flexible.

The hallway helped me adjust. At home there was room for imagination. In church there was no room for imagination because what occurred in church was beyond my wildest imagination. I needed imagination at home. I couldn't have imagined what I saw in church. This required adjustment. As I passed through the hallway, regardless the direction, I was reminded to adjust. Adjust what I was doing to what I should be doing. Adjust what I was thinking to what I should be thinking. Adjust how I was acting to how I should be acting.

Later in life, I learned this flexibility and adjusting was called wearing two hats. The hallway taught me to naturally change hats. It provided a physical location that reminded me which hat I was wearing and which hat I should be wearing; how I had been behaving and how I should be behaving.

The hallway taught me to review and reflect. In the hallway I had to think about where I had just been, how I had just acted.

The hallway taught me preparedness. In the hallway I had to think about where I was going and how I better act when I got there.

The hallway taught me I would always be between things. In the hallway, no matter which way I was going, I always knew I wasn't there anymore and wasn't there yet.

The hallway taught me to concentrate on other people. No matter where I exited, I had to be prepared to act according to who was there. I learned to think about who was going to be where I was going.

The hallway taught me perspective. Every time I walked through it, the hallway demonstrated how a change in my position changed how I saw things and how I was seen.

The hallway taught me to make decisions. I didn't have a lot

31

of time in the hallway, it was only about ten steps between the doors of home and church. In between I thought, I decided, I did.

For all these lessons in the hallway, I was alone. This helped me develop independence.

Unlike home and the church, the hallway seemed to be my private personal tutor. I didn't think that odd. I heard of kids who had invisible friends they talked to. Now that was odd.

THE ADVENTUROUS MEAL

There was a hint of excitement in the air. I felt it as soon as Olga made her announcement. It came out as a proclamation that tonight we were going to share a specialty meal. With her sense of whimsy there was no predicting who, when, or what was going to be special about supper.

I knew better than to take the bait so casually thrown and went about some business in the back room. But I was listening for any further hints. She knew she had me listening. I knew she knew.

In time, speaking to no one in particular since no one was there, she added to the excitement. We were going to eat as the Serbs in the mountains back home. We were going to share their adventurous experiences by duplicating this special supper.

She didn't say anything else. She was letting her comments sink into my little head. The only sounds coming from the front room were those of her rattling around with the utensils. The excitement level increased as she started humming some Serb ditty.

Now the bait was swallowed and she was reeling me in as questions raced through my mind. What did the Serbs back home in the mountains eat for such a special meal? What kinds of adventures were in store? Would I have to do something to earn the right to partake? Would I be able to eat the food? Oh, I'd have to eat, but that could be hard. I had eaten some Serbian dishes that I wished I could forget. But this was a meal eaten on an adventure in the mountains. Suddenly, I realized I had walked into the front room and, when I looked up, she gave me that smile only the victors may flash. I was caught, cleaned and filet-of-Ron.

She was gentle. If I were older I might have called it condescending. She started explaining. Of course we weren't back home in Serbia. That was just a phrase. This was our home. Of course we weren't in the mountains. But, we had imaginations, didn't we? The two of us and our imaginations could make this place, anywhere or anything.

And so it was that with our imaginations we were in the mountains of Serbia. The terrain was harsh and the surroundings ominous but we had our faith and wits about us. Due to the dangers, we were not going to be able to have a fire. We had to remain undetected till morning when we could get home safely.

Wow, this is an adventure. But how are we going to fix this special meal without a fire?

In Serbian Olga explained, "Zoran, we're going to use techniques proven long ago. You get the potatoes and onions and I'll start here."

It made perfect sense that since we were among the rugged peaks of Serbia we would speak Serbian and she would call me by my Serbian name. I foraged in the drawer, found a few potatoes and onions and brought them to the campsite.

She had already unpacked the raw bacon and bread. Neither one of us was surprised that the bread was really hard. After all, it had been carried in our packs all over these mountains.

Next, as she was organizing the condiments of salt, black pepper, and paprika, I got the plates, cups, and hardware that would be needed, and set them up on the tree trunk we were using as our table. Then I took the goatskin and headed for the brook we had noticed as we stopped. In no time I was back with fresh water.

As the night settled in around us and the sounds of the mountains grew steadily louder, we began to eat. The raw bacon was smothered with paprika and the raw potatoes and onions salted and peppered to taste. With such a specialty meal it was the proven routine to take a bit of bacon and bread and chew thoroughly. The next bite should be of potato or onion or both. Then the bacon and bread, then the potato and onion, and so on. We reminded each other that on such an adventure it was important to eat correctly. The key was to chew everything completely. This insured getting the maximum energy from the meal which was critical. Neither one of us knew what emergencies might face us before morning and the safety of home.

We were cautious of the surroundings and circumstances but not fearful. We talked and pointed out the sounds made by the various types of wildlife, just out of sight, beyond the clearing we had made. The overhead moon was bright and we had no trouble seeing each other or the meal.

When the meal was finished, there was not a crumb of bread or grain of salt, pepper, or paprika anywhere to be found. As for the bacon, even the smell had been eaten.

Olga offered to clean up the campsite if I would get ready for sleeping.

We agreed that the Lord would have the security watches during the night.

It had been an adventure and I was tired. I was cleaned up

and asleep under the stars, before she had finished cleaning up the campsite.

We shared this meal on one of the nights when George was overseas, the gas was turned off because we had no money to pay the bill and, no parishioners had managed to bring us any food.

CONGREGATION

Well he's here again. He not only makes both Sunday services, he's here every Wednesday night. I still don't know his name. I've seen him in the neighborhood but don't know where he lives or anything about him. He's absolutely not a Serb. It's amazing, no matter what the weather he always has that sort of sweater on. He's nice enough but never looks me in the eye. I don't understand why his nose seems bigger than it should be or why it's so dark red, almost purple. He coughs a lot, yet still tries to sing the hymns. He comes in just before the service starts and leaves just as it ends. I wish I had something that he needed, so I could give it to him.

OLGA: DAUGHTER, SIBLING, WIFE, MOTHER

For Olga, God was everything. She was committed, dedicated and satisfied giving her life to Him. Everything and everybody, separately or collectively, could never be more than a distant group of lesser importance.

The first of the lesser was her mother. The Matriarch was the first person to receive Olga's attention.

Her sisters and brother were next. The loyalty they had to each other was fostered by The Matriarch. They were "The Vukich's." However this familial commitment was limited to the five of them and did not include all relatives named Vukich. Olga's loyalty and support of her siblings went beyond Baba's influence and was a result of her own decisions.

George had no priority. Her behavior made it clear that The Reverend Olga Marksity and the parishioner George Marksity worked together. The fact that he was her husband was extraneous. The fact that he was also a Reverend, immaterial. She was the senior Pastor. Neither the Reverend S.G. nor the husband George were offended or hurt by her attitude and behavior. They were happy to be near her and working with or for her. I never saw her give my father a present or as much as a card. I am unaware that she ever did so. She was a terrible wife.

She was not much better as a housewife. The demands on her time were her explanation, not excuse, for her performance in the home. She didn't make excuses, they were beneath her. I believe she refused the concept of housewife and never noticed that Baba, George, and I fulfilled her job description. Oh, she would take over cooking from Baba, when she felt like it. She would help Baba and me with the laundry, when she felt like it. She would show interest in George's handling of the administration, when she felt he needed her to be interested. She would work in the yard, when she felt like it. She would grocery shop, when she felt like it. She would fiddle with the garden, when she felt like it. As for any cleaning, she never felt like it.

Her basic character was entirely upbeat. Her behavior was full of fantasy and constantly celebrating the joy of life. This was priceless for a Pastor and in the face of tragedy. It was something else on a day-to-day basis. She loved to sing and had a repertoire of favorites but she was just as likely to go skipping into a room singing "tra-la-la." She was as bubbly as a child and her childlike qualities made her happy and others happy to be around her.

The positive impact of her character on people was echoed with animals, they loved her. No matter where we visited, if there were animals, Olga became the center of attention. When we moved to places with yards, all kinds of animals adopted her. Red Birds were particularly attracted. They would feed from her hand and she from their spirits. Together they seemed to be a special kind of family. I don't know if Cardinal chirping translates to tra-la-la-la.

Her character was not always the easiest to share or understand.

Her siblings said she lived in her own world while Baba thought she was just preoccupied. Whatever the diagnosis, the affliction had its impact. One day she was driving and I was responsible for reading the directions. We were approaching the side street where she was to turn right and she asked, "Ronnie, is this where I'm to turn?" I answered yes. She immediately turned right. Right into the front lawn of a house. She didn't miss a beat. She put the car in reverse, backed out and headed to the intersection. She honestly didn't notice the tire ruts or mud she left in the yard.

Olga was an avid reader. The Bible first and anything after that. When it came to novels, she followed her own way of picking a book. This started with waiting for a book to jump out at her. When that happened she would catch it and no matter what the book, that was the book for her. Next she had to find the right place to read. This meant a comfortable seat, good light, quiet and no interruptions because she had to feel what she was reading. In such a place she would start. After some time she would feel she knew the people and could sense the places. Once she reached those feelings she would turn to the end of the book, read what happens and then return to the front and complete the book. I never saw her read a book any other way.

She had a way with sweets as well. She saw them as mysterious because of the power they seemed to have over her. However, a box of chocolates was not a mystery if you could find the key. She could. The key was to take a piece out, poke a hole in the bottom to see what it was. If you liked the filling, eat it. If you weren't looking for that taste, put the piece back. Someone else will eat it, probably never knowing there was a hole poked in the bottom. How often do you look at the bottom of a piece of chocolate you've picked from an offered box?

When it came to disciplining me, Olga's Program Of Subtle

Discipline had three levels. The mildest was being aware. I would be somewhere and suddenly feel her gaze. Searching, I would eventually see her. She would look at me long enough to let me know she was watching. Never long enough for anyone else to notice. This told me she was aware, she was watching. Was I watching myself? Was I aware?

Level two was offering suggestions. She would shift her eyes to the person I should acknowledge or thing I should do. She would close her eyes to tell me to stop what I was doing. She would take a breath and close her eyes to reinforce the last suggestion she had offered. She would incline her head slightly to point where I should go. She would purse her lips, making others think she was thinking and making me think what she was going to do if I didn't follow her suggestions better. When she dropped her eyelids and curled the corners of her mouth downward so she looked as if a cloud were descending, that cloud would be descending on me.

The highest level of Olga's Subtle Discipline was hand control. To an outsider, the mother affectionately caressing her son's neck was sweet. "Ah, here comes The Reverend Marksity with her son. Look how she's pretending to lean on him for support." "Yes. And look how he seems so proud to be helping her." "He's such a good boy. He's so attentive and respectful and quiet. He acts like a real little gentleman." From my point of view that was not the hand of affection resting on my shoulder, it was the claw of death gripping my neck. If I failed to stand straight, walk tall, smile, and play the role, the claw tightened. When I felt pressure from the thumb, I better turn in that direction. When I felt pressure from the fingers, I better turn in that direction. When I felt pressure down, I better stop. Pressure up, I better go. I'd be real glad when we got to her destination and I got away from her claw.

Olga's Program Of Subtle Discipline was a mystery to others, but not to me. One Sunday, visitors from India were arriving to spend the week interviewing her. I was excited about seeing Indian Indians and not at all under pressure because of it. On the way to church I missed her signals. When we arrived the Indians were waiting and she was fed up with my being unaware and missing her suggestions. She clamped onto my neck as we were leaving the car. After some time, one of the visitors asked if I was ill. Olga had been so focused on the conversation that she forgot about me and I was turning blue. I got a lot of mileage out of that particular claw grip.

I loved when she read to me. These were events and she was the producer, director, every character, and the musical accompaniment. They always began the same way. "Zoran, you know that book we've been working on? We're going to have to make time for it." This was both the general advertisement of the coming performance and a reminder for me to review what I had heard so far. I'd replay the story in my head and wait for the specific announcement.

"Ronnie, how about eight o'clock tomorrow evening? Will you be free?" Translated, this meant I'd better have everything I'd ever been told to do done before eight and be able to answer her questions. "Did I have enough to eat? Did I get something to drink? Have I visited the restroom?" In this way she emphasized this was our time and woe be it to anyone who interrupted.

Okay. Now it was a matter of waiting. As the time of the performance neared, my excitement grew because she always left the hero in a real fix. I would arrive early to be sure I got to watch her arrive. Time would drag as I waited. I would or would not hear her in the other rooms but just before the appointed time she would make her entrance.

With her entrance, the overture would begin. This always centered on the book and included the following movements. Bringing it with her or locating it in the room. Looking around to see if everything was settled before carrying it to her chair, sitting down and placing it on her lap, unopened. Adjusting the lamp shade, the overture would end as she would look over to me for the first time and ask, "Well, should we begin?" Please. Please! With that encouragement she would open the book and, with all the promise of a Broadway opening night, cradle it into that perfect position for reading and speaking that the best soloists use for their songbooks.

The curtain would go up and the performance would begin. Using the pace, pitch and volume of her voice she created a masterful soundtrack that incited all the nerves of my imagination and brought the words to life. Her pronunciation, enunciation, emphasis, and pauses made me close my eyes so I could see the living picture better. But, I couldn't afford to keep them closed because her body language, gestures, and facial expressions made the story bigger than life. With sideways glances, sniffles, a raised eyebrow, guffaws, a hand to her throat with her eyes wide open, tears, and the gift of creativity, we lived the stories as she read.

Finally, like the best producers and directors, she was a master of the ending. I always marveled that when she would close a book I would feel completely satisfied, to include that physical fatigue after a good exercise, and at the same time anxious with anticipation of the next performance.

Olga the daughter, sibling, wife and mother, and I, lived together from my earliest memories until I left for the Army. These four were not the only Olgas I lived with during those years.

64 E. MCMICKEN: THE NEIGHBORHOOD

All of 64 East McMicken was part of the surrounding neighborhood. The part I called my neighborhood had boundaries. Boundaries I set and was comfortable in.

Looking out of our building to the right were a couple of buildings, a small street, a few more buildings and then the brewery. I'm not certain what brand of beer they made but the boss's parking slot had a two toned snazzy little Crosley convertible. A little past the brewery were the library and fire house. These marked my neighborhood's north boundary.

To the left was a grocery store where I could get a little brown bag full of assorted candy when Baba gave me a penny. We had a mini Christmas discovering what goodies had been put there by the grocer. The grocery's exposed wall marked the start of the playground and the unlimited outfield of baseball games as fair balls hit off the wall were in play. The playground was my neighborhood's south boundary

To the east, pushing against the back wall of our building was the hill. I never went up the hill.

To the west, the neighborhood boundary was Findlay Market.

Within these boundaries was a constant hubbub. Something was going on which interrupted a something and something else began before that something was done and other somethings were doing the same thing all over the place. The neighborhood was alive and throbbing. When you couldn't see the somethings, you could feel them. The energy of the neighborhood didn't stop and didn't slow, it just pulsed. Frequently this pulse would spike.

In the neighborhood I experienced America as melting pot. The place was an imagination's worth of differences. Optimism lived on the first floor with pessimism on the second. Name a Slavic nationality and representatives would step forward. As soon as they did, smaller numbers and individuals would raise their hands to insure their nationalities were recognized. Educated and illiterate shared the playground. Faithful and faithless shopped at the grocery store. Hope and despair with every nuance in between could be heard hunched on the stoops, leaning against the buildings, sitting on the steps and fire escapes, smoking, drinking, living.

Findlay Market reflected the neighborhood. An incredible mixture. Any nationality. Any product. Farmers coming in at sunrise setting up their stalls next to the local stores. The surrounding streets turning into store aisles on Saturdays. The Spice Store's mysteries from India, China, South America, and places I couldn't pronounce. Just get a world map and all the recipes you can find and head to Findlay Market.

With all its life, energy, activity and differences, the neighborhood was proud. If a man were lying in the gutter he was taken in. Not to be out of the gutter but to be out of sight in the neighborhood. I was never afraid to walk anywhere within the boundaries of the neighborhood. I have no memory of ever seeing a single police officer.

I have unlimited memory of the library. I spent more time there than anyplace but home. Never hot or cold, steady even comfort. Never loud or throbbing, quiet and serene. A refuge from the world of the neighborhood. A gateway to the world beyond the neighborhood. A mirror of the present, picture of the past, and promise of the future. I had the same sense of reverence among the books of the library as among the pews of church.

In and among all the diversity and life around McMicken, there was one shared constant, we all lived in poverty. The only distinction was to what degree. That didn't mean much to me but there were periods when people around me were making comments I didn't understand. "It's a shame how they have to struggle." "Really, three adults and a youngster having to use the one toilet and hand sink built for a store." "When I dropped off the vegetables she put them in the drawer and there was nothing else in there, nothing." "Brother goes off on those long trips and Sister is so busy ministering. He's alone a lot. That's not so good for a child." "We're just glad we can bring them some of the slaughterhouse leavings but how often can you eat brains, tongue and innards." I didn't understand these comments because, although they seemed to be about me and my family, they were nothing like what I saw when I looked at my family and me.

Let me make one thing clear. I have absolutely no memories of being poor, going to bed hungry, or the deprivations of doing without. I enjoyed a personal relationship with The Almighty Wonder. I was busy with what I knew, engrossed with learning what I didn't know, husky and happy. I lived in the back of a church, which used to be a store and was now regularly visited by all kinds of people from all over the world. I had a comfortable, exotic and exciting life at 64 East McMicken.

Many of the people and events I experienced in the neighborhood molded my life. Not just big dramatic things by folks larger than life but also the little obvious common and fleeting events and people. Some of the people and events are unforgettable and it enriches me to share them.

S. G. MARKSITY:
THE REVEREND

He had worked hard to become Reverend Marksity. Now, he worked harder to be Reverend Marksity. But he was neither a pastor nor a minister. He did not have the personal character or interpersonal skills needed to serve a congregation. This was not his calling. I felt sad for him. I knew how hard he worked to be what he was not. The reality of The Peniel Missionary Assembly was that the head of the Church and acknowledged leader of the congregation, individually and as a body, was Reverend Olga Marksity. It was the first part of her gift to surface.

But he too had a gift. He had an incredible singing voice. When he exercised his gift, the impact was amazing. His lean frame produced a powerful, resonant, perfectly pitched baritone that seemed more for concert halls than congregations. When he would let himself go he had the same effect Olga had when she was preaching, total attention of those gathered and reverence for a clear gift from God. Unfortunately, he rarely let himself go. The reason was more unfortunate. Olga was never happy when he let himself go and made certain he could see her displeasure.

49

As always, whatever she wanted, he provided. There were times when I thought she was jealous that he could get the congregation to admire his singing. In any case, we frequently missed the pleasure of rejoicing in his gift.

This was not the only awkward area. As time passed I could see more clearly and more often that Olga was the preferred one. People could not identify with Reverend S. G. Marksity. In retrospect, I really saw this first when we visited the Assembly Of God where they were ordained. The people were polite to see him again but were anxious to see her. The conversation was not away from him but was directed toward her. He was missed because he was with her and she was sorely missed. They may have been equally accepted but she was the one respected. This attitude and the resultant behaviors only became more obvious as years passed. It was awkward between them in such instances. I could not understand how he felt. I knew how I felt. He was not so much my father, as the husband of my mother.

In the meantime their work was rewarded. Their start-up church provided the platform for her ministry and a congregation developed. A congregation of displaced foreigners, poor, lost and needy locals, and others, all looking for peace and love. A congregation, with no other place to worship, turned the store front into a Church. A Church where The Spirit of The Lord dictated the course of a service and the direction for the future. The Reverends Marksity took only what was needed to get by and everything else went to those who needed it more. They had their Church and it was a ministry, not an organization.

In this setting, he decided to answer his calling. He was certain he was to go to Yugoslavia as a missionary and spread the Gospel. In the political climate at the time, his missionary work could put him in physical jeopardy. He was determined to accept whatever happened. He was convinced it was his destiny to die in this endeavor. It was on this point that we had our most significant conversation as father and son. I had to understand his calling. I had to face the reality that he might not return. I had to know, as he knew, that I would be able to take care of the home front if this should occur. I was five at the time.

He had no trouble getting time off from his tailoring and was always welcomed with open arms when he returned to work again. I don't know how many missionary trips he made to Europe or his itineraries. But I do know each trip included three identical parts.

First, his packing. What he could put in a two-suiter suitcase, briefcase, shopping bag, and his pockets, astounded me then and has yet to be surpassed. He used one bed in the back room for staging and the other to hold the containers. He arranged all his clothes, shoes, belts, hats, gloves and boots. The first time I watched him empty every drawer, box, and make-shift closet, I wondered what he would leave behind. When he was finished, he had left nothing behind. And, he still had room for his Bible, notebooks, alarm clock, and maps.

Second, seeing him off from the marvelous train depot with its huge rotunda, gorgeous mosaics, leather seats, glistening metal fixtures, shiny floors and more. For these goodbyes it was always the same group, Olga, some people from the church, me, and The Missionary. As the train pulled out, Olga and I knew it would be a long time before we heard from, or about, Reverend Marksity. Watching the train disappear down the tracks, I knew it was my time to take care of the home front. Oddly, I don't remember our ever going to the depot to welcome him home.

Third, regardless where he had been, how long he had stayed, who he had worked with or what he had accomplished alone, his attitude upon returning home was always the same. Negative. But his was not the routine negative. He had a relationship with negative. Their relationship was intimate and boundless. He would clearly be physically drained. He would frequently be depressed to the point that I could feel his condition. He hated himself. He would spend considerable time asking God to forgive him for being such a failure. This railing against himself would continue long after his return and frequently became more intense as time passed. His self-abuse was difficult to witness and impossible to understand.

I wanted to ask him what it was about his trips that so demoralized him. But I was hesitant. I had no idea what could make a person so full of self loathing. My imagination concocted all sorts of odd devilments, but I knew I had no idea of the real reason. I was afraid that he had done something horrible and once I knew about it I would have to live with it forever. But I knew I had to have some understanding of what was going on and determined to ask him.

It was on a calm afternoon and we were sitting in the sun in the tiny courtyard outside the back room at 64 E. McMicken. We were polishing shoes together. After I asked him, he stopped polishing and began to stare at the ground. Finally, he looked up. I still remember the look on his face because it was the first and only time he let me see his true self. "Ronnie, I keep coming back. I keep coming back. I'm not supposed to come back. I'm supposed to die over there doing God's work." When he turned away he seemed to disappear under a black cloak. We went back to polishing our shoes. So, for him, living was failure. I still had no understanding of what was going on and determined to never ask him again.

At home he filled his life by working as a tailor and being a Reverend. The Peniel Missionary Assembly was thriving with general service to the congregation and specific help to the needy. Support was provided whether the need be spiritual, secular, physical or mental. Two pastors were certainly none too many and they divided the workload to suit their talents.

Olga led the congregation, delivered the sermons, ministered at tent meetings, revivals and camp meetings and to the constant flow of visitors who came to see her.

Reverend S.G. handled the schedules, classes, materials, supplies and administration of the church. Most importantly, he handled her every need. He would make all the arrangements and see to it that she was where she needed to be when she was supposed to be there. She considered what he did as lesser activities. I don't think she ever knew what it took to get her to, and from, a camp meeting or revival. All she had to do was get in the car and he'd take care of everything else.

He was The Reverend S. G. Marksity, my mother's husband. He lived like this from my first memories until my thirteenth year.

WORDS TO LIVE BY

The Reverend Olga was regularly visited by remarkable personalities and renown ministers from around the world. Nick Gruick was my favorite. In fact Brother Nick was one of my favorite people. From the adult point of view, he ministered in Eastern European and Middle Eastern countries with a spirituality that consistently reaffirmed The Unfathomable. From my childish point of view, he was a smile I couldn't respectfully hide before being overcome with happiness and laughing out loud.

Brother Nick saw life as few others did and was generous in sharing his views. During one visit, he was amazed by our '48 Buick. He kept muttering how it wouldn't fit in the streets of this place or that place. Places I had to look up on the globe in the library. One day, as he put it, "I offered the appropriate request and was granted permission to drive the four door monster."

On the way there was a traffic jam. After waiting just a minute, he began to nudge the Ford in front of us with our Buick. When the commotion subsided, he explained his action to the assembled participants, police, witnesses, and passers-by, as if explaining gravity to a group of youngsters. "In a traffic jam with camels, it is appropriate, and in fact helpful, for the camel behind the recalcitrant to nudge it and in so doing encourage its forward movement." Watching them watching him, I saw the purity of his gift. He had a positive impact on everyone there, even the driver of the Ford.

When I first met him I couldn't ignore his briefcase. He seemed to be guarding it. He had it with him all the time. When asked about it he said it held things he might need at any moment. I came to learn that all the time and any moment, his briefcase held a case of Double Bubble Bubble Gum which he shared as generously as he shared his views. He said the foreign kids loved it. As a sort of foreign kid, I can tell you, he was right. You had to laugh out loud.

It was during a meeting full of hard work to find an answer that Brother Nick stood and announced, "It is a simple answer. 'Don't lie.'" Everything stopped. The group that had been debating sincerely for hours was done. Nothing was added. There was no summary. Everyone had complete understanding. Everyone completely agreed.

That was the first time I witnessed that certain things that were said had a different impact or status than other things that were said. When such a thing was said, whether in Serbian or American, there was immediate understanding of, and agreement with, what was said. I wanted to know more about such sayings and listened for them.

After a prayer meeting, I listened while Brother Neville and a group of men talked about something to do with business. I didn't understand anything about business. But I did understand one man was in trouble and the group of men was being very sensitive with several different opinions. At a point, Brother Neville offered, "If you feel to make a loan do so, but do so without the expectation you will be repaid just because you should be." That was it. Just like before, complete understanding, total agreement and the group broke up. I had another example of what Brother Nick had demonstrated. I wanted more.

More came from Baba Maria. One afternoon, I walked into home and a very heated gathering. There were a lot of Serbs and they were unhappy. I took to my corner under the sink, all ears. They were all complaining about the same man but everyone had a different explanation for his behavior. Taking stock of their feelings, Baba waited while they let off steam. In the lull that followed, she calmly made a comment that literally translated was, "What the drunk says, the sober thinks." I thought it would have been better to say, what the man says when he is drunk is what he is thinking when he is sober. In the time it took for me to have that thought, the gathering was done, everyone leaving in understanding and agreement. These sayings had power.

On this particular afternoon I had been sent to Findlay Market where I dawdled so that I got home later than expected. As Baba took my package for the cooking, Olga remarked, "You know, if you're not careful, you're gonna end up with the same words to live by that I grew up with."

During the course of the meal that evening I learned about words to live by. There was actually a title for those things that were said that had greater impact or status. Everyone knew about them. Most people had their own private list. Baba was shocked that I thought her comment about drunks was special, she heard it from her grandfather. George wondered what I thought the Ten Commandments were? Olga tried to help me understand the origin and usefulness of words to live by and told me that the first for her were, "You should be back from the errand before I remember I sent you."

Over the next several years I heard and learned the words to live by that guided the world around me.

God keeps score. The good you do is balanced against the bad you do. Make sure the good outweighs the bad.

You have to earn your keep.

The world is hard. Be harder.

Protect yourself and be prepared at all times.

Never give in. Never give up.

Don't strike back. Strike first.

Be independent. It is better to have nothing but your independence, than to have everything and be dependent.

Don't Lie. Tell The Truth. Be Honest.

Never ask for help. Receiving help makes you indebted. It is not under your control how, or when, such a debt will be recalled.

Whenever you can, maintaining yourself, offer and provide help. But do this without the expectation that you will be able to recall such a debt.

What the drunken man says, the sober man thinks.

Obey your parents and the law.

Trust no one except family.

Blood is thicker than water.

Believe in the Lord.

Have faith in God.

In the course of learning these maxims I discovered one, "Children should be seen and not heard" was never applied to me because I didn't have to learn it, I lived it. Born into the world of The Matriarch and Reverend Olga, I was hearing and seeing extraordinary things. I had nothing to say. I naturally became a listener. It was not an accomplishment. I had no choice. Living in water, fish have to swim. Living as I did, I had to listen.

My being seen and not heard was very much appreciated by adults. It was not long until I was permitted to witness activities beyond my years. It became routinely accepted that I could go anywhere and see everything. This increased the wonder of my life. I was to learn that's not always fun.

An obvious by-product of my being seen but not heard was I never asked questions. This solidified my acceptance by all adults and turned out to be the source of benefits I would only comprehend years later.

Since I didn't ask questions, I had to develop other means of gaining understanding and satisfying my curiosity. The other means were a sense of subtlety, innuendo, reading body language, intuition, being totally aware of the surroundings, and discernment. During my childhood, these senses were developed at an accelerated rate to an exaggerated degree.

Circumstances promoting my development occurred routinely around Baba and Olga.

The examples with The Matriarch occurred in the front room of home and were carbon copies one of the other. Someone would come in. There were always reasons for such visits, from requests for opinion to being summoned. A discussion would occur. A decision would be made even if that decision was to put off a decision. There was always a conclusion. The someone would leave. I would have formed my opinions based on what I had observed. The Matriarch and her attendants would then discuss what had happened. I would compare what I saw with what they saw. For the better part of my youth, I learned that my observations identified only splinters of the forests before me.

Examples of my development with The Reverend Olga occurred anywhere and everywhere and involved individuals and multitudes. No matter the circumstances, suddenly there would be a focus of the moment. Only rarely could reasons for these events be identified, they just occurred. The focus was followed by the presence of The Spirit. You either felt this or you didn't. What was seen was not the key, the key was faith. Everything about these events was in the control of Something Greater. What was to be, emerged. Most of us felt the presence of God. Afterwards I would not listen as people explained what they saw. What I felt was more important.

Whether only seeing a splinter of the forest or overwhelmed, I was developing my senses of subtlety, innuendo, observation, intuition, awareness and discernment. These were the foundation of my approach to daily life.

Eventually I could recognize, list, and define words to live by. Not too long after, I could discriminate those that were important to me. That was when I realized they had become a part of me, my dogma. They were no longer words to live by, they were the words by which I lived.

UNCLE LOU AND AUNT ROSIE, THE BAKERS

They did not appear in my life in any fashion normal to a child becoming part of a family. Except for Thanksgiving, Christmas, New Years Day, and Easter, The Bakers and my parents spent no time together. As a result, almost all of my first impressions of Uncle Lou and Aunt Rosie were second hand, derived from watching and listening to the impressions they had made on others.

Most of what others said and did regarding Uncle Lou and Aunt Rosie convinced me that they were not part of, yet different from, the things around them and the biggest difference was that they were not seen as individuals, they were seen and related to as one. Anytime anyone mentioned The Bakers, words and actions became respectful to both Rose and Lou. Anytime anyone approached Lou and Rose they did so with deference to both, regardless if the matter related to only one. This two-are-one mentality included all the relatives. Considering that I was just a child, yet could see the treatment they received, points up just how significant was the position they held.

There was a much more powerful reason that I saw Rosie and Lou as one, Baba. From day one Baba spoke of Them, not of Rose or Lou but Them. She referred to actions They took that were of benefit to individuals, their church, the community, the family. She pointed out the merits in the way They got things done and emphasized that They were respected. But she almost never referred to either as an individual. This behavior of my Baba, you know—The Matriarch—was an endorsement from on high and I followed her example. The net effect of the preceding was that my Uncle Lou and Aunt Rosie were The Bakers and shared the same pedestal.

As mentioned, my family felt a family tree was something to be manipulated to one's advantage, regardless the advantage be real or imagined. So all I got about The Bakers was variations on the obvious theme, they were the perfect couple.

Before they met, they each worked hard, managed their monies, and saved with a vengeance. When they got married they joined their assets and behaviors. Not long after they got married they bought an all brick two family home, rented the second floor and had the tenants provide a steady cash flow. Things went well and a son, Ronnie, was born. Things went very badly when Ronnie died before he was three.

With the loss of what was to be their only child they may have been childless but their behavior was like the best of parents, they were open to help those in need and were generous to a fault. They lent money to family members and enabled us to have cars we couldn't afford. It was as if everyone in need became their duty and in time I came to see they were a soft touch. I also came to see that my Aunt Rosie and Uncle Lou enjoyed life and others enjoyed them.

With both working full time and with their talents and work

ethic, The Bakers enjoyed even better rewards. Put bluntly, in my eyes they were rich with a financial status I couldn't imagine. Neither could I imagine their unrelenting willingness to give, and not just money. They participated in a structured manner with formal commitments to those around them. For instance, she was an Eastern Star and he was a big time Mason. They also participated with those around them in supporting traditions such as being godparents, which in the Serbian culture was a serious position of esteem and carried with it responsibilities to help the godchildren. Having Lou and Rose Baker as your godparents was to be envied.

The Bakers maintained their extended family by staying in contact with the relatives in Europe. They went to visit, hosted more than a few to come and visit, and saw to it that the immediate family made at least one pilgrimage home to Yugoslavia.

They were often the subject of conversations among Baba, George, and Olga but were never there to participate. They were a most popular topic of conversations among others. However, no matter the group or situation, whenever Rose and Lou joined conversations, others seemed to listen somehow differently.

They came to our home on 64 East McMicken but did not ever enter the Peniel Missionary Assembly. They were Serbian Orthodox and attended their own church. Rosie sang in the choir and volunteered with gusto. Lou was part of the Church's secular administration. Together, The Bakers represented the church in certain Regional and National venues. Finally, as if it was their signature, they maintained a level of financial support that was uncommonly generous. People made it clear that The Bakers were among the mainstays of that church.

No one went to their house uninvited or on the spur of the moment. An invitation or a positive response to a request to visit was required. Until junior high, when I went to their house it was either for a holiday or when Baba went to watch television and took me along, she was crazy about 'I Love Lucy'. The Baker's standards applied to people coming and going. Stay too long and Lou would stand up and announce, "Rose, I think it's time we went to bed so these people can go home." And darned if he wasn't always right, the people were ready to go home.

I can't explain why I felt that their house was a step up from the houses of our other relatives. They did nothing to promote my feelings. However, in my mind I somehow knew they were significant and I think the house took on substantial status just because The Bakers owned it.

On the other hand, I can explain why the male half of The Bakers, Milutin Baken, was a significant presence in my eyes. He was a significant presence in the eyes of anyone with an ounce of sense. That he was born in Rumania and his father died when he was young are all the details I have of his history before Cincinnati. But, whatever his history, it was the subtleties of his appearance and his behavior, how he dressed, moved, watched, and spoke that could bring both people and situations up short. He was a man's man and if one looked closely it was obvious he was not restricted by the normal boundaries of routine life.

As my first impressions of The Bakers were primarily second hand, my first impressions of Uncle Lou were primarily third hand. With one exception, when he took me to my first major league baseball game at Crosley Field, we did not spend time being uncle and nephew. I could relate to my other aunts and uncles as their nephew but Uncle Lou was different. He had a unique relationship with Baba that I could only sense and never understand and to me, that relationship felt more ominous than curious. The result was that I related to my Uncle Lou Baker because we were both related to Baba.

Lou was average height, well proportioned, coordinated, and moved with the surety of those who always seem to be in shape. In all things he was a gentleman. His hair was silver, not white, shiny silver. If cool was a degree for measuring charisma, Lou Baker was frigid. Just as one extreme is people who look sloppy naked, Lou Baker looked dapper smoking on the steps of his front porch in a wife beater undershirt. He loved to tease anyone and anything and had a good sense of humor. Watching Lou produced pictures of happiness and comfortable moderation. Watching Lou produced feelings of anxiety about what was under that moderation.

He was full of surprises. One day, when I got to his house he was going through a closet, from way in the back he pulled out a box. It turned out to be a commemorative box with a fifth of The Glen Livet, a fifth of Crown Royal and two crystal tumblers. I wondered how it got in the closet. He had put it there. When did he put it there? A long time ago. Why? He knew the value of what he had been given and was appreciative but he didn't prefer these special drinks. He was a shot of Seagram's 7 guy so he put the box away, believing eventually someone who would really want them would get them. I did and did.

If smoking was a habit, for Uncle Lou it was a ceremony. From the beginning he noticed my fascination with his smoking and I was in the fifth grade when it finally happened. "You want to try it." Oh my yes. Could I? If I had been paying attention things might have been different but I wanted to smoke and didn't care that we were alone in his living room. He took his time and demonstrated his full seven-course ritual for lighting a cigarette. I was mesmerized as he handed me the lit Pall Mall and didn't waste a second to pull a huge drag. Along with air, a full third of the tobacco in that cigarette came shooting down my throat and into my lungs and stomach. He had cut the cigarette so that on the second drag it came apart. As I choked, the living room filled up and Lou led the charge of relatives wondering what in the world possessed me to take one of his smokes. I thought I was going to die. Lou almost died laughing. I didn't smoke cigarettes.

Uncle Lou worked as Service Manager in various high-end automobile dealerships until he retired. Packard was his favorite. After he retired, to keep busy, he sold products related to the auto industry on routes that were a pretext to visit his old buddies. He loved his work and loved cars and every year or so Aunt Rosie would call and tell me to be ready for a ride. We'd end up sitting on the wall in their backyard with real anticipation in the air. I am talking about genuine Christmas like excitement. In time, we'd hear a car pulling into the driveway and heading toward us which made the driveway a Christmas tree and the brand new car coming around the house the present underneath it. As the car came into view, my chest would leap and I would fall in love again. Once parked, we would go over everything until Uncle Lou would ask Aunt Rosie if she approved. She never knew what car he had bought until she saw it in the driveway. She never didn't approve. Of all these events, the 1953 two tone, green and crème Buick was my favorite.

On another occasion, Rosie was looking through their dresser to get me a hanky when she felt something in the back of the drawer. It was a watch box and she laughed and murmured, "That Bake, I wondered where he hid it." She opened the box and handed it to me. Inside was a top of the line white gold Omega wristwatch, untouched since he purchased it years ago in Switzerland. Aunt Rosie gave me the details. Lou didn't want anyone to know that he had it, it was just important that he had it.

He loved boxing and was disinclined to miss his Friday Night Fights on television. I had the feeling he had a relationship with boxing that was something special, something he was not showing me, and that was that. But, even if it happened that we talked together, I certainly had no desire to ask him questions he didn't want asked.

Uncle Lou's yard, house, cars, equipment, were always like his person, tiptop. I couldn't help but wonder how he managed this because I never saw him doing anything physical. More wonder was that he was clearly comfortable having others do things. Uncle Lou used his brother-in-law whenever he could but he had a laundry list of artisans and fix-it guys eager to work for a man who would recognize their efforts and paid them well. In time, I grew to understand that ex-Sergeant Baker and Uncle Lou The Service Manager provided my first real glimpse of management. More to Lou Baker's character, he had no qualms acting like he needed help.

However, he did have qualms about secrets. Over the years, Uncle Lou taught me that he had lots of secrets but trusted only one person with them, the other half of The Bakers, Ruzitsa Vukich. Like the rest of the family, I called Aunt Rosie, "Fufu." I'm sure there is some cute tidbit of who couldn't pronounce Rosie, but could pronounce it as Fufu, go figure, but I never heard that tidbit.

Anyone and everyone meeting Rosie for the first time came away with the identical first impression, she was the incarnation of nice and the reason for this impression was that she was just that.

As I was growing up, only the two of us knew the amount of attention and caring she showered on me. She would pick me up and go for rides during which she taught me how many other drivers were jackasses, in American and Serbian. It was her taking me downtown for Christmas shopping that planted the seed of how Christmas can be the celebration chronicled by Norman Rockwell, as well as the awesome spiritual experience of the season. In truth, I spent most of my grade school years wondering why she was so nice to me.

As for her background, the only thing anyone needed to know about Ruzitsa Vukich was that she was Serbian and The Matriarch's first born. What more could anyone need or want to know about her? Put another way, who would want to interrogate The Matriarch about her daughter, or later, probe Lou Baker about his wife? Not this kid.

Rose Vukich was born in Kikinda, Yugoslavia. She was Serbian to the core. From her very early years she helped her widowed mother Maria rear her three siblings, Viola, Olga, and Botta (Charlie). This included several relocations back and forth between America and Yugoslavia until they settled in Cincinnati. Once settled, not yet a teen, she started working in tailor shops and did so until she retired. School was not a highly rated option for Rose. She was a young girl when she met Lou and a teenager when they were married and became The Bakers. Rosie loved America and became a citizen but never abandoned her lineage or homeland. This respect and loyalty to her past remained a constant in her life and was often evidenced by her behaviors.

Rather than recall the harshness of her youth, she embraced what she called the privileges of her childhood. Fresh chicken was one. No matter the mountains of Serbia or the suburbs of Cincinnati, available chicken was proof of blessing. It was routine for Rosie to buy a live chicken and start the evening meal at the stump in the rear driveway. There she would cut off its head with a small hatchet and release the cluck. To her, this was great fun and she insisted that I see the reality of, "Running around like a chicken without its head." Whether this was ceremonial or just to keep in contact with her roots didn't matter, it meant fresh chicken and that made Rosie happy. As for me, I hated plucking the feathers and couldn't stand the smell of the water.

As a Serbian, Rosie was from the soil and determined to remain close to it. It was perfectly natural to her that she act like farmers the world over. No matter the size of the yard, in the suburb of Bridgetown she grew tomatoes, peppers, spices, herbs, fruits, and more.

As The Matriarch's eldest, Rose Vukich saw incredible toughness routinely demonstrated by her mother. No detail of the things she witnessed escaped the grasp of her Serbian blood.

Every person who related to Rosie, everyone, was surprised by how long it took to notice that she was missing two fingers up to the first knuckle of her ... which hand was it? She just made it impossible to notice or, after noticing, to ever again think about her hand. And yes, she worked in tailor shops, often as a seamstress, until she retired.

When her brother Botta took a flyer down his basement steps and landed in a coma, she reverted back to her youth as her mother's helper. Botta remained in the coma until he died. Rosie walked to the bus stop, rode to the bottom of the hill of his nursing home, walked up the hill and fed him, shaved him, bathed him, took his clothes and bedding home to wash and exchange the next day and then reversed her walks and bus ride home. She did this every single day for all the many years he lived. If you wanted to see Rosie, you planned your visit around the nursing home. Christmas, Thanksgiving, Monday, any day, every single day.

Rest assured that Rosie was not all toughness tooth and nails. Neither was she all loving nice and kindness. Underestimating her as too hard or too soft could put one on the wrong side of Rosie and that was a precarious position. From her beginning to her end, Rosie Vukich was her mother's daughter and from when she met Lou she was the female half of the Bakers.

Okay. But I had a brain full of things I wanted to know about my aunt and uncle as individuals and as one. Unfortunately, my aunt and uncle had no interest in me even asking questions. When I tried to get answers from Baba, she made it crystal clear that I had no need to know even what I already knew. These rebukes convinced me that there were secrets being kept and I committed to uncovering them.

I always wondered what it was about Lou that convinced The Matriarch to let him marry her firstborn. I suspected there must have been any number of gentlemen eager to marry the lady Rose. Was Lou the best prospect? Baba's response was that I knew nothing of marriage but allowed that Lou was a hard working Rumanian, loyal, honest, tough, and dependable. Well, that's a fine endorsement but how did she know so much about Lou? It took a long time but I was insistent and one day, using her annoyed voice, she filled me in. Baba, The Matriarch, knew Lou was hard working etcetera because they had worked together making and distributing bathtub gin.

I got the heck out of there and later thought about it. Sure enough there was no question. Running gin demands a whole lot more trust in, and a whole lot better knowledge of, the partner you're working with than almost anything you might think of. On the other hand, what you learn about whoever it is being sincere when he drops by under his hat with flowers to court mommy's eldest, can't measure up. She knew Lou alright.

From the beginning, Baba never referring to Rosie and Lou as individuals was unsettling. It just didn't feel healthy, more contrived than reasoned. Guess what? Maria Vukich treated Lou and Rosie as one, rather than individuals, for a very, very rational reason. She had arranged their marriage. Rosie and Lou were joined at the hip from the time Rosie was thirteen. The whole truth is that Baba saw to it that Lou and Rosie became The Bakers.

In fact I really didn't understand Uncle Lou and Aunt Rosie or our interactions until my teens. In this way they were in my life, in the background, felt but not seen. In time I came to feel their influence and recognize their handiwork. And now it's time to tell my secret, pay my respects and set the record straight. Starting in the third grade, for a considerable length of time, I thought The Bakers were my parents. That was the only way I could explain the way they made me feel.

The Bakers had one passport. When I saw the picture of the two of them sitting together smiling for the Government, it gave me a warm surge and for that instant it seemed the joint passport was made available just for the iconic two-are-one Bakers of The Matriarch's realm.

Finally, managing the closing of their estate, I came across a small, old, if not antique, case. It's hard to share the feelings that confronted me when I looked inside. The contents were impossible to challenge. Here was the truth about their most important secret. They were married well past fifty years when Lou died. They spent their lives together except for his Army service in Panama. The case contains their letters, one to the other, and the cards for any and all occasions, one to the other. Due to the number, it may very well be that this was every letter or card they had shared. In these glimpses of their love they called each other "Bake." Bake to Bake to Bake in a never-ending circle. I felt privileged to have found the case but after reading just a few samples, I felt I was intruding and never looked into them again.

Truly, The Bakers were one and continued to be after Lou died as Rosie chatted with him routinely until she joined him.

CONGREGATION

Last Sunday morning's attendance was a worrisome surprise. Some of The Regulars were missing.

The older ladies I called The Regulars included Serbs and other Slavic nationalities. 64 East McMicken was not in the center of any Slavic ghetto. In fact, the Serbian enclave was on the other side of Findlay Market by Central Avenue. So getting to church was not easy, yet the ladies managed to do so regularly. For one of them to be absent could mean sickness, or worse. So three of them being absent concerned me. They had taught me a great truth and I cared about them.

Visually there were interchangeable. Short heavy old women dressed in black, usually to include black babushkas. The weights of their lives were visible in their physical selves and heaviest in their eyes. In church they were on their feet with their arms high, singing and giving praise. They rejoiced so all could see their thankfulness to be alive. In church, their weights were removed and their spirits soared.

I was not alone in witnessing their worship. They were hearty as they prayed, listened, sang, and took part. Anyone could see and share their joy. I was able to see more because I was bilingual.

Our church services were not conducted in Serbian, Hungarian, or any Slavic language. At the Peniel Missionary Assembly all services were conducted in American. Few of The Regulars spoke any American. The ones who did, spoke only the barest broken bits. The truth they taught me had to do with worship. The truth of worship is not what is said or heard, it is what is felt.

The Regulars also taught me something about myself. I was uncomfortable with their appearance, particularly when they lifted their arms to sing or give praise. When they did so, the loose flesh under their upper arms would flop back and forth. I felt convicted that their appearance made me uncomfortable. No matter how I tried, I couldn't control my feelings. So I learned, for me, at this time—how people looked hindered my ability to see them.

Anyway, it's good to see all The Regulars are here for this Sunday's service.

SUMMER VACATIONS

Sometimes in the summers, when it would get hot and humid as it can in Cincinnati and tropical jungles, the fireman would open the hydrants and let us play. It was a wonderful treat. A better treat was once a summer, maybe twice, never more, when Baba would throw a party. It would be held in the all-purpose kitchen, dining, and on such occasions, party room of home.

Preparation was required for her party. First, the big galvanized wash tub was placed on towels in the middle of the room. It must have been three feet across and almost two feet deep. Next, one of the big standing fans from church was wheeled into the party room and positioned behind the tub. Finally, four folding chairs from church were arranged in front of the tub. However, the success of the party depended on the caterer. This responsibility was not granted lightly. The caterer who supplied Maria Vukich's party was gaining the highest profile referral.

On this occasion we were waiting for the caterer. I was nervous and excited as I knew that pomp and ceremony were coming. Finally, the noise from the street alerted us he was on his way. Baba waited until we heard his cart stop and then, with the style that only The Matriarch could carry, she headed to the street. As she approached the waiting caterer, a hush fell over the crowd that was gathering.

Baba was not one to rush decisions. With so many observers from the neighborhood, it was important she maintain her decorum. She acknowledged several bystanders and spoke to a few before she stopped at the curb.

The caterer was prepared. Looking back I imagine he was rehearsed. He acknowledged my grandmother and stated his appreciation for the opportunity to be of service. Today he had a special offering and only hoped it would please her.

Having paid his respects, he set about making a production of looking over his wares. He stretched up, down, side to side, forward and back, until finally he settled on the prize. Presenting it to Baba, he and the crowd waited to see if his offerings would satisfy her standards. She hesitated just long enough, and then gave a slight nod of approval before turning and entering the narrow covered alleyway to home.

With her nod, the fate of what was sure to be the longest lasting of all the blocks of ice in this load was sealed. The proud Iceman used huge tongs to grip the monster and manhandle it through the crowd and side entrance and ultimately into the tub. Before leaving he was gracious with recognition of Baba. She in turn offered her thanks which was more than he could have expected. He left, the door was closed and we were alone in the party room.

The fan was adjusted so that it blew across the ice. Baba and I sat on the folding chairs in front of the cold air coming off the block. I don't remember how long the ice lasted or how long the rooms stayed cool after it was gone, but I savored every moment. They were my summer vacations.

THE MATRIARCH

Friday night was a time of excitement and accountability. It was payday. A day for the family to get together at the Reading Road residence. Earlier the family lived on Reading Road. A day for meeting one's responsibilities.

It always began the same way. As family members arrived, they would be happy to greet each other and more happy to greet Baba and discreetly give her their pay. Rose and her husband Lou Baker. Viola and her husband Nicky Golusin. Olga and George. Baba's son Botta and his wife Lena. Then it was customary for the men to gather around a bottle of Four Roses with their individual shot glasses while the women chatted together. Jokes, gossip, the normal language of families at the end of a long hard work week filled the air.

After everyone had arrived and had time to mingle, Baba Maria Vukich would make a gesture. Then, as if both were choreographed, the position and mood of those gathered would change. Participants would be seated around the table in the pecking order she determined, which usually reflected respect for age or length of time at the residence. As people took their seats, Baba would return to them those monies she allocated from their incomes. From this they were expected to manage their lives and build their homes, families and futures. She kept what she kept.

With the completion of this payday ritual, the visiting continued. These times together were spent many ways, from suppers of major proportions to casual chatting around cold left overs. But regardless the menu, the atmosphere was familial and full of accomplishment and recognition. The mood optimistic. The spirits buoyed.

The preceding was told to me in almost the exact words by each of Baba's daughters and Rosie's husband Uncle Lou. I never heard this from her son Botta. There was something else exactly the same about their recalling the paydays. For each of them, it was one of their happiest memories. For all of them, those were the good old days.

I was never in the residence on Reading Road, but this picture of Baba as The Matriarch made it easier to accept her other roles. As mentioned, it was common for her to call meetings with members of the Serbian community and common for them to ask for her time. However initiated, these meetings generally involved fact finding, clearing up misunderstandings, guidance, and judgements. From all such meetings I witnessed, the following remains the strongest memory.

I was five years old and in the front room at 64 East McMicken. I was seated on the floor leaning against the cabinet next to the sink when he was brought in. He was stocky and strong. His clothes were wrinkled and spotted. His shoes dirty. His huge muscular hands made it impossible to miss the dirt around and under his fingernails. He appeared to be growing a beard and his hair was rumpled. He seemed full of energy but as time passed, I recognized it was anger.

Lou and some other men I didn't know were escorting him. I

had never seen my uncle in such a serious condition. Something about him was foreboding.

The man was led to the chair across the table from Baba. He made a point of avoiding her gaze. She made a point of not saying a word for a very long time. The man fidgeted, played with his hands and did his best to avoid looking up. The room was dead quiet.

Finally, she said his name. He stopped fidgeting and became immobile. She waited. I don't know how long she waited but it was very clear she would have waited forever. After some time the man must have sensed this because he looked up. She asked him if he knew why he was there. His first reaction was not to answer. From where I was sitting, I could see that it quickly went through his mind that it was in his best interest to speak. As this flashed across his face, he said no, he didn't know.

She said she would tell him. She had been told that he had beaten his wife. Had he beaten his wife?

In the spirit that answering was his best action, he attempted to answer immediately and started to explain.

She cut him off and asked again. Had he beaten his wife?

Again he began to explain and again she cut him off. Had he?

He said no he hadn't beaten her but he had hit her.

I realized everyone in the room was extremely tense. I was glad to be on the floor near the underside of the sink.

Then, my grandmother Maria Vukich did something I never imagined. She reached across the table with both her arms extended, making it clear she wanted him to join hands with her. I can not explain the look on his face as he put his hands in hers. She began to speak in a soft, knowing voice. I didn't understand what she meant by the affects of drink but I could feel she understood his circumstance. As she continued to speak, I saw her exhibit a maternal admonition more caring than I had ever seen her express to any of her children. By the time she completed offering him guidance, she was treating him with an understanding I had only seen her extend to one other person. Me. Her final admonition was that he must stop this behavior. She believed he would do so. With this, she sort of shook his hands, released them, and motioned that the meeting was over.

The man was unable to speak as he got up. I couldn't understand how his eyes could be so full of liquid yet not one drop escape to his cheeks. As if he were a criminal given a reprieve and astonished by his good fortune he began to thank her and thank her and thank her while, in a tentative way, he backed out of the room, into the back room and out into the courtyard. By the time I adjusted to his leaving and returned my focus to the room, I found that everyone and everything was back to normal, except me. This was going to take a long time for me to digest.

Time passed. How much I'm not sure, but enough that when the second meeting occurred I was taken by surprise. The setting and circumstances were the same as the first time but the man's appearance was different as he had shaved. This time he knew where he was to sit and made no attempt to avoid her eyes. His face was full of pleading and remorse.

Unlike the first meeting, she started as soon as he was seated. She said his name and as he looked up she put her palms flat on the table and began. "You were here before and I believed you would stop hitting your wife. I've been told you have done it again. Have you?"

He didn't attempt to avoid or explain, he merely lowered his head and said yes.

She barked his name and his head sprang up, his eyes wide

and locked with hers. She said, "This is the only time I will tell you. Do not touch your wife again." She paused and the look on her face was one I had never seen before and didn't want to see again. I turned my head and realized my hands were sweating and I couldn't swallow.

She motioned for Lou to stand him up and move him out. He was escorted out and I could hear muffled sounds as Lou and the other men led him to the street. When I looked up I realized everyone in the room was maintaining the position and look they had when she made her final comment. They were all waiting for what she would do next. When it was clear he was gone, she raised her palms from the table and everything seemed to go back to normal. My heart was beating very fast and my stomach hurt.

Again time passed and again I don't know how much. He was brought in so unexpectedly that I hardly had time to get into my safe spot by the sink. It was clear he had been in some sort of accident as he had red blotches that were sure to be bruises and cuts about his face. He was summarily dumped in the chair and there was true fear on his face.

Maria Vukich said his name and he didn't react. She said it again and before he could react, Lou grabbed his head and jerked it straight so she could look him in the eye. In a voice that terrified me, she said, "I told you not to come back."

That was it. He was escorted out and the session was over. Everyone left and Baba went into the other room. I didn't know what to do. I stayed by the sink.

Not too many days later, but enough that my body returned to normal, I was running an errand to the spice store. As I was waiting for the spices, I thought I saw the man outside the store but he was so short he must be sitting down. What was he doing?

As soon as the spices were ready I hurried out to see if it really was him and why he looked like he was sitting.

Outside I saw it was the man. He was sitting in some kind of funny chair and both his legs were extended straight forward. Then I saw that he was looking at me and as I stared he yelled, "My knees are broken." I ran back home with the spices, left them on the table in the front room and continued running back outside and over to the playground where I found a little corner where I could sit — and be alone.

CONGREGATION

Hey, I can't believe it. That's the guy from the playground. What's he doing here on Sunday morning? Is that his mom or older sister? It must have been two weeks ago when he was talking with some other guys and I heard the word church. I got a little closer and heard he hated going to church. They noticed me listening and all of a sudden I was included. He was Catholic, one was a Methodist and a couple others were other things. They asked me what I was. I said I was a Christian. For some reason that wasn't enough because they wanted to know what kind of Christian? I answered, non-denominational. They looked at each other and then at me kind of funny and asked what the heck was I talking about? I started explaining about The Peniel Missionary Assembly. In no time they agreed, "Oh, you're a Holy Roller" and the conversation was done and they were on their way. Now, here he is. I'll go say hello after the service. I wonder what a "Holy Roller" is?

MY AUNT VIOLA

My Aunt Viola was the first branch of the family tree I became aware of after Baba, Olga, and George. She was Baba's middle daughter, between Rose the oldest and Olga the youngest. I knew absolutely nothing about her childhood, young adulthood or marriage to Nicky when Viola Vukich became Viola Vukich Golusin.

My first memories of her are from church. She attended church in blocks, there for months or a year, not there for months or a year. When she attended she played the piano, led the singers, and did all kinds of things to help Reverend Olga and the church. Aunt Viola was typically Serbian in appearance, prim and proper in behavior, and the model of a Christian in belief.

I never felt close to her. Maybe it was because the backdrop of our relationship was church. Maybe it was because we spent no private time together or because she had two kids of her own, Gloria and Donald. Maybe it was because she never drew me close. She had an aloof air about her, circumspect. According to Olga, she was loving. I wasn't sure about the loving but she was nice and seemed kind. I just couldn't get a feeling of her. Maybe

85

it was because, in my eyes, she was the image of a real Lady and I was just a kid.

I had a clear feeling about her house on Glenmore, it was my favorite. A huge frame Victorian with rock basement, coal and root cellars, ten foot ceilings on the first two floors and a finished attic. The first floor had a solarium and I could walk into the fireplace in the dining room. There were closets, stairs, nooks and crannies all over the place. It was the perfect house for exploring and pretending and at Christmas it had a tree with a train set running round.

During one visit to Glenmore, a man was taking pictures of Donald on a pony. A real live Paint. Donald had two outfits and they took pictures of him in both. One, a cowboy rig of hat, shirt, bandanna, vest, gun-belt and chaps. The other, Indian buckskin leggings and jacket with rawhide fringe, moccasins, quiver with bow and arrows, and a chief's headdress. The headdress was authentic with real feathers. Viola saw how I felt about the outfits. When Donald got too big for them she asked him to give them to me. He said no. In time she saw to it I got most of the cowboy rig and the headdress. She said it was our secret. I had the headdress till Olga pitched it after I left home.

I made another visit to Glenmore and we shared another secret. It was a fall afternoon and Olga, George, Baba, and I were dividing our time living on East McMicken and Orchard Court, which was off Herbert off Glenmore. I was riding my bike when the local bully spied me. I knew his reputation and had made up my mind I wouldn't become one of his victims. So as soon as I saw him I did some quick figuring. Going home was useless because no one was there. My only hope was to make it to Aunt Viola's. But that was a long way from the bottom of Herbert. I had no choice. I pointed up Herbert and started pumping.

He started pumping after me. I never worked as hard on my bike but he was bigger and stronger and as we raced up Herbert he was steadily gaining on me. Could I make it to her house before he caught me? When I turned left on Glenmore he started yelling what he was going to do to me when he caught me. It seemed he would catch me as he was closing fast and when I finally reached her driveway he was right behind me. Then he just stopped. I was glad but couldn't understand why he quit.

He had seen her before I did. Aunt Viola was raking leaves in the front yard. She was happy to see me and sensed there was more going on. She asked if my friend wanted to join us. I answered he wasn't my friend and had been chasing me. She started toward him with her rake and in a loud voice asked what kind of bully was he, picking on a kid half his size. He looked like a coward to her. A coward who needed a lesson. She yelled for her son Donald to come on out and give this cowardly bully a thrashing. He needed to know Donald was about twice his size. As soon as she started toward him he got nervous and by the time she called for Donald he was falling all over himself to get out of there. Seeing him go she turned back to the yard saying, "Always attack a bully. They're mostly just fraidy cats."

I didn't know what to say or do. I asked if I could help with the leaves. She said of course. A little later she told me not to worry, she was sure he wouldn't bother me again. Still later she told me to stop looking for Donald, he wasn't home. She had made that up to scare the bully. She was right, he never bothered me again and I never forget her lessons about bullies and the value of making things up.

When I left home in 1965, these were my only memories of Aunt Viola. From '65 to '80 my contacts with her were memorable for the other people or topics involved, never for her. She was there, in the shadows, an indistinct, non-participative observer who disdained unpleasantness.

In 1980, a relationship began between Viola and my wife and boys. They spent time together and later Nicky was included. By the mid '80s Aunt Viola and Uncle Nicky were pleasant additions to our family. Then Donald died. Then Nicky died. Aunt Viola carried on.

In the early '90s she was hit by cancer. She fought hard and long, but this Christmas she was sick and felt it was to be her last. As we were getting organized to move into the dining room, she asked that we sit by the fire together. She had a request. Once settled, she started.

"Ronnie, this isn't easy but it needs to be done. I have let it go too long. I know I should do this. I know I should have done it long ago. Never mind." She paused and looked at me as if seeing me for the first time. Studying me she made a face I took to mean she'd realized something. She continued. "Ron, you do know I trust you?"

She saw I had no clue. Not easily, she reached over and took my hands in hers. This was the most caring physical contact we ever had and she meant it to be a clear message. She smiled. "I have always been proud of you, starting at McMicken. All of us respect you."

I was astonished, speechless, touched. I knew when she said "All of us." she meant The Vukichs and Lou. She was surprised if not shocked by my reaction. She started again.

"I don't know how you couldn't know but now you do. It is because of who you are that I am asking you this favor. I want you to promise me something. Promise me you'll see to it Saka never gets another cent from Rosie. Not one penny more of the Baker's money. She has taken enough already. I know what she has been and what she is. I know she will take anything and everything from anyone and everyone. Protect my sister. Protect Rosie from my daughter. Promise?"

That she referred to The Vukichs showed she was back in the good old days when The Matriarch demonstrated facing one's responsibilities was the honorable and only option. That she called her daughter Gloria by her Serbian name, Saka, authenticated this as a Serbian edict, not a favor. That she verbalized what was never said before—Gloria had been receiving $200 a month from Rosie and Lou forever and more whenever she could—showed just how much Aunt Viola trusted me.

More words were unnecessary for me to understand the following. This is what she had been carrying over the years. She knew what was going on from day one. She just made it her life's work not to validate evil by admitting its existence. Of course she was circumspect. Not participating was her way of diminishing the negative things that filled her life. Her way to live with the ugly truth about her husband Nicky, her daughter Gloria, and her son Donald. She stayed in the shadows with her own misery. She had never confronted her daughter and couldn't do so now. She acknowledged she and Nicky had played the biggest roles in making their daughter what she was. They deserved the pain that resulted from genuflecting to Gloria's every whim and desire while ignoring Donald. They deserved the loss of self respect and the loss of the respect of others. She knew all this and lived with it.

I was humbled by her trust but didn't like the assignment. It was none of my business. It was destined to be ugly, dirty. No matter. I didn't let Aunt Viola know how I felt. I promised I would comply. Of course I would. The only question was when? As we moved into the dining room for Christmas dinner, in a voice only I could hear, she gently offered, "Silly boy. I've always loved you." That was the first time she ever told me those words.

She was no longer in the shadows as I finally had a feeling of my Aunt Viola. The respect I had for her playing the piano in the church resurfaced as an epitaph. Prim and proper in behavior, the model of a Christian in belief, the image of a real Lady.

Viola Vukich Golusin died the next year.

RED HOT WINTER

I loved the four seasons. They were my friends and completely different, each looking and acting totally unlike the others. It was never easy to say goodbye to one, even while welcoming another. I developed opinions about each. I found they were equal in my eyes, but not in the eyes of most people. Oh most people liked them well enough but for most people spring and fall played second fiddle to summer and winter. It was not easy to guess which season anyone liked the most. Almost everyone liked winter the least.

Winter at 64 East McMicken was cold.

The large pot-bellied stove in church was not lit during non-service days. The church was cold by Monday morning and kept getting colder till preparations for the Wednesday evening prayer meetings. For those meetings and Sundays, George would start the stove early and by service time it was fine.

The obvious reason church was cold was the big front windows. In the daytime, with the sun streaming in, it could be considered warm but without the sun … forget consider … it was cold. The darker the day the colder the church. Regardless the day, at night it was bitter cold. On nights of the days when the church was not used, it was Arctic cold.

During winter, water was a problem in church as people's coats and feet were wet. The large rug inside the front door did its best but ended up soggy. When attendance was high, the rug would become soppy, the floor more than damp. During the course of a winter, more than one rug was pitched, tattered and torn victims of winter water.

Snow was not a problem. It was easy to clean off the front sidewalk and four by five foot stoop and this was done regularly. Only when it really blew and drifted against the door did snow make it into church.

Ice was another matter. Ice on boots and shoes left footprints on the floor that went from bold to barely as worshipers took their seats. Ice sitting defiantly on rubbers and leathers. Some ice gave up early, some later, some lasted to the first hymn but no matter the length of defiance, all ice ended up in puddles on the floor. Ice on hair, hats and coats, stuck until it would just not be there anymore.

Ice on glass could only be experienced sitting by the front windows and door. It was extra cold but worth it. I saw ice slowly show itself at edges where the windows met the frames. It would spread, slowly. It was very thin. So thin I could write in it. I learned that what I wrote could be seen later unless I smudged it out with my hand. This was not a cheap lesson. I became an expert smudger. As ice continued slowly spreading, it became thicker. If I looked closely, I could see it had cracks or lines that were like patterns. Each growth of ice had its own design, its icyprints. It would keep growing and get so thick you could pick off a chunk if you worked at it. Such chunks had a metal sort of taste and made me more cold but I still popped them in my mouth. It was pretty normal during the middle of winter that on Wednesday mornings, when the stove had been cold the longest, the ice would be thick around the entire window frames and thin toward the centers. Sometimes there was only a hole as big as my head that I could see out of, all the rest was ice.

During services, the only cold places were up against the windows and door. Every place else was comfortable and near the stove it was too hot.

The temperature of church had no impact on the temperature at home as warmth or cold from church was dissipated in the hallway.

At home, water, snow and ice were not a problem. Plus, "…in the middle of the back room on a round metal sheet that it thought was its throne, the black iron stove dominated the scene and demanded to be looked at first." It was during winter that the stove got its attitude. In winter it did not have to demand. We all looked after it first. I clearly remember being taught how to treat the stove.

Since the only heating in the front room was from the cookstove, we spent a lot of time in the back room. As near the throne as possible was my position. Of course we had other techniques for keeping warm. I slept wearing woolen socks, a knit cap, long johns and pjs. Baba and I warmed each other. If it was wicked cold, we put hot baked potatoes under the covers by our feet. They kept us warm for an amazing long time.

During the coldest times it was normal for parts of the stove to turn red. This was common after the stove was stoked. Waking up during the night and seeing the royal stomach or chest glowing was itself warming. But no matter how bright the glow, it dimmed as I watched.

On the night of this experience, all four of us were home and it was plenty cold outside. I woke up in the middle of the night and the stove's stomach and chest were glowing. Wonderful. But wait? I had never seen this before. This time the pipe going to the ceiling was also glowing. In fact, that brightness is what woke me up. As I watched, the stove and pipe glowed brighter. That was different. This continued until all of a sudden, at the top where the pipe went through the ceiling, it began to smoke.

I called out and George woke first. He got Olga and Baba awake and they made a great ruckus.

I layed in bed watching the stove and pipe get brighter and then the spot where the pipe hit the ceiling had a flame in the middle of the smoke.

Baba told me to get my boots, coat, and blankets and follow her.

This was distracting. I was fascinated by the way the glow had turned to a smoking glow and then a flame appeared. The pipe was burning like a really big candle that is sputtering because it's about to go out. Baba called and I lit out after her.

It was really cold out in the courtyard. I kept wondering why we didn't just go into the church. Baba was not as proud of my common sense questions as she usually was.

George had gone off to get the firemen who were just down the street.

I went back inside for a peek and could see the flames. They were not sputtering now. They were solid and happy. It was really exciting. Baba ordered me to her. I had heard her use that voice before and decided I'd go by Olga instead. Once there, I asked if she thought we were going to be able to get back to bed? I hoped this question explained to her and Baba why I went to Olga. They knew what I was up to but let it pass.

Back to the action, I saw a lot of people had come out to watch and then a whole bunch of firemen showed up. In the commotion I took another peek inside. I saw the red hot metal of the stovepipe and melting linoleum and roof tar. Then one of the firemen yanked me out of the way and Olga about choked me to death with her claw of discipline. I knew I wouldn't get another peek but the smells of the metal tar and linoleum told me what was going on. The firemen set to work and in no time had everything under control. The crowd broke up and that's about all I remember. Where we went that night, what happened next, I have no clue. But the thrill! The feeling of adventure! Oh it was neat.

For the record, it turned out the cause of the fire was the coal. It was too good. George stoked the fire as usual with coal donated by someone in the church. But this batch was a better type and burned hotter than anything we had before. We didn't know anything about better types of coal. When your coal is being donated, you don't specify the type. We were very happy just to get coal. The type was never a concern. I will admit the amount was sometimes a concern.

OLGA: PASTOR OF THE PENIEL MISSIONARY ASSEMBLY

By this time I had a pretty good idea of what was what at church. The Reverend Olga Marksity was what was what. She was the life of the ministry. She was the spiritual leader of the congregation. She was The Pastor of The Peniel Missionary Assembly. The Reverend S.G. was her assistant. All the other ministers who participated, were visitors; apostles passing by.

Her consecration to God was complete. He was her life. Whatever He wanted her to do, she would gladly do. No being or thing, encroached or approached her relationship to The Almighty.

At this point, He wanted her to be The Pastor of The Peniel Missionary Assembly. To shepherd the flock at 64 East Mc-Micken and to help other shepherds, as called. Everything she did related to and derived from her fulfilling her ministry. She ministered with joy in her heart. And that was it. She did not look to the past for what was done. She did not look to the future for what she might do. She ministered in the moment and everything else she left to faith.

Her efforts began with focus on the three events of each week, the two Sunday services and the Wednesday prayer meeting. I could never tell if she was reviewing the last week or preparing the next week. Whichever, both involved reading, meditating, writing, and a lot of praying. Beyond this basic focus, Pastor Olga's weeks were filled with categories of activities.

Ministering. As a preacher, she was irrelevant. She made it clear that everything that came from her was from Him. She was an incredibly gifted teacher. She caused understanding. As a counselor and leader, she gave precisely what was needed, in the perfect sized doses.

Meetings. With individuals within her flock, from other flocks, or those that were all alone. To offer help, support, time, or sweat. To receive help, support, time, or sweat. Of the meetings, my strongest memories are those involving finding food, shelter, work, and some hope for a future for displaced people. These DPs were mostly from Slavic countries.

Visits. As much as possible, she visited anyone and everyone who needed help, or only thought they needed help. The fact she would go anywhere to minister, amazed me. The fact she never went anywhere just to socialize, didn't.

Deciding. What were the most pressing needs? Who can we solicit for what? How will we collect what is given? How should we allocate?

Evaluating. When faced with a spiritual matter, Pastor Olga was all patience and thoughtfulness. When faced with a secular matter, Olga shot off an answer before the question was complete. She switched spiritual and secular hats quickly. In doing so, she made it clear she didn't like the secular hat one bit, it took time from her true priority. As The Pastor, Reverend Olga knew and kept her life's priorities better than anyone I have yet to meet.

98

Living with The Pastor was serious and very quiet. I attended a lot of church related sessions, seen but not heard. Church related activities such as reading, studying, and contemplating, don't generate much noise. Praying, even less. Conversations were muted. I learned to occupy myself, and to do so, quietly.

CONGREGATION

It's always neat when kids attend. Donnie and Kathy Christoff are my favorites. Their mother Selma lets them sit with me in the back while she sits up front. She's very nice but sort of confusing. She's not a Slavic baba, wears colorful clothes, has light skin and isn't old, but she's heavy like a baba, maybe even fatter. I never saw any Mr. Christoff. Me and Kathy and Donnie always have a good time together. I don't know if we are friends. Probably not really friends. Maybe playmates. More like churchmates. Yeah, churchmates.

ORCHARD COURT

Sometime during kin-knee-garten, that's the way it was pronounced at home, we began transitioning to Western Hills. We split our time living on East McMicken and Orchard Court in a rotation reflecting the church schedule and my going to kinkneegarten. My report card shows that during kinkneegarten I was absent 24 days. The transition was not real smooth.

Orchard Court was a picturesque eight house side street off Herbert off Glenmore. I didn't know it was in the suburbs. We lived on the second floor of a two family owned by friends of Brother Nash, the minister at The Assembly Of God where Olga and George were ordained. It was no surprise others helped us improve our living conditions but the picturesque part needs some explanation. It was picturesque to me coming from East McMicken. To everyone else, it was a lower middle class dead end.

During the first grade I lived almost exclusively on Orchard Court. Sometimes the four of us were there, sometimes there were combinations of two or three of us. A lot of times just Baba and I were there. From the second grade on, all four of us lived together on Orchard Court. I lived there over three years, but it never became my neighborhood. I continued to attend The Peniel Missionary Assembly regularly and 64 East McMicken remained my neighborhood. Orchard Court however, became my campus. Its curriculum was Americana. I began learning right off that the suburbs were not the ghetto and Americana was not Serbian.

The kitchen exit is the only memory I have of the interior of our apartment. This detail remains because I didn't like heights and the back steps, outside the kitchen, were three floors up due to the way the ground slanted from the street to the back yard. Those sets of wooden steps were a constant call to courage. Maybe I don't have a detailed memory of the apartment because it was too much better than East McMicken. Too big an adjustment. Too hard to accept that I now lived in such a place while others, the majority of the people I knew, didn't.

The outside of the building was light colored clapboard. The roof of the first floor porch was our uncovered porch with the fancy railing. Neither apartment in the building was back of a church that had been built as a store. Both apartments were built for how they were used, as homes. Like the downstairs apartment, our apartment had windows. In this suburb all the houses were built as homes and all had windows all over the walls.

There were driveways leading to garages. Personal parking slots like that of the brewery's boss with his two toned snazzy little Crosley convertible. But there was no brewery or fire house or Findlay Market or library around our house, there was nothing but houses. Houses with front yards and huge back yards.

Everywhere I looked on the Orchard Court campus, wonderful things were growing. There was grass, flowers, bushes, shrubs, hedges, and trees. Trees of all sizes, from little to big-old-timers that maybe the first Indians planted. Trees that had beautiful flowers. Trees that had leaves that changed to the most amazing colors in fall and then fell off to be raked into piles that I jumped into. Trees that didn't have leaves, they had needles which never changed color or fell off. There was grass everywhere, even between the curbs and sidewalks.

The place was a fantasy and I was living in it, but at first I was uncomfortable. All the neighbors were constantly yelling. They sounded like they were angry with each other. At 64 East Mc-Micken, had we heard voices like those on Orchard Court, we would have gone to see what the ruckus was about. They were so loud you could hear everything as you walked by.

This was way different from our house where whispers and low volumes were normal and I knew never to air our dirty laundry in public. Baba, Olga and George never talked loud enough to be overheard. If Olga and George thought they were overheard, they'd change languages. Of course this fit the church, but for us, no matter the place, quiet was a mark of dignity. I was told I must have mastery of myself and keep my private self private. As for our new neighbors, they aired their laundry, dirty or clean, and let their private things be public.

In time, the campus of Orchard Court taught me the neighbors weren't yelling, they were talking normally. We were talking abnormally. These people had nothing to hide. They didn't care if a passerby overheard their conversations. They weren't careful, suspicious, paranoid. They didn't practice those behaviors. They weren't Serbians. This Americana curriculum was strange. Strange and hard.

The curriculum may have been strange and hard but living on campus was wonderfully strange.

Once I got used to the noise, I could see more. It was astonishing. Our neighbors had so much food and money they could feed and take care of animals. Animals! And not for food. I learned these were called pets. Fish, birds, cats, dogs, a turtle, all as pets. I was living with the rich.

Then there were the animals and birds that were not pets, they just shared the neighborhood with us. Squirrels, they weren't afraid of heights. Chipmunks, rabbits, raccoons, birds, bees, bumble bees, wasps, crickets, lightning bugs, daddy long legs and more. I'd never seen anything like it.

Neither had I seen anything like these adults. There were no men around during weekdays. They all had jobs. There were no women around during weekdays, they were all busy as housewives. Well, all except Olga, we already know about her relationship to being a housewife. The adults didn't show up till the weekends. Then they were all over the place, cutting grass, cleaning cars, working in yards, shoveling snow, whatever, yet at one point or another they'd stop to chat in the middle of the street. They didn't act like they were good friends or knew each other well, they just lived together. Compared to Serbian, Americana was straightforward.

As I listened to the neighbors when they chatted, it was nothing like East McMicken. This was not a place where hope and despair, with every nuance in between, could be heard. They stood in the street and yards and were making plans. This was not where they were going to end. This was just where they were now. They all had better places in mind. For me, I couldn't imagine a better place.

Another difference between my neighborhood and my campus was the proximity to Aunt Viola. From our place on Orchard Court, all I had to do to be in her back yard was cut through the dead end, turn right and go up the steep street to the corner. This is not to suggest I was a frequent visitor. Orchard Court was teaching me Americans didn't expect or offer invitations for every visit. Americans just dropped in on friends or relatives and were okay when friends or relatives dropped in on them. But I was Serbian and so was my Aunt. So I'd go up and take a look at the place every now and then but never knock on the door. If Aunt Viola were outside, I'd wave hello in passing. If her husband were outside, I'd head back home, I hadn't fit him in my life just yet. I never saw their daughter or son. No matter, it was neat to have relatives so near, even though as long as they lived there I never just dropped in. Sometimes I learned the lesson on campus but just couldn't practice it.

Here's something else about campus. Every family on Orchard Court had a car! Every one.

Sounds began to teach me more of the differences between the ghetto and suburb. First the sounds that were not there, trucks, traffic, street vendors, hustle and bustle. Then sounds never heard before. Dogs barking, cats meowing, so many different bird songs and one, Olga said they were doves, that sounded like a warm bed on a cold night, a cool shade on a hot day, soothing I guess you'd call them. Wind in the trees in all kinds of faces, gentle wafting to fierce howling. Insects I could hear but couldn't find, of course the bumble bees I could find real good. I lived in a symphony of life.

I learned even more from the sounds of people. During the late afternoons and early evenings, I began to hear parents calling their children. Time to come in and do your homework. Let's get going, it's time for supper. Okay, it's time to stop playing. There was no calling around East McMicken. I knew what time I was supposed to be home and it was my business to make sure I got there before that time. The American approach was a lot easier, all a kid had to do was wait to hear the call.

Then I began to see that being a kid here was just too easy. On Orchard Court, "Children should be seen and not heard." were not words to live by, they were words nobody used. In this suburb, kids were the center of attention. They all had everything they could possibly need. They seemed to have everything they could possibly want. And to have all this they didn't have to do anything but act the way they felt. I knew I'd have to learn to play with these kids so they could teach me how they finagled such a situation.

Then suddenly one day my campus gave birth to a gift I have enjoyed ever since. Church bells. Think of it, I lived in a church with other churches downtown but had never heard church bells. Okay, our church didn't have bells, very few retail stores have church bells I'm sure, but there were churches downtown with bells, yet I had never heard them. Church bells, how can gonging be so serene?

When I started playing with kids, the door to their world opened. I went in real slow, it was too much for me to handle. For example, where we played. The playground downtown had swings, a teeter-totter and a slide. Orchard Court had swings, teeter-totters, a slide, sand boxes, ladder things to climb on and hang from and the geography of all cowboys and Indians. Downtown had a concrete structure of benches to sit on and toilets that stood on two sides of the pool. Orchard Court had all kinds of chairs, lounges, rockers, tree stumps, yards, porches and steps to sit on and toilets in every house, but there wasn't a pool, or the adults and bigger kids to keep kids from using it. Downtown had lost its grass and the concrete structure provided little shade. On Orchard Court the grass was greener and trees provided shade a-plenty. East McMicken had a playground. Orchard Court was a playground.

It was not my imagination. The hottest summer day on Orchard Court was never as hot as that same day on East McMicken. It was normal to see the heat waves downtown. It was normal to see the grass wave in the suburb. It was never as cold on Orchard Court as it was all winter downtown. It never snowed as much downtown as it snowed in the suburbs and McMicken didn't have a Herbert Avenue, the best street for sled riding in the world. A huge V with Orchard Court running off it at the bottom.

I didn't like rain on East McMicken so when I got caught in the rain coming home from school I was surprised I didn't mind it. It was different from the rain downtown. The next time it rained I went out and had another dose of difference. I did this a few more times and finally went for a purposeful walk to understand the difference. The rain on McMicken deposited things on me, film, greasy goo, grit and left me feeling dirty. The rain on Orchard Court was pure, fresh, and left me feeling clean. From that day I have loved rain.

Of course I was attending Westwood Elementary School and really loved it. The building was so clean and fancy with huge windows, big rooms, a gym, an auditorium, playgrounds and trees all around, a field for baseball and huge long steps up to the big front entrance hall. I couldn't believe it, they gave me my own desk to use! That's not all, there was a monster library right across the street. I wished my old library downtown could have seen me in this one. There was even more. Every year before school started I'd get all kinds of presents, you know, paper, pencils, a pen, a notebook.

The lessons going on in the big rooms were nice and I did my part, but my focus was on other things. I was much more interested in learning how to go to school with rich American kids.

I spent all my time watching them, how they walked, how they dressed, how they talked to each other, what they said about their families, the bikes they rode, what they ate for lunch, and most importantly, how they thought. It wasn't easy. For example, they actually said they got money from their parents every week, for no reason. They called it an allowance. Baba would have gotten a kick out of that. She'd give me an allowance! Trust me, studying the other kids at Westwood Elementary was all the education I could handle the first three years.

As Orchard Court was my campus, The Fletchers, who lived next door, were my tutor. Mr. and Mrs. Fletcher, their oldest daughter Lucy, and Lynn and Doug who were about my age. There was absolutely no family or person or experiences even close to them on East McMicken. Years later, when I saw television at Lou and Rosie's, I immediately related to Ozzie and Harriet and other such shows because I had lived next door to them on Orchard Court.

My tutor's differences were easy to spot. They all lived next door. All of them, all the time. Lucy, Doug, and Lynn were my first look at brothers and sisters who weren't "Brothers" and "Sisters." They were actually blood relatives. Mr. Fletcher had a car and a truck. How could that be? Why? Doug and Lynn explained both to me but all I heard was what I always felt, he was a boss.

The specific tutoring by Lynn and Doug started the day they saw me from their sandbox and called me over. It was the first time we played together. After a time, they asked me why I hadn't come over before? When I explained our habits, that I had to wait for an invitation, they were curious and quiet. They thought about this for a while and then announced, "Look, just consider yourself invited from now on. We haven't got time to come looking for you instead of playing." Over the next few days I

110

cogitated on their comment and concluded, to my utter amazement, they were serious. They really wanted me to come over and didn't care about invitations. They made it seem so simple and sensible. I didn't share my opinion at home.

The more we played together the more what I saw baffled me. They didn't drink all the drinks their mother gave them. They left their toys out. They had their own rooms. They shared everything, their sand box, their sand box toys, and all their other toys with each other and with me. I didn't have toys to share but they didn't care. They didn't keep score like Serbians. They didn't eat all their food. They got new clothes on days other than Christmas. By the time I graduated from Doug and Lynn, they had taught me how to play with kids.

The Fletchers were great tutors, but I had great limitations. Some things they taught just had no place to go in my life's card catalogue. For example, on more than one occasion, I saw Mr. and Mrs. Fletcher holding hands. Here's another example. You may not believe this, I had never seen anything like it before, but one time, honest, I saw them kiss.

So the next thing I realized was that, in this world of plenty if not too much, I felt I was missing something. What could I be missing? Americana was exposing me to selfishness and materialism. Had I already mastered those faults? If I had, that really stinks. YES! Stink is what I was missing. I can't describe the smell of my first neighborhood, sour, rotten, spoiled, tart, it is a mixture that leaves my nose hairs cringing and my spirit numb. I came to call the stink "McMicken-smell." Until I got away from it and got used to the smell of the suburbs, I had never smelled it. Over the years, I was surprised to find "McMicken-smell" in Baltimore by the old docks, on 42nd Street in Manhattan, and in certain areas of Amsterdam. I was surprised not to find

"McMicken-smell" in Okinawa, Vietnam, or Thailand. I wonder if "McMicken-smell" is the smell of poverty in a rich country? In a poor country it isn't smelled. Just like I didn't smell it while I lived downtown.

As I learned to wear two hats in The Hallway, Orchard Court introduced me to the American hat and started teaching me how to act like an American. Sometimes it held out the hope I could become an American. At no time did it hold out the hope I could think like an American.

As far as I could tell, the entire time we lived on Orchard Court, the campus had no Matriarch.

CONGREGATION

Well, that was a great meeting. I really mean after it ended. It was an okay meeting but what happened afterward was best.

That couple and their three kids have been coming to prayer meetings every Wednesday night for I don't know how long. George kept saying there was something wrong, but Olga wouldn't get interested. Once she did, she found he was right. So, she put her mind to it and things changed.

I had a hard time understanding the man and lady. Why didn't the man just tell us he had been hurt and out of work? Why didn't they admit they were having trouble making ends meet? Why in the world wouldn't they take the few things George offered them the first time? I mean, they aren't Serbian. No matter. This was the second Wednesday in a row they stayed 'til everyone was gone and then accepted the box of food, clothes, and little things George had put together for them. That's what was great about the meeting.

It was funny, George and Olga always managed to find things for others no matter how pitiful our situation. More often than not, as soon as they would give someone half of the little we had, someone else would bring us two times what we had.

I just wish I had some toys to give the kids. I know my pocket knife isn't one, thanks to The Matriarch and her friend Esa Borazard.

ESA BORAZARD

I don't remember Baba asking me if I wanted to go. If she did ask, the fact it was she who asked made it a direction not an option. I do remember she told me he was the best on the subject. I also remember not asking, "What was the subject?"

Street cars validated Harrison Avenue as the major route from Western Hills to downtown. As befitted a major thorough-fare, Harrison was lined with stately houses. We had stopped in front of one. It was way back on a field of perfect grass. Yellow brick! A giant porch and huge house, all yellow brick.

Then we were inside with ten foot ceilings, huge windows, glass double doors, gorgeous woodwork, and crystal chandeliers. It was wonderful. This was my first time in a home of the wealthy, yet I made no mental picture to review in wonder later. I couldn't. I was stunned.

Baba was chatting with the owner, Esa Borazard. Ee-sa bo-RRAZ-ard helps me hear his name but nothing helps me picture him as more than a typical Serbian male. I learned he was a butcher. Not the owner of a butcher shop. Not a butcher in an upscale shop. Esa was a meat cutter for a large packing company. How does a meat cutter own such a place? This was only one of the many questions rushing through my mind at the time, but I don't remember any answers. It's the sad truth that my only memory is of the subject.

Knives. There were dozens and dozens. All shapes and all sizes. Some clearly fit into sets as if families. Others were aloof as if announcing their independence. Some pranced at the end of wonderful bone, wood, or pearl handles. Others stolidly blended with their utilitarian handles. Some were shiny as if gleaming with pride. Others refused to show even a spark, as if hiding what they were premeditating. Some were displayed in cases and boxes. Others were mingled in community drawers. But regardless their characteristics and differences, they shared one thing exactly. All were sharp.

Esa handled each knife as if it were an old friend whose every whim he understood. He explained the use of each type and the reasons for its design. To help me understand the various methods of application, he took some meat from his Frigidaire and gave me demonstrations. As he worked, his hands, arms, and at times entire body seemed to be choreographed with the knife and application of the moment. As each knife was different, so Esa's dance was different. The differences ranged from huge to tiny but always perfectly reflected the purpose and use of the knife. In this way he was everything from a sugar-plum fairy dancing with a stiletto to a focused dervish wielding a cleaver.

During his entire performance, he was so at ease with his subjects I wondered if he forgot their potential for harm. To me all his knives were menacing. All made me feel they, not me, would determine whether their use would result in artistry or mayhem. He sensed my apprehension and gave me guidance. He taught me how to respect and handle knives and replaced my fear with realistic confidence. Baba was right. Esa Borazard was the best on the subject.

Months later, I was playing marbles on the porch at Orchard Court. At a certain moment I sensed I was being watched and, looking up, found Baba standing in the door frame. This was not unusual. She kept her eye on me and often watched me play. At that point she said, "That, is something to play as a game." Before I could make sense of what she said, she turned and closed the door.

Time passed and her comment nagged at me. What did she mean? A few days later it was still nagging at me. I needed an answer. However, it wasn't that easy. You didn't just go up to Baba and ask a question for free. No. First, you had to try to figure it out yourself. You'd better figure good and hard. If you didn't figure it out and had to ask her, she would check to see if you should have been able to figure it out. If you could have figured out the answer she'd educate you, and then, she would put a boulder on your back for you to carry till it hurt.

So I figured. Real hard. Real hard but not so good, nothing.

I just kept at it. Nothing.

Then one day while I was looking for something in my private shoe box, I noticed my pocket knife. George had given it to me and it was one of my favorite things. I couldn't remember the last time I had played with it...oh boy! That was it! I loved playing Mumbley Peg. You know, the boys game of throwing knives to stick in the ground near various targets that sometimes included feet and toes. I hadn't played that game in a long time. Not since our visit to Esa Borazard.

The Martriarch was like that. She didn't tell me not to play with knives. She took me to see Esa Borazard.

OLGA: HER GIFT

Just the memory of the day makes me cringe. Olga had called ahead to tell her sister Viola we had some fresh corn to drop off. Aunt Viola said we were very more than welcome to stop by. The two sisters loved fresh corn. Olga was very particular, Silver Queen please. It was a great visit because as soon as we got there I set off playing with my favorite toy, the house on Glenmore. Way too soon it was time to leave and we headed to the car.

George got in the driver's seat while Olga, in the passenger seat, and Aunt Viola, leaning against the open door, commenced goodbye-ing. For some reason, Olga wanted me to sit by her during this phase of the visit. George and I could tell this was going to be a long version of goodbye. At a certain moment I got bored and started waving goodbye, knowing full well it was nowhere near waving time. It became a game. Could I wave pretend-goodbye just long enough so as not to get yelled at. I was a creative little guy, it was a nifty game. I kept winning. Then I lost my concentration. I was waving pretend-goodbye with my right hand between the windshield post and the open door, when it was real-goodbye. Olga yanked and Viola pushed and the door slammed shut.

Our car was a big old four door Buick built like a tank and weighing about the same as one. The fingers of my right hand were smashed between the door frame and window pillar. Between Olga and Viola, I don't know who started crying first. Whoever it was, was crying after me. It really hurt. There was blood. Then Viola thought to open the door. The blood flow increased as I pulled my hand toward me. It really hurt. My fingers were totally smashed. The thumb looked normal but it was hard to see for sure because of the blood. It was easy to see my fingers were pointing in all different directions. They really hurt. George had gotten to us and gave Olga the hanky she asked for. She wrapped it around my hand. There was a lot of blood. It really hurt.

Olga directed us inside and to the kitchen sink. Standing behind me, she held my hanky wrapped hand on the edge and waited for the tap water to reach the temperature she wanted. Then she asked us to join her in prayer. After her prayer she took off the hanky and put my hand under the water. The water slowly washed away the blood and, as it left, so did the pain. After some time, Olga asked Viola to turn the water off. When she did, there was no more bleeding. Olga asked for a white napkin and wrapped my fingers in it and then for another to wrap my whole hand. We all headed back outside and the goodbye was quick. I got in the back seat and then we were home.

The next time we were together Aunt Viola mentioned how great the fresh corn had been.

Incidentally, the morning after my fingers were crushed, Olga took off the napkins. There were what looked like cuts all over each finger but no bruising. Only if I held my hand up directly in front of you could you see no finger matched any of the others.

Each was bent in different places in different ways, the middle one the most. By that afternoon I could use my hand normally and the next morning the cuts were gone.

Yes, absolutely, I believe in God.

CONGREGATION

Doesn't it get to them? I mean, this is the...I don't know how many. Too many. I know attendance goes up and down, fluctuates as George calls it, but this is way down. There can't be eleven people in this church and it's a beautiful Sunday evening. It makes me feel bad for them. Where did all the so called Brothers and Sisters go?

I have to hand it to The Reverends Marksity. They hold all three weekly services no matter the attendance. They act the same whether the place is empty or packed. How are they able to keep it up when there's almost no one here?

I guess an even harder question is how does she do it when he's in Yugoslavia? It's hard enough keeping their spirits up when there are two of them, they can support each other. But when he's over there she's all alone.

That was a bad guess. One thing I know about The Reverend Olga, she's never alone.

SO, WHO IS MY PARENTS?

There were three of us on Orchard Court that night. I was alone in the room Baba and I shared. Baba was my maternal grandmother. She was spending a few days downtown. I was about to do my evening prayer, when Olga and George interrupted me. We sat together on the edge of my bed. Me between my mother and father. They wanted me to understand their decision. I was in the first grade.

Olga started. "The main reason for our decision is that we both have callings. I have been called to lead a church, to minister to people and to share, whenever possible, the healing gifts that God has given me."

George took over. "I have been called to be a missionary. I am to go back to Yugoslavia and spread the gospel. I fear, or accept, that I may not return from there. The point is that I will not be with you. Certainly not on a regular basis."

Olga built on this point. "With the responsibility that goes with the tremendous gifts I've been given, my time will not be my own. The way this affects you is that I may be here physically but will not be available as a normal mother might be."

Then, in unison, "It is for these reasons that we have made our decision."

They stopped a moment, as if to give me time to digest what they had decided. I didn't know what to say or do. I felt I should not tell them I had no idea what decision they were talking about. So I looked back respectfully. This seemed to do the trick.

Olga started anew. "There is another side to this. A side we didn't think you needed to know. Now, we feel you have to know. You are our fourth child. Mary Ellen, who would be your oldest sister, lived for only a short period of time and for whatever reason was taken from us. She is buried in Spring Grove Cemetery. After her were two others, but they were taken immediately."

George picked it up from there. "We prayed, asking God to give us one offspring. He answered our prayers by giving us you."

Olga took over in her manner that meant she was about to say something extremely important. "But, when we made that prayer, we promised that we would not let the granting of our prayer interfere with the fulfilling of our callings."

Now it became a sort of tag team, as each wanted to make sure I understood.

George: "In effect we made a deal with God. If he would bless us with a child we would give that child to the Lord and we would follow our callings."

Olga: "As you can see, putting this all together, you were really not ours from the beginning."

George: "You were God's."

Olga: "That is what we want you to understand tonight."

George: "He is with you."

Olga: "He is your father."

George: "He is your mother."

In unison, as if they rehearsed it, "He is your parents."

With this last announcement they became silent.

I continued to look back and forth from one to the other. I still didn't know what to say or do. The respectful look still seemed the best action.

After a time, Olga hugged me and said, "We are glad to have you. We love you. We know you are not ours."

George put his hand on my knee and gave it a squeeze.

This meeting explained much. It explained that their behavior was not abdicating their roles as parents, but fulfilling their roles as 'called people.' It explained why Baba played such a dominant role in my rearing. It explained why I spent so much of my time alone. It explained why from my earliest memories I always felt that Something Bigger was there for me.

Rather than feeling deprived, cut off, or abandoned, I felt called, special, blessed. I slept soundly that night. The Lord was more than my shepherd. It made Our Father make more sense as My Father. It gave me a relationship that has sustained me, enriched me, completed me and fulfilled me. I was indeed a son of God. The Lord was my parents.

MORE THAN A HINT OF PRIDE

It was a beautiful spring Sunday. For some reason, The Peniel Missionary Assembly was closed and we were on our way to The Assembly Of God. George and Olga used to go to this church. I had heard a lot about it but had never been there before. When we got there it looked exactly like churches in books, like a cathedral. It was clearly designed and built as a church and looked nothing like a converted store. I couldn't wait to get inside and see what it looked like.

But we couldn't go inside because a lot of people seemed to know Olga and George and were stopping to talk. I had heard they were both really liked and that Olga was a favorite of the chief pastor and all the congregation. Now, as I stood and listened to the conversations, I heard that The Reverends Marksity were more than liked, they were respected and missed.

With time to look around, I began to appreciate the setting. The church was across the street from a beautiful big park. The blooms of spring were decorating the place and it was glorious. Across the park was a huge reddish building that was inscribed, Music Hall. The people were dressed much better than those coming to our church. A lot of them pulled up in cars to let passengers out before going to park. I could only think of four of our congregation who had cars.

Now that I was engrossed in the setting and surroundings, Olga and George decided it was time to move inside. As we walked up the stone steps to the huge double doors, I felt I was entering a castle. The entrance way seemed half as big as the entire Peniel Missionary Assembly.

The inside was shocking. A grand altar and pulpit. Built-in places for the choir. No black cast iron stove sending its pipe through the roof. All the people in the choir were dressed in the same kind of robes. Flowers. Lights on the walls. No folding chairs, wonderful solid wooden pews with pockets on their backs for Bibles and Hymnals. Stained glass windows. Candles. My head felt like it was on a swivel trying to take it all in. Suddenly an organ started playing and I must have jumped three feet straight up.

The sound came from everywhere within the church. I wasn't finished adjusting to the organ when the choir let loose. It was amazing. It sounded like I was standing in the middle of them. As the hymn unfolded, the beauty of their voices washed over me in a way that the water in our galvanized tub never did. The hymn ended and the minister, in a wonderful costume, much fancier than the choir robes, began the service. During the service I got used to the scene and the sounds. I began to notice details.

There were more people in this church's choir than there were in our congregation. They had a host for a choir backed by, or dueling with, an organ. We had Aunt Viola on the piano surrounded by Olga or George and two to four of the congregation, depending on attendance.

Our church did not pass a collection plate. In this church they passed what looked like collection platters. The one that went by me had more money in it than I had ever seen.

Some people seemed not to be concentrating on the sermon. As time passed I realized that more than half of the congregation were not concentrating on the sermon. This was in stark contrast to The Peniel Missionary Assembly where everyone in the building was riveted to the message.

One thing looked exactly like our church, the display board behind the altar with numbers for weekly attendance and offerings. But on closer study it was nothing like the board behind our altar. It was beautifully crafted, big enough to be read in the back of this cavern, and the numbers displayed for last week would be our numbers for last year.

My observations stopped when, what seemed to be suddenly, the service came to a close. It felt odd, like there should have been something else. I was sure I hadn't missed it. But I didn't know what it was, so I might have missed it. But something was missing.

On the way out, Olga and George were again the focus of attention for a bunch of people. It seemed that the ones who hadn't spoken to them on the way in were going to be sure to speak to them on the way out. Since I knew the drill, I waited and watched. The feeling that something was missing would not go away.

I was amazed by the number of kids coming from the Sunday School classes. We had maybe five or six. Next, I was surprised by the number of older kids picking up things that had been dropped, putting the Bibles and song books back in their little pockets, taking care of the candles and flowers and generally straightening the place up. We didn't have any candles. Flowers only showed up on Easter when Brother Neville brought them.

There were no pockets for our song books and Bibles on the backs of our folding chairs and I was the one who did all the collecting and cleaning and straightening.

In time, we were able to leave. As we were walking down the steps and heading back to our car, I decided that this Assembly Of God was a much easier church to attend than The Peniel Missionary Assembly. As if reading my mind, Olga asked, "Well, what did you think of the church?"

Now I wanted to be careful. The Peniel Missionary Assembly was their church and very special to them for reasons I really didn't understand. The Assembly Of God was their old church but they had left it for reasons I really didn't understand. This lack of understanding made me feel I needed to be careful. But this had been a neat experience, flowers, candles, fancy clothes, music, pews. I wasn't sure how to keep it from sounding too good. I decided on a broad answer.

"Well, I'm really glad you brought me. It was a good experience. The park is sure beautiful. The place looks like a church from pictures in books and the inside is grand. I really like the way the sun came through the stained glass window. That choir can really sing and they have neat robes and the ministers robes are super." I stopped. That was too much. Then I had an inspiration. I turned directly toward George. "Of course, I did notice as I'm sure anyone who's been to our church would, that there wasn't a single voice in that choir that was even close to yours." I hoped that helped because I was worried I sounded like this church was better than ours. We had gotten to the car and as we were getting in they said, "Good" and "We're glad you liked it."

On the way home I began to think again about what was missing. We got home and I got out of my Sunday go to meeting clothes. As we prepared for Sunday lunch the feeling that something was missing from the Assembly became stronger.

I'm not sure whether it was during the mashed potatoes or while I was dunking graham crackers in milk, when I spontaneously blurted out, "I know what was missing." The two of them looked at me as if I had just dropped out of the sky. I sensed that Olga was moving into one of her interrogations. Specifically her, "Take your time and think about this. I want to know what's really going on inside." I wasn't ready for that exercise so I quickly volunteered an explanation.

"It's about that church. When I was there, I got the feeling that something was missing. That they had left something out of the service. As the day has passed, it kept coming back to me that something was missing. But since I've never been in a church like that before, I didn't know what was supposed to be there and I couldn't figure it out. Then, right now, it hit me what was missing. It didn't have anything to do about where. It's all about what." I paused and, when I saw they were listening, continued.

"What was missing was the feeling of people participating, people feeling better because they were there. I didn't see anyone's face shining as if a light had just been pointed at them. I didn't see anybody who's face looked different after the service than it did before the service. I didn't see people shaking hands or hugging each other as they left. And nobody was sitting around talking after the service. Everybody got up to go. What was missing was the feeling I feel and see during your Sunday services and Wednesday prayer meetings."

When I finished my explanation, I looked up and found George and Olga looking at me in a way I had never seen before. They looked at me with an appreciation for my understanding, obvious self-satisfaction, and maybe even a hint of pride.

George nodded his head and said, "Very good."

Olga demanded we maintain eye contact and said, "There is a lack of spirituality. You were missing the Spirit of the Lord. That's what was left out."

The moment passed. We finished eating and life went on. And, as it did, I began to question more and more why my parents were no longer associated with the Assembly Of God. The more time that passed, the more I wanted to ask questions. But I didn't want to look like I was nosing around in their private business or, worse, that I preferred the Assembly of God.

I needn't have worried. My outburst and explanation during that spring Sunday lunch had earned me special treatment. From then on, my questions were treated differently. I was permitted to ask my questions directly and they answered directly.

I learned that Olga had been saved through the ministering of Reverend Nash, who was the head pastor of the Assembly. He told her from the beginning that he recognized she had a special gift. He was unable to tell her what it was, but he knew it was there. He followed this up by supporting and encouraging her to first become ordained and then to join his staff as an assistant pastor. She was, in fact, preaching at the Assembly when George came to Cincinnati and spotted her. Her work in the church is what drew him to the church. Subsequently, he was saved and ordained as if following her example. They were married there and worshipped together.

I thanked them because it felt good to get a straight answer. Particularly an answer so full of information. But as time passed, I realized I still had a lot of questions. They made it sound like the perfect place, so why did they leave? I had seen that most of the congregation knew and liked them, so why weren't they ministering there? Plus, there were a lot more people to minister to and the physical set up was clearly better than at 64 E. Mc-Micken. So why not preach there? Why couldn't they minister there as they did here? Why couldn't they help people there like they helped people here? I wanted, and then needed, to have my questions answered.

By this time it was late fall. We were sitting at the table after a cold supper. For whatever reason, it seemed the right time to ask my questions. It was just that simple. They answered.

They both were thankful to be saved and loved the Lord with all their hearts. She was not saved from working in a tailor shop and candy factory as a child. Her salvation was the opening of her spiritual understanding and the filling of her soul. At that time, she felt she had a special gift, a calling. Even though she didn't know what it was, she was determined that when it surfaced she would not hide it under a basket. He equated his salvation with his spiritual awakening and the finding of his true love. He too, had a calling and knew what it was, to be a missionary.

Although they had very specific goals and plans for reaching those goals, work toward those goals was not what The Assembly of God had in mind. Supporting a recently ordained minister as a missionary to Yugoslavia was not included in the Church's annual plan. Were it to be included, it would be at a very low priority. As for Reverend Olga, it was clear she had some special gift that would in time reveal itself. But, in the meantime, she needed to concentrate on the objectives of the Church. She spent too much time with people, some of whom were not even members of the Church. She spent too little time attracting new members. Frequently, when delivering the sermons, she forgot the administrative responsibilities of having the pulpit. She did not encourage generosity in giving or mention the current promotions. She needed to understand there was business involved with running a church.

Well, she wanted to minister and he wanted to missionary. And if this church would not support them, would the Assembly Of God system franchise them to open up their own church? The Assembly would be happy to see a new branch begin to sprout. They received a comprehensive package outlining the costs of affiliation, the specifics of the relationship and other requirements from both sides for the growth of the new church.

It was in this period that they learned what was driving them away from the Assembly Of God. They were not willing to run a church by the numbers. They investigated other denominations and found each demanded numbers. In the end, it seemed perhaps the Assembly of God was the least demanding. They found, regardless the denomination, success, and therefore the support that is given to successful churches, was determined by the size and growth of the congregation and the collections. When either of these numbers began to slip, demands would increase and support would decrease.

In the cold reality of their discoveries, they made their decisions. The Reverend Olga would leave the safe, secure position as a staff minister at the Assembly. Together, they would open a church that was not run by the numbers. A church that would enable her to minister to anyone who needed it and him to missionary as he was led. He would increase his tailoring to help fund the effort. God would run their church and direct their lives. The Spirit of The Lord would be constantly sought after and always welcome. That Spirit would dictate the course of a service and the direction of the church. Without that Spirit, they only had an old retail store. With that Spirit, they had the keys to the Kingdom. They would take only what was needed to get by and everything else would go to those who needed it more. The number of people and the number of dollars would never be the measure of their church. It was a ministry, not an organization.

Thus the relationship with the Assembly of God died and the non-denominational Peniel Missionary Assembly was born.

Olga and George had never been as open with me as they were during this conversation. But the moment lives in my mind for another reason. When they were finished, I realized I was in the presence of two heroes. The Reverends Olga and George Marksity were tough. They had guts. They had the guts to drop the safe, big, secure church. They had the guts to open an independent nothing with no support. They had the guts to drop the church and go for God. I wondered if the people, who so wanted to talk to them before and after the Assembly Of God service, also admired The Reverends Marksity as heroes? I looked at them with understanding, appreciation, and more than a hint of pride.

ANOTHER OLGA

It wasn't a big deal. It was just a demonstration of another Olga.

I was playing outside when the girl who lived on the other side of the Fletchers came over to see what I was doing. It was the first time she talked to me. She asked if she could join me and I said sure. We started playing and she decided she wanted to do something else. I didn't. She wanted. I didn't. After the third time I said no, she grabbed my arm and bit me.

I headed inside and told Olga what happened. She didn't react much but I learned later that she talked to some neighbors and found the girl made a habit of biting others. She told me the next time I saw the girl I should walk up to her and tell her never to bite me again. And, I had better be aware. Fine. I knew about being aware.

Well, I was less aware than I should have been and the girl bit me again. I remembered Olga telling me to talk to her. I hadn't done that. I decided not to report the incident. No chance, Olga could read me like ...it was scary how she could read me. Once she got the story she went to talk to the girl's mother. The lady felt Olga was making a mountain out of a mole hill. Further, was Olga sure her daughter was the one who bit me? Had anyone seen the incident? When Olga mentioned it was incidents, the lady was not impressed. My direction was to be 'aware' better.

On this day, Doug and I were playing outside when Biting Girl joined us. Things were going along fine until she wanted the truck I was using. I said not until I was finished moving all the sand for my project. You know you can't just leave a project half finished in a first class sand box. Well she wanted that truck and she wanted it now. Before I finished saying no, she bit me on the arm. I let out a yelp and told her never to bite me again. She bit me again, twice.

Doug took off for his house while Fangs kept demanding the truck. In the meantime, Olga heard the commotion and was coming down the steps. She didn't say a word but motioned me to join her as she walked over to the Little Cannibal, took the girl's arm and told me to bite it. I did. The girl turned white and started screaming. Olga motioned me to our house while The Little Darling kept screaming bloody murder.

In no time, the girl's mother, with her screaming monster in tow, was hammering on the front door. Olga was totally relaxed and told me to let the lady in. As I opened the door the woman called me an animal and kept glaring hate as she yelled for Mrs. Marksity. My mind went into fantasy mode. I couldn't wait to see what The Matriarch's daughter would do. Would it be, "It seems to me you're making a mountain out of a mole hill." No, wait. It would be, "Are you certain Ronnie was the one who bit your daughter? Did you see him do it? Did anyone else see the incident?" Instead, Olga welcomed the two as if they were missionaries that had come from China to see her. The lady yanked her daughter's arm so Olga could see the bite mark and yelled, "Can

140

you see this?" Calm as the dead, Olga answered, "Of course."
Then she pulled me over, pointed to the three bite marks on my
arm and said, "I think he owes her two more." The girl never bit
another person as long as we lived there.

MY UNCLE NICKY

Nicholas Golusin was my aunt Viola's husband and the father of Gloria and Donald.

He was taller than anyone in the family. He was proportionately large with a big frame. It was said he had been a good baseball player in his youth but I have no picture of him as a young man. He had no distinguishing physical characteristics and in a line-up of any number of Slavic types, all seated to appear the same height, he would be impossible to pick out.

I don't know where he was born, about his parents, if he had brothers or sisters, if he was the alcoholic he was rumored to be, how he met Viola, or anything else about his background. I know he was a cutter, not a tailor. A cutter and a minister. I only saw him in the ministry when I visited London, Kentucky where he was the pastor of a local church. There, I saw a functionary in a lifeless ministry. It made sense. A cutter takes the pattern and the cloth chosen by others and produces the pieces. A seamstress assembles the pieces. All this, including design and fitting, is under the direction of a tailor. Uncle Nicky did not have the vision for design. He could identify the pieces of the church but lacked the spirituality to sew them into a mantel of faith. He was the

143

administrator of a bureaucratic church. He was a cutter, not a tailor.

When I was little, Uncle Nicky didn't like having me around and when he couldn't ignore me would merely say, "Ronnie, vatch." He did this strongly rolling the R and in a heavy Slavic accent. He did this for two reasons. First, to make fun of people who spoke with an accent. This included me and most of the family on certain words. George for instance, had a hard time getting Wine and Valnut Streets to be Vine and Walnut Streets. Second, to poke fun at my being well behaved, as this was the phrase Baba used to caution me.

But Uncle Nicky was not treating me special. He didn't like having anyone around. He had trademarked a personal stockpile of unpleasant behaviors. He had a special one just for visitors. No matter when, why or who came to their home, Viola might answer the door but if she couldn't, you better let yourself in because he wouldn't. He sat in the far corner of the living room in his easy chair, with his feet on the non-matching ottoman, reading the paper. Once inside, you could say hello, but he wouldn't answer. You were better off putting up your coat and looking for Viola. No matter what you did, Uncle Nicky remained in the same place. It was normal for Nicky to read the paper while the family and guests for Christmas dinner arrived and sat around talking with each other in his living room.

His communication with me never went too far past "Ronnie vatch." But I listened to him. And, I watched him. He taught me a lot. He taught me the subtleties of making others look and feel awkward. He taught me the craftsmanship of embarrassing others and bringing them to the verge of tears. He taught me how to make other people feel inferior. He showed me techniques for disabling and maiming the self-image of others. He taught me how to distinguish the weak, who could be preyed upon, from the helpless, who could be devoured. He was a master and could turn anything into a weapon to hurt others.

Take his newspaper. We have the picture of him in the corner in his chair. But there's more to it. He has his long arms extended spreading the paper so it covers him like the curtain of a stage. People arrive, let themselves in as Viola is in the kitchen, say hello to each other, hang up their coats and say hello to the paper. Uncle Nicky doesn't move. People get refreshments and move about. His only movement is to turn the pages of the paper in a way that makes them look like bed sheets flapping on a clothesline. People come and sit in the living room around him and talk to each other. He doesn't notice. At the right moment, when perhaps someone would ask, "Nicky, do you want something?" he would let out a sigh. A sigh of The Important being interrupted. The room would always get quiet. I never understood this because he always did the same thing.

Dramatically, he would fold the newspaper together, then fold it in half and finally, fold it one more time. The paper made a lot of noise while he did this. Looking like he had just been called away from saving the planet, he would place the paper, as if it were the Magna Carta, on his non-matching ottoman, look up, take a deep breath and seem honestly surprised that bodies had invaded his living room. The person who had asked the question suddenly became a target. Nicky would stare at them and ask, "Now, exactly what was it that you felt was so important?" Some people would laugh at this. I wouldn't.

Nicky may have been the first sadist I ever met. But he was not a slasher with a broad sword. He was not a slicer with a carving knife. He was not a doctor with a scalpel. He was a pin point technician who found the weakness, no matter the type or size, and stuck a needle in it. He stuck his needles with such consummate skill that he caused dismay, discomfort, pain or horror, as he wished and to the degree he wanted. I often saw him pick the smallest imperfection and dig at it until it became an open running sore.

The family seemed to accept his actions as part of his character. Baba had nothing to tell me.

He was an accomplished actor. When someone would object to his treatment, his "Who me?" was an innocent theatrical masterpiece. There was no possible way the person could be talking about him. Seeing his "Who me?" the first time, anyone could be forgiven for feeling sorry for poor Nicky, who was obviously the victim of misunderstanding.

In time, Nicky and Viola moved to California to be with Gloria. When they did, Donald moved into their home in Bridgetown. By that time, I knew my Uncle Nicky to be a mean, joyless person. Devious, vicious, and able to be so while smiling as a cutter or a minister.

In 1965, I was driving from Fort Benning, Georgia through the Grand Canyon to Fort Lewis, Washington. Olga reasoned that was close to California and asked me to drop by Modesto and say hello to her sister and Nicky. Once nearby, I called the numbers for the parsonage and church where Nicky was the pastor but got no answer. When I got to Modesto, I tried again but got no answer so I found both the church and parsonage. They weren't there. I talked to several people and discovered I had the wrong phone numbers and nobody knew a Reverend Golusin or a Viola. I tried other churches in the area but had no luck. I left without finding them. I was not a happy wanderer. But, it made sense. Nicky was devious. Who knew what he was really up to? I figured he was somewhere sitting behind a newspaper.

A year later when I left for Vietnam, I wondered what I might not see again. I thought of people, places and things, but never Uncle Nicky.

In 1974, nine years after my fruitless detour to Modesto, I was in L.A. on business and looked up my Aunt Viola and Uncle Nicky. On the way to see them, I remembered their huge three story frame house on Glenmore where, as a little boy, I could stand in the main fireplace. I thought of their move to the cozy two bedroom brick in the quiet suburb of Bridgetown. I wondered what their California house would be like when I realized I was in a huge industrial looking complex, loud, crowded and shabby. When I got to their address it was a one bedroom apartment.

They were both standing at the top of the front steps waiting for me. They couldn't have been more hospitable. Not only was Uncle Nicky not reading the newspaper when I arrived, he didn't pick up a paper the entire time I was there. He offered me his easy chair and pushed the non-matching ottoman close by. He made me feel he was honestly overjoyed I was there.

It was okay to see them after so many years but I was confused. Why were they living like this? We did the small talk but it was a miserable experience. The apartment would have been comical if it weren't so sad. A tiny one bedroom apartment, where what little furniture they had taken with them looked out of place, as if someone put a new front seat in a rusted wreck in the junk yard. Only Nicky's ancient chair and non-matching ottoman fit the surroundings, but even they were too large for the space. They were embarrassed. I was embarrassed for them.

I realized I was meeting an Aunt Viola I had never seen before. She was not a wife. She was a caretaker for the father of her children. Finally, she pulled herself together as if caught in a crime and blurted out they had been living like this since they moved to California. Then proudly, because she had started to cry, she added, "After all, we have a paid off home in Cincinnati." She went on to explain they lived like this to help Gloria. Now I was more confused. She filled me in. They were spending their golden years helping Gloria rear her children. They lived below the standard of living they had worked all their lives to enjoy, so Gloria could live above the standard of living she could afford.

Nicky and Viola were relieved to get this off their chests. I realized there was a pain in what they had been doing that I could not imagine. I also realized my Uncle Nicky had lost his haughty superiority. He was beaten down, humbled. I thought I saw fear in his eyes. I wondered if he was afraid of being stuck by needles?

When we finished talking about Gloria I agreed I would see her the next time I was in L.A. I fully expected Nicky would want to be along and mentioned the place I had in mind. That he was a broken man became evident when he declined the meal and admitted he couldn't handle such a meeting with his daughter. In fact, "Ron, I'd be grateful if you would do it alone." That he, "…would be grateful." was unimaginable. This was an infinity from "Ronnie, vatch." In this way, my Uncle Nicky demonstrated he had changed.

Odd, they had the perfect house for making everyone feel at home, and didn't. Now they had the most improbable facility for making anyone feel at home, and did. I believe any visitor would have felt welcome and would have been welcome.

In 1975, I took Gloria and her son and daughter, Mark and Mary Anne, out to supper. The facts were Gloria wouldn't accept the facts. She knew better than everyone. She wouldn't change her behaviors regarding her divorce, work, or social life. She refused to ask her ex-husband Glen for help but would continue taking money from her parents, aunt, and uncle. The other facts were that I was unable to help Gloria or her children.

When I visited Viola and Nicky to report on the meeting, I soft pedaled the reality. I couldn't see any benefit in telling them their grandchildren recognized the true ugliness of their mother. I didn't know if they knew their daughter lied to herself with premeditation, expected as her right the monies from Rosie and Lou, and was a conscious leach who intended to suck them dry. Even if they did know, I wasn't going to confirm it.

Uncle Nicky's reaction was too difficult for Viola to witness. As he started speaking she went into the bedroom. Nicky wasn't wielding needles. He wasn't being stuck by needles. He was being impaled on huge spikes. He was embarrassed by his daughter, his son, his residence, and himself. There was only one similarity between this Nicky and the one I had known years before. They were both joyless. But they were joyless for different reasons. My first Uncle Nicky was joyless from inflicting pain. This other Uncle Nicky, was joyless from enduring pain. I believed heaven and hell are here on earth and he was in hell.

I visited now and then over the next several years when on business. They were so pleased when I took them to the Del Rae. They had both heard of it and were gracious in their thanks. It was uplifting to see Uncle Nicky appreciative. Thereafter, they were very generous with gifts. A hand inlaid wooden tray one Christmas and artistic shell hanging for an anniversary became part of our home decor.

Over the years my wife had been exchanging cards as polite, but not close, relations do. She kept up with Viola and Nicky through bits and pieces, usually supplied by Rosie. The biggest development was when they moved back home. Back to their paid for, cozy little two bedroom brick on Grace, one house up from Rosie and Lou. My wife and boys spent time with them and a nice relationship developed.

By 1982, Nicky and Viola had become pleasant additions to our family. In the fall, they agreed to stay with the boys while my wife met me in Europe for a vacation. Very early in the trip they called about the boys. At one point, after we left, Nicky told Drew to do something that Drew felt was not right and therefore refused to do. They had let that pass but a similar situation occurred and Burke told Nicky, "You're not our father and we only take directions from our father." Nicky called Europe and I told the boys he was in charge while I was gone. On his own, he wasn't able to manage my five and three year old sons.

Nicky's eyes were no longer full of fear, they were merely sad.

When we got home, we learned that after the phone call the boys had been their usual well behaved selves. Viola was very complimentary about the house. All Nicky said was, "The toilet paper holder in your bathroom is hard to get to." My wife and the boys were surprised at his comment. I wasn't. I remembered the Nicky I grew up with. The one who never said anything positive, ever. After spending over two weeks in our home, he was only able to complain about a toilet paper holder. With our background together I heard what he said but knew what he meant, he loved the place.

As time passed, we talked more and more. One day he told me that when I was a boy he had attended the City Class C Little League All Star Game and saw me hit a triple. I remembered the triple but didn't remember seeing him. He said I didn't see him because he didn't want to see me. It was a sort of apology. Strange. And unimportant, because now Burke and Drew would have been shocked if Uncle Nicky wasn't at their soccer games.

In 1987, Donald died and Uncle Nicky's eyes went from sad to tired.

In his older age he still had a stockpile of behaviors but they were no longer trademarked, they were common. He had to be every place early. Nine o'clock church found him in the front pew at eight. Two o'clock Thanksgiving at our house, found him at the door by noon. He complained about the same things, the same way, over and over. He would not ask for directions. He was not unpleasant, rude, mean or vicious, he was a typical old man.

An old man who added to my understanding. He taught me there is no upside to being negative. No aspect of our existence benefits in the least by negativity. He taught me that people could change. That he had changed was demonstrated every time we were together. That how people see us can change was evident by how my family saw Uncle Nicky. That I had changed was confirmed as I accepted him the way he was now, just as I discarded him the way he was then.

In 1989, Nicholas Golusin died, but I felt two people were buried. One had died fifteen years earlier. Which was the real Nicholas Golusin? They both were. One was a cutter. The other an uncle. This was the end of both my Uncle Nickys.

THE TENT AND THE
DONUT LADY

Olga and George told me we were going to a different kind of Church meeting. It was going to be outside under a tent. I was excited and eager to go.

We had been riding along the road by the river for some time when all of a sudden I could see the tent. It was big. The closer we got, the bigger it got. By the time George turned off the highway, the tent was huge.

We drove into the parking area, which was all the fields next to and around the tent. That tent was giant. There were almost no cars and we parked very near the main entrance. Once we got out of the car, George and Olga showed me around the tent. There were three large poles sticking out of the top along the middle of the tent. All around the edges there were smaller poles sticking out. All the poles had ropes going from them to pegs in the ground. The tent was monstrous.

We walked in the front entrance to find what looked like a sea of wooden folding chairs. There was no floor covering, just grass and dirt. We walked down the right of two aisles leading to the altar. The altar was a large raised platform that filled the front of the tent. There were four steps at the end of each aisle that climbed to the altar. On the altar there was a place for a choir, a long row of wooden folding chairs and a podium, which served as the pulpit, where several people were talking. We went up the steps and one of the people came over to welcome Olga. He welcomed George and me as well, but it was Olga he was waiting for. George and Olga went over to the pulpit and I went back down the steps and sat in the first chair on the aisle.

There were very few people sitting in the wooden chairs. They were all dressed in their Sunday best, even though it wasn't Sunday. It was Friday night. As time passed people came in randomly. There were couples, groups, and individuals, all of different shapes and sizes. But no matter the differences, they were all dressed in their best. By the time the service started, the altar chairs were full but the choir area and sea of wooden chairs were more empty than full.

With the exception of the number of ministers on the altar and the place being a tent, the service didn't seem much different than any of the others I had attended. But the tent had my attention. It was big. As big inside as it looked outside. I was amazed at the ropes and metal things and holes and how it all hung together. I wondered how it was put up? How would it be taken down? Would it be folded and if so, how in the world would that be done? What would they do with the poles? How would it all be moved once apart? Where would it go next?

I don't remember who spoke or what was sung, but by the time The Reverend Olga Marksity got up from her folding chair, it felt like most of the service was over. Olga began to speak and, as always when she spoke, the entire congregation was soon mesmerized.

After a time, I noticed a lady walking down the aisle. She had a very strange neck. When she reached the steps leading up to where Olga was speaking, she stopped. She stopped right next to where I was sitting. Now, I could see she had a big fleshy thing around her neck, as if a huge donut was growing out of her shoulders. As I stared I saw that the donut wasn't even round. It was misshaped, larger in the front than back. It looked like her head was stuck in the hole of the misshaped donut.

I turned away, embarrassed. Not embarrassed by the lady's condition. Embarrassed because I had been staring. I had been taught better than that. Plus, I bet it was easy for others to see me being so rude. Right after these thoughts I again started staring at the lady and, at that exact moment, Olga stopped speaking. I jumped. I hadn't been listening. I was sure Olga was going to reprimand me for staring at the lady. But geeez, I had heard her more than one time and I had this donut lady standing two feet away from me.

Everything became extremely quiet. Only the crickets could be heard outside the tent. Olga turned to the lady as if she had just noticed her. She walked over to the steps, came down, reached out and held the lady's hand. They seemed to be talking but I couldn't hear a thing. Soon, they closed their eyes and Olga began to pray. I could not hear what Olga prayed, but as she prayed, she put her free hand on the woman's head and the donut began to disappear. It shriveled and got smaller and smaller until the woman began to cry.

A couple in the front row also began to cry. A woman three rows back fell to her knees. A man very close by was frozen with his mouth open. Then others, from all over the floor, began to cry, kneel down, sing, or just stare. It must have been the singing that made me understand they were crying from joy and kneeling in respect.

I looked back at the lady. She and Olga were no longer holding hands and their eyes were open. The donut was gone. The woman's neck was totally normal. This was easy to see because the neck of her blouse was now oversized for her new shape.

A sigh came from the people gathered under the tent and low murmuring prayers could be heard as Olga turned, went up the steps and over to the pulpit. She waited. It seemed to me she waited the perfect amount of time because, when she raised her right hand, the silence was immediate and this time, included the crickets. She said a prayer of thanks to the Lord, asked for His blessing on all of us assembled, said Amen, dropped her hand, turned, went to her seat and sat down.

The man who had welcomed us was the minister in charge. He was as taken aback as the rest of us and it took a moment for him to realize he needed to conclude the service. He did so by inviting the people to come back tomorrow night and bring their family, friends, neighbors, and strangers.

As he talked I looked at the lady again. I was staring again. I couldn't make myself stop. The misshaped fleshy donut was gone. Her neck was normal.

Once more, under the tent, the presence of Something Bigger, beyond my comprehension, was pacifying, nurturing, and guiding. A peace covered us all. A peace beyond my understanding.

The next day Olga made a point of educating me about the fleshy donut on the lady the night before. It was a goiter and it was caused by something and a bunch of other factual stuff. I was glad to hear the explanation but couldn't really concentrate. It was too bad I couldn't think more clearly because she also explained some things related to her gift. I missed a lot of what she told me but got the general picture.

Last night was not the first time she had been led to exercise her gift. God had been using her in episodes of healing for several years. This was just the first time she felt I was ready to bear witness. Further, she now knew I was ready to go along with her and George whenever she was called to minister.

She was not the only one with such a gift. She pointed out that I had already met one minister used by Something Bigger in the same fashion and she knew both Brothers and Sisters equally blessed.

It was a lot for me to digest. I spent the rest of the day thinking, or at least trying to think. I had a million questions. When did this happen? Where did it happen? How did it feel? Could she tell when she was going to be used for healing? Was it always so wonderful? Did she ever ... and on and on. Of course I didn't ask The Reverend Olga Marksity any questions. I was having enough trouble listening to her, what with my emotions and the shock of it all. Most imposing was that I really had no idea how I was supposed to talk to someone The Unfathomable used as He used her.

I didn't figure much out with all my thinking but knew for certain that ever since I saw the goiter disappear, I felt different. But I couldn't decide how I felt different. Things around me seemed to be some distance away and in my head there was only room for the picture of that fleshy growth shrinking and shrinking and being gone.

That night we left home the same time as the night before and were again on our way to the tent. When we got near the tent we had to wait in a line of traffic. We found the traffic was turning into the tent parking areas. As we drove in I was not so focused on the tent as the night before and saw the sign that announced Reverend SoAndSo and his congregation were hosting a two day Tent Meeting. On the list of ministers who would be participating, The Reverend Olga Marksity was printed in the largest and boldest letters. I hadn't noticed that last night.

We had to park in one of the back fields. As we walked to the tent the flow of traffic continued. We didn't try to go in the main entrance because it was backed up with people. We went to the rear of the tent, behind the altar, and were let in by one of the participating ministers.

When we got inside the tent, the sea of wooden chairs was gone, replaced by a sea of people, all dressed in their Sunday best. The tent was so full that the sides were being rolled up and people were starting to stand in the openings. The altar had another row of wooden chairs behind the row that was there last night and all the chairs except the two in the front middle were full. Even the choir area was packed. As we approached the pulpit, all the participating ministers gathered around Olga and they began to talk about the evening's agenda. The only place I could sit was on the ground next to the steps on the left side of the altar.

Just as the size of the tent amazed me last night, the number of people in and around the tent amazed me this night. Past the rolled up sides of the tent I could see the cars backed up in both directions of the highway, waiting to get into the parking areas.

At a particular moment I realized I couldn't hear anything going on around me and was replaying the shrinking of the goiter. That picture would not leave my head. Normally, I was able to control my thoughts, but not tonight and not much of the entire day. Things were different. I was different. Then somehow I felt it was okay. With this thought I seemed to rejoin everything around me and the sights and sounds made me happy to be there.

I recognized the sense of anticipation that filled the tent and surrounding area. I had seen and felt it many times in The Peniel Missionary Assembly, but this was a hundred times bigger and this was not our congregation. As Reverend SoAndSo got up to begin the service, the tent seemed to be alive with a pulse of its own.

The Reverend started the service, led us in a hymn and introduced the first participating minister. While this gentlemen was preaching a lady got up, way across the tent, and made her way down the right aisle. When she reached the bottom of the steps leading to the altar she stopped and I could see she had a goiter. Not too much later a man took his place next to the steps where I was sitting. He seemed okay to me but was really sweating. When the first participating minister was done there were five people standing at the bottom of the altar steps.

By the time The Reverend Olga Marksity was to minister, a slow and steady flow of people had formed two lines that stretched up the aisles, half way to the rear of the tent. There were men, women, and children of all ages and descriptions. For some, it was easy to see their afflictions. Others seemed perfectly normal. As Reverend Marksity rose and moved to the pulpit, the tent and surrounding crowd became very quiet. But the pulse of the gathering increased so that the whole place felt like it was swaying.

When Reverend Marksity finished her opening prayer, the participating ministers and various church elders stood up and moved to what were clearly predetermined positions. There were two men at the bottom and top of each set of altar steps and four men either side of the pulpit. While they were moving into position, Olga explained that all those waiting would be welcome to join her, escorted one at a time, alternating from the two aisles.

She went on to congratulate the crowd for its participation and acknowledged the faith and hope of both those standing in the aisles and those who had brought these Brothers and Sisters. She did this in a manner I had witnessed many times before with the same results. Even though she spoke to the crowd, she was heard by each individual personally.

She asked that the first lady, who had walked to the right hand steps during the start of the service, come up to the pulpit. The lady was escorted by one brother after another until she was standing with The Reverend Olga, who began to pray. The lady clasped her hands and closed her eyes and as she did so The Reverend Marksity laid her hands on the woman's head. The woman's goiter seemed to quiver and then began to shrink. As all eyes focused on the scene, the goiter got smaller and smaller until there was nothing but a proportioned neck. The woman tried to thank The Reverend. But the man from the opposite steps had been brought to the pulpit. As The Reverend smiled at the woman and turned to the man, singing spontaneously broke out and the crying for joy was uplifting and infectious.

As one after the other of those who had come in faith moved across the altar and were healed, exaltations to the Lord and a general uproar of thanks, praise, and wonderment swept over and across the crowd.

This went on for several hours but I am not a good witness to that time. The night before, after the first goiter, my mind was jammed. Now it had two images of fleshy donuts disappearing right in front of me. As the lady's goiter disappeared I seemed to retreat to a quiet corner where my mind and spirit needed to be. I felt safe and secure. I felt the presence of God. I gained balance as I came to the understanding that my life would never be the same. I still couldn't explain how I was different but knew it was a fact.

In time I returned to the reality of the moment and was able to see and feel the experience. It was as if God was roaming around the tent in a Casual Magnificence, touching humans here and there and giving all a glimpse of Himself. I couldn't describe the power of His Presence, but knew that anything that was to follow in my life would always be second. At that moment, in that tent, surrounded by the miracles I had witnessed, I had no clue how far behind second could be.

CONGREGATION

What a crowd. We don't have enough chairs. People are standing along the walls and sitting in the display windows. How did all these people find us?

It was full houses most of the weeks after a Revival, Tent Meeting, or any instance where the Reverend Olga Marksity, was being used by The Almighty Wonder.

There were other things that routinely created crowds at The Peniel Missionary Assembly. For example, when Brother Frink visited, his flock would follow to our store front. He had a following across the country. He also had the need to visit with The Reverend Olga regularly and when he did, the parts of his flock in the vicinity suddenly appeared. In his case, vicinity meant two States away.

Similarly, referrals would bring crowds that strained the seams of church. Referrals from ministers, gurus, teachers, skeptics, theologians, and those who had simply heard someone talk about the feeling they experienced in our church.

How long would these crowds continue? Not so long. Like George said, attendance fluctuates.

THE MATRIARCH

Baba and I went places together. Sometimes she had to drag me, sometimes it was a matter of convenience, sometimes I was eager to go. This time, I was more than eager to go.

It was early afternoon when we left McMicken. It took a long time to make the trek to Central Avenue and up the three flights of stairs to our destination, a small apartment in a tenement. Sparsely furnished, clean, with the Serbian trademark crocheted doilies everywhere you looked. We were very welcomed at the door. This is what I had been waiting for since I don't know how long.

There were four babas, dressed in black, plus mine in black as well. This was not her habit but this was not a routine visit. Baba introduced me and as she did each baba hugged me and patted me on the head. I didn't hug them back. Something made me feel I didn't have the right to do so. I did thank them for allowing me to visit. They were glad we got to meet and then excused me to make myself at home.

I took up a spot by the window. As they began to talk, I once again thanked The Almighty for giving me what I needed. My reputation as a child who was seen and not heard, who didn't ask questions and repeated nothing, enabled me to witness activities

beyond my years. Those experiences developed my senses of subtlety, innuendo, and awareness of the surroundings. I needed all
of them at their best for this encounter. My language problems
in school, resulting from Serbian being my first language, were
unimportant and worth the aggravation. Sitting on that floor, I
was very thankful Serbian was my first language.

As mentioned, Baba Maria Vukich controlled her history.
She told me almost nothing about herself. Her four children
were part of her history but knew she didn't want them to say
anything. They knew who was in control and kept their mouths
shut. In time, I concluded there was another reason they didn't
talk about her. They didn't want to share her, not with each other
or anyone else, including me. The plain truth was, no one in the
family, congregation, neighborhood, Serbian communities, no
one, ever talked about Baba. Now, I was going to learn about her
in a manner that could only be described as a gift.

These babas grew up together. The one visiting Cincinnati,
after recently arriving in America, had been presumed dead for
years. She had been one of Baba's friends. Now, she was the last
living friend Baba had from her homeland.

The five ladies were reminiscing about home. Childhood in
Serbia. Their memories were not childlike. They reviewed no parties, excitement at school, family get togethers, youthful infatua-
tions, celebrations, secrets shared. They were not little girls forced
to grow up very fast. They had never been little girls. They shared
no memories of light heartedness, fun, or laughter. Their memories were of lean years, scraping by, the flash flood, hanging by
a thread, sixteen hour days, deaths of loved ones. I was surprised
they were neither bitter nor sad. They were neutral. Almost happy, in a mood of acceptance that their lives started hard and got
harder. "Yes, that's the way it was."

Then right in the middle of this, they stopped to have a drink. When they asked if I wanted anything I almost blurted out that all I wanted was for them to continue. Fortunately, I didn't embarrass myself or Baba and politely declined. They mentioned I seemed very hot. They were right, I had been sweating. I hadn't noticed. I was hearing privileged conversation.

The baba who lived in the flat brought me a drink and told me to climb out the window and sit on the fire escape. I thought she didn't want me listening and my face must have shown I was hurt. They all laughed and told me to sit outside and not worry, I'd be able to hear their boring tales. They were uncertain why I would want to listen to such things, but listen I could.

I climbed out to the fire escape. It was pretty high up. Worse, it was not solid but grill work that was way too easy to see through. I was none too fond of heights but lo and behold, there was a breeze moving upward at a steady pace. Compared to inside the flat, the fire escape was a pleasant place to sit, if I just remembered not to look down. The move outside and all this thinking took about a minute and then all my concentration was back with the babas. I would have stood on a board or clung to the bricks to hear what they had to say.

Finally, they got their lemonades and waters and Vichy's and began again.

As the afternoon turned to evening, I saw my Grandmother in an entirely new light. She was not The Matriarch during this experience. In fact this was the only time I can recall her being one of those around her. She was one of a group, one of them. The black outfit was an early clue to this reality but I had missed it. She wanted to be one of this group. They were all glad to be one of them. They were glad to have each other. They were gaining strength from having and sharing the same history. A group where each member perfectly understood the others.

I have mentioned that being accepted to go anywhere and see everything increased the wonder of my life. It wasn't always fun. This, was painful. I hadn't imagined what their lives had been. Something Bigger had given me experiences so I could understand their stories, but the hardships that were the routine of their lives made me humble.

It was late when Baba and I said "laco noich" and headed back to McMicken. We didn't speak a word, but she knew. Knew and would have preferred it were not so. It didn't matter what she preferred, she had become an even larger figure in my life.

I had been taught the word respect. That day, listening to those babas talk about their shared experiences, where they had come from, what they had been through, my concept of respect matured. Those five black clad babas established a new benchmark by which I measured respect from then on.

As for me, I was hearing privileged conversation, first-hand accounts of life beyond my realm. I was learning history from those who made it. But it wasn't fun and haunted me long after. I was haunted by the questions, would I ever have the strength, could I ever find the courage, to live a life such as theirs?

There was one more result of that day. I learned, clearly and with resolution, that I was exactly like those five babas in one way. We all had faith and believed in A Greater Power. That is what sustained them and for a glimpse I knew, it had and always would, sustain me.

CONGREGATION

It's nice that Baba Mitza finally dropped in at The Peniel Missionary Assembly. It took long enough for her to get herself here.

She's the "some sort of Aunt" George came to see when he moved to America. I just can't understand what "some sort of" Aunt, Uncle, whatever, means. George and Olga won't let me pin them down to explain the matter. Their most usual ploy is, "Zoran, we're all of the same family, everyone in the world, we're all God's children." The fact they didn't satisfy me one iota, didn't matter to either of the Reverends, one iota. Remember what I told you about our family tree?

A lot of relatives, both the "for real ones" and the "some sort of ones," don't attend. People come from around the world to see The Reverend Olga while her blood can't make it across town.

Anyway I'm glad Baba Mitza is here. Of course her husband Elia just won't attend.

THE PLAYGROUND

While we lived at 64 East McMicken I spent a lot of time at the playground, watching. I stayed by myself. I don't think I was shy but I knew adults not kids and I sure didn't know how to play. Also, I didn't sound like the others and didn't know how to swim. I didn't even have a swimsuit. But I watched everything. I learned about non-Serbs, boys, girls, and the differences between church, home, and playground.

My favorite person to watch was a guy everyone watched, he was a pure athlete. I don't know how old he was. He sure wasn't a kid and he sure wasn't a man. Olga would probably have called him a young man. He was tall and played with a natural coordination. He moved like liquid even when he wasn't playing. I watched him anytime I could. The girls were always watching him too. I heard them say he was handsome. I wasn't sure what that meant. They all hoped he was watching them.

My least favorite person was a guy I made myself watch to be sure he never got too close to me. He was a bully and sneaky mean. At least as tall as my Favorite and twice as wide. He was clumsy, fat, greasy, and seemed older than everyone else. The girls

171

never watched him. They said he was ugly. They hated when he watched them.

I ended up watching them both because most of the time, when I was watching my Favorite, Sneaky Mean was there. He was always trying to compete with Favorite. No matter throwing, running, hitting, catching, sitting around talking, he competed but couldn't win. Everyone saw Favorite as good and Sneaky as bad and loved having good beat bad. And swimming? Forget swimming. It was the Dolphin and the Beached Whale. No matter, Sneaky Mean kept competing and always looked the fool he was. He was hopeless. They were white and black, hero and villain, and as the girls said, handsome and ugly.

Favorite didn't notice. He was just himself. He had no competitive feelings and shouldn't have. There was no one in his class. He was the hero of the playground.

As for the villain, he was sneaky, mean, mad, and full of hate. He was the only one who saw himself as Favorite's competitor. Everyone else saw him as a funny fatso. Not me. He was dangerous, and dirty. He made me feel worried, like something bad was just around the corner.

So the game of choice on the playground was egg-on Sneaky to compete and lose. Over time, Favorite didn't notice anything but sport—while Sneaky just got meaner.

I was in the second grade, between seven and eight years old, and we had been living on Orchard Court for some time. For some reason this particular week the four of us were staying downtown. It was a late summer evening and I went over to see what there was to watch at the playground. When I got there I found people hanging around poolside, even though the pool had been empty for days.

It was extra special because Favorite was there, standing in the empty pool with his strong arms crossed on the concrete pool deck, chatting. Everything was pleasant when, like a snake from the sewer, Sneaky Mean was there in the pool across from Favorite. He started saying things and kept the words going. Favorite didn't notice and that's when Sneaky made his rush.

Favorite dodged the rush of rhino as nimbly as a matador. Sneaky kept chasing Favorite and Favorite kept making him miss and everybody cheered.

After a time, Sneaky had to rest between each rush. People yelled at him. He rushed. He missed. People yelled. Sneaky took a deep breath and made another rush.

It was a swimming pool and even empty there were damp spots. As Sneaky charged, Favorite slipped on such a spot and Sneaky caught him on the shoulder. The blow knocked Favorite off his feet but Sneaky couldn't get stopped and turned around before Favorite was up.

Everything changed. The crowd was silent, stunned that Sneaky hit their hero. Sneaky had finally connected and wanted more. Favorite was now aware of Sneaky's power and knew it was a fight. It became a boxing match.

The boxing match was all Favorite. He had the moves and was working Sneaky's face into a pink then red glow and balanced this with regular hard shots to the body. But Sneaky wasn't going down. His fat absorbed the punches. His nose began to bleed.

Sneaky connected now and then and he packed a wallop but it wasn't enough to have an effect. When Favorite hit him flush, it hurt but hurt was not enough. Sneaky just kept coming. His lip began to bleed.

Favorite kept up the boxing lesson and eventually Sneaky doubled over. His nose and lip were bleeding freely. Favorite waited and Sneaky wanted more. The next time Sneaky was on a knee and Favorite gave him time. The third time Sneaky went down Favorite went to him and asked if he'd had enough and that's when Sneaky got him in a bear hug. With Favorite in his grasp, Sneaky bit his ear, face, and almost bit his nose off. By the time Favorite wriggled free he was bleeding all over.

Favorite now made Sneaky chase him and Sneaky did just that. Someone yelled, "Get out of the pool." Another voice, "He's got you trapped in there." But Favorite didn't seem to hear and stepped up the pace of his blows. His face and shirt were red with blood from the bites. Sneaky's nose and lip kept bleeding and his left eye began to swell. The pool was splotched with blood.

They went on. Favorite was tiring, his shirt was blood soaked and his pants were turning red.

Sneaky's left eye was swollen shut, his lip and nose bleeding.

They kept at it. Sneaky taking everything and only getting crazy. Favorite's punches were losing power. He was wearing red soaked clothes. His nose was gone and the ear Sneaky had bit was half off. Every time a punch landed a mist of blood sprayed those closest to the pool.

Then Favorite missed a punch and was off balance. Sneaky hit him flush on the right cheek. It was the first time he connected flush and it sent Favorite sprawling across the slippery floor. Sneaky was after him and hit him mean before Favorite got his feet going. Sneaky hit him with all his weight behind the blow. Favorite was lifted off his feet and flew against the pool wall. Blood flew on the crowd. People screamed.

Before Favorite could defend himself, Sneaky was on him. With Favorite against the concrete, Sneaky hit him in the side. On the second hit there was a crack like when a bat makes perfect contact with a ball. Favorite let out a scream. Sneaky pulled back for another blow and somehow Favorite lurched away. Holding his side he couldn't seem to breathe. Both were drenched with blood.

Sneaky was after him. Now there was no difference in their speed. Sneaky hit him in the back, driving him against the other wall and down on one knee. Sneaky moved in on the slumped Favorite and raised his fist to strike. Somehow Favorite was ready and swung from the pool floor with all his weight and legs behind the blow, catching Sneaky flush on the jaw. Blood sprayed the crowd again.

Sneaky staggered back and people cheered, certain that was the knockout uppercut. Sneaky staggered backward across the pool. He came to a stop against the opposite wall. On his feet.

The place went silent. Favorite was too hurt to follow Sneaky. It was plain Sneaky had some left but Favorite was done. The crowd went limp. It was over. The hero had lost. All over. People started to leave.

Not Sneaky. This had only fed his hate and anger. He had tasted blood. Now he was on Favorite. He hammered away. First in the mouth sending Favorite's teeth and blood flying all the way to the swings. Next in the mouth and Favorite's jaw seemed out of place, caved in. Next in the ribs, the same spot where the sound of bat hitting ball came from. The sounds were horrible as Favorite threw up a baseball sized hunk of red and black goo. Again to the face. The sound of Favorite's head bouncing off the concrete was loud yet dull. Blood was everywhere.

Favorite was unable to defend himself and Sneaky was glad. Another punch and Favorite was limp against the pool side. Another punch exposed the bone on the side of his face. People yelled at Sneaky to stop. This only fueled his meanness. The next punches sent Favorite's ear into the crowd. The men, pool and crowd were splattered with blood. Blood ran in rivulets to the drains.

Finally a bunch of guys jumped in the pool. Before they could control him, Sneaky kicked Favorite again. They got Sneaky on the floor and I realized I was crying. I must have been crying for some time, my shirt was all wet. I took off running in the neighborhood and kept running and crying and running and crying and running until I stopped crying—and the wet could be taken for sweat.

The next year Sneaky was there but no one else, even when the pool had water again. I don't know what became of him, one day he didn't show up and was never seen again. Not too long after he disappeared, Favorite showed up. He didn't move like liquid, he could hardly move. No one watched him, no girls called him handsome and most people had a hard time looking at him.

I tried to forget this as it was happening but couldn't. I tried to forget it afterwards and couldn't. In time, I began to see that the carnage and gore were more than a memory, they were a haunting. This haunting never left me.

CONGREGATION

Now that's a special couple. The Tollivers are about as different as I can't explain. They live on a farm. Someplace in Kentucky. They drive all the way here to attend church. Troy, what a keen name. Joyce, beautiful, blonde, American, with some sort of accent. I don't know how or when they started doing it, but they go anywhere The Reverend Olga goes. They worship like they seem to be. Troy is serious and concentrates, trying to get it just right. Joyce is smiling and carefree, like a shining light.

Boy is she pretty.

MY OWN ROOM

In 1951, after the second grade, we moved into our first house.

I had my own room.

It was a brick, two story, three bedroom on Daytona Avenue. I didn't have to share a room with Baba.

I had my own room.

The big front bedroom was for Olga and George. The left back bedroom was for Baba. The other bedroom was mine. All mine. There was a window on each of the two outside walls of my room. There was a closet in my room. It was my own room.

Unlike the move to Orchard Court, this move was not a transition. It was the way normal people move. We lived on Orchard Court in the morning and on Daytona that night. All of us.

That night was the first time in my life that I slept alone in my own room.

Just as it did after we moved to Orchard Court, McMicken remained my neighborhood after we moved to Daytona. It was several years before Daytona took over as my neighborhood.

Soon I was very busy with chores, my paper route, and school. I couldn't go downtown with Olga and George as before. Instead,

I began riding the electric street cars to attend the Wednesday evening prayer meetings. We'd all come home together.

Did I mention I had my own room?

ART DUPPS AND THE
NEWSPAPERBOY

I started working for money right after we moved to Daytona. Art Dupps was the newspaperman. He gave me the job of delivering The Cincinnati Times-Star, Monday through Saturday afternoons, on Daytona between Glenmore and Boudinot. These were the busy streets and, since I lived on Daytona, this route avoided my having to cross either. It was the perfect route for a third grader.

Five foot five, wiry, slight of build, and in excellent health, Art was always in motion. But not just physical motion. He could deliver a route, train a new carrier, collect a past due bill, calm a dog, tell a story about the area, say hello to everyone who passed, and make pencil notes to himself, all at the same time and all at very high speed.

He made notes in a small thick book that was held together with two big rubber bands. It was very special to him. Slips of paper were always sticking out of it. His notes were always in pencil. I can't recall him ever using a pen or without his book.

His hands were permanently black. His clothes looked like

the work of an artist who was learning about shadows. Everything was clean and sharp but anywhere there was contact with the papers, there were shadows.

What I remember most about his face was that his eyes were always shiny. In fact they weren't shiny, they were happy. And he should have been happy because he made anyone around him feel good.

I still can't figure out why I didn't call him Mr. Dupps. For me, anyone who wasn't in school was either Mr. or Mrs. or Brother or Sister, depending on whether they were from outside or inside the church. But Art was never Mr.

I didn't know if he was married. I thought he was. I thought everyone over a certain age was married. I didn't know if he had kids. I didn't know where he lived. I didn't see him in any other setting than as the newspaperman. In this setting, he was magic. So magic that in a few days he had turned me into a newspaper boy.

I would wait on Daytona, at the corner with Glenmore, dressed for action. My canvas sling on my right shoulder crossing my chest and riding on my left hip. Right on time, Art would pull up in his station wagon, park and open the back. My stack of papers, like those for all his other carriers, would be counted and staged. I'd pull my sling open and Art would slide my stack in, fold up front page upside down facing my body. During this time Art would ask me how I was, say something that made me feel good, tell me of any changes to delivery, wish me good day, close the gate, get in the wagon and be gone. Loaded and trained, I'd turn to my route.

The secret of the job was an Art specialty, the 'five-fold.' As I'd walk I'd pull the sling slightly apart with my left hand, reach across my body with my right hand and pull a paper out and up to my chest. First, fold the front page in half lengthwise. Second, fold the first third of the bottom of the front page to make a forty five degree angle. Now turn the rectangle over, so the corner fold was against my chest and the crease facing up. Third, fold the one third of the paper with the rectangle. Fourth, fold another third. Fifth, fold the last third and tuck it into the pocket formed by the forty five degree angle. Five folds, one tight square, locked into a thing of beauty.

Except when the paper was too thick, the five-fold was the ticket. When it was too thick we used the roll and tuck, a minor league trick that anyone could do.

As I folded and walked, it was less time consuming than preparing the papers before starting to deliver. However, the real genius of the five-fold was placement. Placement was the name of the game. The closer to the door, the more personal satisfaction. Placement was what earned the distinctions, The Newspaperman, The Newspaper boy. With the 'five-fold,' I could knock a frog off a stump, hit birds on the fly, or drop the paper in the dead center of Mrs. 3443's welcome mat.

Truth is, from my perspective, Art gave me money for taking a daily walk through wonderland. The trees on Daytona were plentiful and large. Their branches formed an arbor over the street. Daytona was a tunnel of comfort in the summer, a tunnel of colors in the fall and a tunnel of glory when covered with snow or ice in the winter.

Art paid me thirty-five cents a week to start. When I got the first little tan envelope with the coins inside, I felt a tremendous sense of security. I could make money. Fairly soon, he raised it to fifty cents. The amount was nothing compared to the recognition it represented.

There was more than the pay. Art was an American adult. A

male American adult. The first with whom I had direct private interaction. He was unlike any adult I knew. He was positive and uncomplicated. He cared about me learning to do the job. He showed me a person could be all business and all human at the same time. He taught me it was my responsibility to have fun working.

Sometimes his fun escaped me. He had some sayings. I'd learn and parrot them, even though I didn't completely understand them. To describe a silly mistake, "Grapefruit, you cantaloupe." which he would make sound like six words. When asked how he was, he'd answer, "Well, if a tree don't fall on me and the creek don't rise too high, I figure I'll be able to live until I die." For no apparent reason, "AB, c d goldfish? L, m n o Goldfish. O s m r."

I worked for Art steady through the summer of my sixth grade. At the end, the paper had undergone change and so had I. I was making a dollar and a quarter and still getting it once a week in a little tan envelope with my name printed in pencil.

Years later, while working in England, I watched smartly dressed people put on white gloves before reading The Times. Their gloves turning black reminded me of Art. Observing how they folded their papers, it came to me I never realized he had also taught me origami. The 'five-fold'.

Fifty years after I started working for Art, my wife and I went to dinner by Siesta Key in Florida. We were seated next to six couples celebrating one gentleman's 75th birthday. It was impossible not to hear them, as they reminisced, comparing their experiences as paperboys in New York and New Jersey. As they talked I realized they were missing something. I went to the Hostess and asked for a soft copy of their big rectangular menu. On the way back to the table, I did the 'five-fold' and before sitting down, pitched it perfectly in the center of the birthday party's table.

They had never seen anything like it. They had to try. "Fantastic, that fold can make anyone a dead eye." "It's so easy to learn to do." "It makes the box tight as a drum." "You say you call it the five-fold?" As they left we offered our best wishes. When we left, the Hostess presented a boxed tiramisu they had arranged to accompany us home.

I miss the wonderland tunnel that was my paper route, and I miss Art Dupps.

CONGREGATION

Oh boy. We're in for a treat. Militza Kosonchich is here.

Brother Benton was not the only artistically gifted person to attend The Peniel Missionary Assembly. There were several talented people. Singers, musicians and music teachers, artists and art teachers. Aunt Viola was an example. She'd just sit down at the piano and let fly. It could be real slow, real fast, or anything in between, but it always fit the song. No matter what it was, when she played, everyone's spirit was lifted. She made me want to learn about music. Sometimes I'd think, maybe I could even play.

Anyway, Militza Kosonchich was a singer.

I didn't know anything about her beliefs. I did know she really loved Olga. She was Serbian but like no Serb I knew. Not that it made any difference at church, but I think she was divorced because her son's name was Val Nicholus. Later, he and I attended grade school together.

Militza was a big lady and very pretty. That's wrong. She was more than pretty, she was beautiful. But her beauty was a kind I had never seen before. I didn't know how to describe it. Later I learned she was wearing make-up. Okay for make-up, from my point of view.

When Militza sang, she gave me goose bumps. She was the only person I ever heard who sounded as good as George when he let it go full out. Maybe even better, but if so, only a bit better. Small wonder, she was a professional opera star.

This time was just like the first time. Her singing was angelic. The entire congregation was affected. Some stared in awe. Some cried silently for joy. Some reflected the peace felt when in the presence of a gift. Aunt Viola was in great form but was working really hard. At a certain moment she just stopped playing, turned around and sat like all the rest of us, listening.

About half way through the service, I had a premonition. I couldn't make it out but as the service progressed it got stronger. Then I turned around and saw the cause. A crowd of passers-by had formed outside. They were standing on the sidewalk and curb, watching and waiting for Militza's next offering. As I saw them staring, I felt I understood what the displays in the down-town department stores windows felt like. When the service was over, the crowd was still there.

Sometime later, Militza gave us tickets to watch her perform at The Cincinnati Zoo. The Cincinnati Opera preformed during the summers at a special place in the zoo. What a thrill. I had never been to the zoo before. There were countless super cars and people dressed all fancy. It was exciting and maybe a little prideful that I knew the lady belting away on the stage. Like our congregation, the audience was affected. Lord, she could sing.

It was years later that I learned every zoo doesn't include an opera.

THIRD GRADE TEACHER
1951–1952

Printed on all Westwood Elementary School report cards, was a "Note to Parents" that included, "The teacher whose name appears on this cover is the one responsible for the general guidance of your child." Little did anyone know how much Eleanor C. Knoechel guided me.

Her appearance and demeanor reminded me of an American Aunt Viola.

She was the first person to make my language her priority. Being reared by Baba and thinking in a mountain dialect of Serbian made my words and pronunciation laborious and nothing like any of the other kids. Previous teachers were not negative to me, they just ignored my limits. Ms. Knoechel didn't ignore anything. She added volumes to my understanding of Americana.

She wasn't Serbian. Her approach was straightforward and simple. She noticed I had a limitation and treated it as normal. She confronted me with the fact I didn't speak correctly. Everybody had some limitation, this just happened to be mine. She had her own words to live by. "If you have a problem, face it. If you need help, admit it. When you need help, take it from anyone willing to give it, and then, forget it." Nope, she wasn't Serbian.

Her technique stayed with me. When I was stuck for a word, you know, you're moving along and you come to a _____ . When this happened to me, she would never fill in the blank. She would suggest a word and have me decide if the word fit the blank. This had obvious benefits for my language skills. It had other benefits, as demonstrated by the following.

Her question had to do with helping our parents clean and how we did so. When it was my turn to answer, I was proud to offer, "Of course I help. I have a regular schedule of cleaning the floors. I use the _____, to, ah ... the _____ ..."

She gave me a moment and then offered, "What do you think of vacuum, or sweeper?"

Vacuum sounded just fine. "I use the vacuum."

Thank goodness. I was happy to sit down. Just let someone else take over. Let me hide.

She didn't miss much. She asked me to come see her after school. When I showed up, I found she had seen this was a crushing incident for me and she wanted to know why. In no time she had me spilling the beans.

"I don't know what a vacuum is. We don't have one. I've never even seen one. I use a broom and dust pan on the wood. I shake the floor rugs out the upstairs window and off the porches. Some days I hang certain rugs on the line and beat them with a sort of stick. I was looking for the word for that stick."

My third grade teacher was the first person outside my home who got me talking about my home. She made talking to her about it — not difficult.

After I advanced to the fourth grade, she let me know where she lived. It was not too far from our house. She invited me to visit her whenever I wanted to talk. Particularly to talk about things American.

She was an American adult and a truly nice lady. She cared about me and my Serbian habits. I'm sure she never realized hers was the first American home I ever entered alone. I visited her five or six times—which meant I spent more time visiting her than I spent in all the homes of all my neighbors and all my classmates until high school. I hope she knew the positive impact she had on Zoran Mrksic.

By her hospitality she gave me my first view of an American home. When I visited, she thought we talked, I knew she taught. Her guidance expanded my mentality so that I began relating to other kids. As you can imagine, I didn't relate exactly like an American. However, thanks to my third grade teacher, I sounded almost exactly like one.

Ms. Knoechel would probably agree with almost.

STEVE KLAJIC

Not too long after we moved to Daytona, at breakfast, George and Olga announced we were going to have a meeting after supper. They wanted me to understand their decision. Great. On the way to school I thought how serious they were about the after-supper meeting. In fact, almost solemn. Then it hit me. During our last solemn meeting, I got new parents. I didn't know whether to be worried or excited. Since I didn't know, I let it go. After supper, as advertised, we had our meeting. They were solemn. Solemn and sincere in explaining their decision.

The Lord had blessed us many times over. Their ministry was providing support, comfort, and guidance for the spiritual, emotional, and physical needs of people who would not be served by any other means. We had our health and strength. We now lived in a wonderful neighborhood in our own home. We needed to show our appreciation. We needed to practice our faith and share our blessings. There were many people coming to America who had no place to go. They were called DPs for displaced persons. Many of them were from Yugoslavia and surrounding countries. We could help them by opening our hearts and home.

Finally, there were two circumstances that needed to be

understood. First, he was more than just another DP from Eastern Europe. He was a relative. Second, Baba would continue to live with us, so he would be sharing my room. His name was Toza Klajic. Americans called him Steve.

So, that was it, I was getting a roommate. Well, this is a nice meeting but there are some things I don't know. How come I never heard this person mentioned before? Ever? What kind of relative is he? Exactly? Where is he from? Originally? Is he coming here from there? What happened to him since the last time you were in contact? How old is he? Is he married? Does he have children? What's his background? What's he do? Not only did I not get answers, I didn't get to ask the questions.

Goodbye, my own room.

After the meeting, the biggest impact on me was that the family tree had undergone another mutation. Toza Klajic was from Baba's side of the family but, since she disdained to acknowledge that branch of the tree, it was not clear where he fit. I figured he had to be Olga's cousin. No one confirmed my figuring. So I decided that my new roommate was a relative who should be on the tree and I would call him Uncle Stevie.

On the day he arrived at our house, as we were being introduced, my first impression was that there was more about him on the inside than on the outside. Physically, he related perfectly with my family. Five foot three or four, he was short and stocky, certainly not fat. He had a round midsection that looked soft but on contact was as solid as rock. He had large forearms and wrists, thick hands, and was well coordinated. His overall complexion was not as dark as the rest of us. He had a considerable head with high cheekbones and wide set eyes. He was balding in the middle of his forehead which made him seem open and welcoming. I liked him immediately.

194

His American was poor so we talked Serbian. He moved in without incident, took the bed I wasn't using and we got along. Uncle Stevie was one of the few grownups who didn't treat me like an adult. We were comfortable together which was remarkable, considering we shared a bedroom with twin beds, a dresser with a mirror, and a small desk with chair. We also shared the single bathroom with Olga, George, and Baba.

Uncle Stevie seemed jolly, never griping, complaining or nit picking. He was energetic and more than willing to do anything around the house. When he offered to cut my hair, I learned he was a barber and he remained our barber. Soon after this he was hired by a local barbershop and we decided we'd start speaking American to give him practice. He developed a unique accent.

One night he came home from work and retrieved a case from our closet. He had not opened the case since placing it there when he moved in. It was his mandolin. He took his time preparing, then started to play. After a few songs he began to sing. I was to learn he could play guitar and other stringed instruments. He loved to sing and was particularly vocal when he came home late. He had a nice voice and played with a feeling that made me recall my first impression of him.

I'm not sure how long Uncle Stevie lived with us. More than a few months, less than a year. While we were roommates, I really enjoyed him. We never had serious or personal discussions but he told me things about Yugoslavia and Serbia. He gave me some idea about where we were from and taught me some songs that still push their way into my head. He was a Serb, yet he was different. I couldn't explain what was different. I just knew there was something about Toza Klajic that I had not experienced before. He laughed and played and sang and was happy. More than that, happy from the inside. No matter how upset Olga became with him, he could make her smile in short order. How did he do that? What was it about him? I just couldn't figure it out.

After he moved out, I would see him at various family holiday celebrations and every time I got a haircut. I would see him if the celebrations were at Rosie and Lou's, or our house. He was rarely present for get togethers at the Golusin's although I thought Aunt Viola liked him. He was never present at Botta's for anything, unless it was to provide manual labor helping Baba's boy. It became more and more pronounced that the family treated him, not like a black sheep but like a black mule. Baba did nothing to mitigate this treatment. She was the Matriarch and had made up her mind about that side of the family long ago. Uncle Stevie was on his own.

On the job, he was enjoying remarkable success. It turned out that his unique accent, enhanced his ability to communicate from behind the barber chair. The accent seemed to disarm his customers so that they were comfortable telling him anything that crossed their minds. Clearly he was a good barber, but there had to be other reasons for the loyalty his customers demonstrated. Barbershops actively recruited him because they knew how much additional business Steve Klajic would bring to their establishments. He did not move casually and thereby demonstrated his loyalty. When he did move, where ever he went, all his customers were sure to go. How did he do that? What was it about him? I just couldn't figure it out.

A few years after he arrived, a new development arrived. Her name was Elfriede. No one wanted to explain who, where, when, how, or anything about the two of them but everyone treated the two of them like lepers. What developed from this point on was a subtle, insidious, and cruel treatment of my old roommate and his lady friend.

In the barber chair I got him to admit he knew her from the war. The only thing he shared beyond that was that he had been working hard to bring her over so they could be together. From these sessions I realized he would always see me as the child he had bunked with and would not tell me his story. I also realized that I knew very little about my roommate. He had never mentioned Elfriede or, being in the war.

I decided to hear his story another way. Baba certainly knew the facts. When I asked her to fill me in, she was absolutely not going to talk about him or anything related to that side of her family. This Serbians 'never forget' thing was really beginning to chafe me. George, as usual, had nothing to say except, "Go ask your mother." Finally, Olga decided to tell me the story.

Toza Klajic became a Yugoslavian Partisan at the outbreak of World War II. He was captured by the Germans and shipped to Germany where he was held prisoner. During this period he met Elfriede. When the war was over, he made his way to America and us, his family, and then worked hard to get Elfriede to join him. There, I had it. Why this was such a secret was beyond me. I was glad to finally learn his story.

In the meantime, his success continued on the job and at home. He and Elfriede got married. I knew he was happy and I was happy for that.

In a couple more years, his success reached the point where I could see, feel, and ride in it. On this day he drove over to show us his brand new Pontiac. It was a big engine convertible. Black and red with whitewalls and a white top. It was gorgeous, plush, loaded and fast. When I saw it, I was happy for him and joyous for me. This was my roommate. I knew him when he came to America and had to share a room with me. I had seen his efforts pay off and felt like I was sharing his success.

It was not too much later when, in the middle of one night, Olga and George woke me and told me to get in the car. We headed down Queen City Avenue. When we came to the intersection with Harrison Avenue, we turned left and started up the hill. At the first curve, I saw the Police lights and the rear of Uncle Stevie's Pontiac. When we got up to the car, it was oddly close to a telephone pole. As we passed and pulled in front to park, I could see that the pole was two feet into the car and had pushed the engine through the dashboard.

Uncle Stevie was nowhere to be seen. I went over to the smashed convertible. Blood was splattered all over and the front seats were covered with it. It came to me, this must be his blood. From the policeman at the scene, we learned that he had already been taken to the hospital.

I don't remember anything after the scene of the accident and the topic was never mentioned by Olga, George, or any of the relatives. Uncle Stevie survived and didn't seem to have any lasting effects from the wreck. At least none I could see from the outside. How did he do that? What was it about him? I just couldn't figure it out.

The years passed and I had little contact with Steve and Elfriede. No matter, because they were doing fine. They bought a house, started a family and had two daughters. Monica, who was full of spirit and energy and Margie, who was beautiful.

During those years, Baba's son and his second wife didn't change toward Uncle Stevie and merely looked down their noses at Elfriede and the girls. Margaret would have probably looked down her nose at their dog, if the Klajics had one. The Golusins, Aunt Viola and Uncle Nicky, were not so blatant but the Klajic's were not welcome in their home. The Bakers were as nice to them as they were nice to everyone, how they really felt was always hard to know. Olga and George were genuine in their affection for Steve, Elfriede, and particularly the girls.

As for me, the time came when enough was enough. I'm not sure how old I was but I was in High School. We were at the Bakers, the whole clan. On this occasion a favorite and particularly dirty little trick was being administered. Whenever Elfriede would try to participate, the family would begin speaking Serbian. Uncle Steve walked into the other room but I spoke up. I described exactly what they had done, reminded them of the untold number of times I had witnessed this before and wanted them to know I thought they were all cowards, prejudiced bigots, and consummate asses. Everyone looked at me but not in shock. What shocked me was, no one said a word while I got my things and walked out.

Steve and Elfriede were just the opposite. They were always upbeat, positive. This was their demeanor, no matter how rudely they were treated by the others in the family. More opposite the rest of the family, was their generosity. In hosting holiday celebrations, everyone was welcome. Botta could have brought his second wife and she could have brought her dog, if she had one. How did they do that? What was it about them? I just couldn't figure it out.

Sometime in 1962, while I was in college, Uncle Stevie was selling his beautiful 1960, wide-track, two door, Pontiac Ventura. He gave me more than a good deal. I had the feeling he wasn't selling it to me, he was selling it to his old roommate.

It was 1966 when I had my next contact with Steve and Elfriede. I was home on leave before departing for Vietnam. Elfriede wanted to talk to me, privately. Most of what she told me is reported as part of her story, but this part of what she told me belongs here, with Uncle Stevie.

She explained what I had seen the day he arrived at our house. As we were being introduced, my first impression that there was more on the inside than on the outside. There was. A lot more. His story was a lot. Captured Serb Partisan. Put in a German prison camp. Meeting a German woman. Getting both to America and having a life and family. But his story was not the 'more'. The 'more' was that they were in love. That's what it was about him. That's how he did it. I had been roommates with a man in true love. Not a love story. A living true love. Right there, in the twin bed against the opposite wall of what used to be, my own room.

Toza, Uncle Stevie, Steve Klajic died in 1983. I truly regretted being in Europe at the time. I wanted to attend his funeral and say goodbye to my old roommate. He is buried in Cincinnati, in the Vukich family area of Arlington Cemetery. He is in a row, with the people who couldn't understand him. People who never figured out what there was about him or how he lived.

CONGREGATION

Olga and George eventually got around to my experience with the boys in the playground calling me a Holy Roller. They explained that Holy Roller was a term used to describe the members of congregations, in those churches where worship was accompanied by a lot of physical exertion. That sure was the case at The Peniel Missionary Assembly. We had all kinds of singing, crying, bursts of excitement, moving and jumping and dancing around and a whole lot of loud love. So, the boys in the playground were right, I was a Holy Roller.

Later, Baba let me know Holy Roller wasn't a term used as a compliment. She added that she very much approved my not taking offense when being called one. I was thrilled to get her compliment, but down deep I didn't feel I deserved it. Why should, or how could, being called a name make anyone take offense?

Anyway, back to Olga and George. They had no problems with labels, so Holy Roller didn't get their attentions. What got their attentions was my lack of understanding of other denominations. Thereafter, Olga saw to it that we attended all kinds of other places of worship.

The Methodists and Presbyterians were very organized. Their

services were mostly serious. Our church was mostly Old Testament, so I knew all about serious in services. But these were a different kind of serious. A serious that made me feel, if I started having a good time or even just enjoying myself, I'd be out of place.

The Greek and Serbian Orthodox were basically the same thing. There was some business about the history between them that I really didn't get. Anyway, even without the history, I was fascinated. Their pastors, make that Priests, had the neatest outfits I'd ever seen. Gold I'm sure and maybe some kinds of gems on the...I don't know what to call those things on their heads. And the places themselves! They looked like art galleries to me, with all the Saints and what-have-you all over the walls and behind...I guess it was the altar. Oddly, what really got me, were the smells. The Priests swung these gold things on chains that gave off a fragrance. The aroma was enough to make me want to attend their services.

The Catholic church was something like the Orthodox. What struck me was the exercise. I felt like a yo-yo, getting up, sitting down, getting up, kneeling down. Maybe it was because we were there at a special service. I figured it had to be special, they gave Communion.

It turned out the Baptist service was the closest to what went on at The Peniel Missionary Assembly.

The Synagogue was not a good experience. If there was anything spiritual about that gathering, I missed it. They were very positive that I needed to know I was different...to know I was not one of them. Now I knew all about being different. Different wasn't a problem for me. Nonetheless, not being welcome in their place of worship because I was different, because I wasn't Jewish, that was a problem. There were a few who pretended I was welcome. Welcome to be impressed by their history and rituals. Welcome to see what was not available to me, because I wasn't one of them. I was glad when it was over and wondered how I could have such a feeling after being in a place of worship. The more time passed, the more I wondered about that experience.

The most memorable church was The Assembly Of God, where both Olga and George had been saved and ordained.

From this period of visits and education I reached two conclusions. First, I had clear confirmation of what I had always believed. No matter the place or pageantry, there is absolutely—Something Bigger. Second, it's not the church that matters. It's not the religion that matters. All that matters is faith.

PINGEEOO

PINGE-e-oo. pin-GEE-oo. Same word. Two pronunciations. pin-GEE-oo had no supporters in our home. For us, it was replace the h in hinge with a p, and take the e and o from Old MacDonald. You know, e i e i o. PINGE-e-oo.

As I've said, studying the other kids at Westwood Elementary was all the schooling I could handle during kindergarten and the first and second grades. After the move to Daytona and the start of the third grade, I saw no reason to change my approach. Watch, don't be noticed. Listen, don't be heard. Learn, don't be known. That was my plan. I learned the third grade had its own plan.

There are some things I'd like to forget. Most of them involve my inhibitions, Serbian characteristics in non-Serb settings or, acting stupid. All of them include me being embarrassed. Real embarrassed. That's what I'd like to forget most, the embarrassments.

We were in a group outside our classroom when it happened. It was a total accident. She felt awful. Her embarrassment was magnified because it happened in a group. Okay. Other people did the same thing. Most were embarrassed. Some were horrified.

At the moment, some saw the chance to add to her embarrassment and had a great time doing so. Still others tried to give her support by pretending it hadn't happened. None of this mattered to her. She was mortified and mortified meant wishing she had a hole she could crawl in and never come out. I knew about mortified embarrassment. I thought I'd help. So I offered, "Ah let it alone. Cryminey, it was just a pingeeoo."

In the time it took to make my offering, she was no longer mortified or embarrassed. She was no longer the center of attention. No, that distinction was mine. And, in an equal amount of time, I was embarrassed and then mortified. The other kids found pingeeoo to be the funniest thing they had ever heard and me, the funniest talker of all times.

Later, standing alone on the playground, I thought of the first time I made a pingeeoo in public. Some adult took me aside and told me it was not a big deal. A pingeeoo was the natural release of gases from the body. It was totally natural and nothing to be ashamed of. However, for big boys who wanted to be men, the polite action was to keep one's pingeeoos private. This was how I saw things, until that day at school.

As the day passed, I learned no one used the label pingeeoo and there were many labels. Cut one, pass gas, poodie, break wind, cut the mustard, toot, the burp that took the basement exit, cut the cheese, silent killer, patootie, the high brow flatulence and, the sort of cuss word, fart. I had never heard any of these. The day passed. The fact she, the originator, laughed the loudest at my crazy word, never passed the Serbian in me and I have never forgotten her.

That night at home, I wanted some clarification. I had some questions based on the fact no one, absolutely no one, at Westwood Elementary had ever heard of a pingeeoo. How could that be? I waited for George to be alone. There was no way I could bring up something like this around Reverend Olga or The Matriarch. Finally he was alone and when he heard what I wanted, he put on his "you bet I'm ready to help" face and told me to fire away.

"Well, how come no one ever heard of pingeeoo?" He didn't know.

"Have you heard it called other things?" Oh, he certainly had. He even gave me a French one that sounded like the sound the girl at school made. That sort of got me off track.

"Okay. Well, why didn't we ever use other labels for it?" He didn't know.

Then he asked me what else did I want to know? I could tell he felt this session was going great.

"How about elsewhere. In the fields, do the cows let pingeeoos?" His answer was confusing. Apparently cows only pass gas.

"How about horses?" Same thing, no pingeeoos from the broncos, they break wind.

At the end of a series of equally useless exchanges, I quit. He left, satisfied he had done good. I left, satisfied that the only living beings that emit natural gas via pingeeoos, were those living in our house.

It wasn't funny. There was more to this incident. To this point, my plan was to study other kids and not be noticed, heard or known. The pingeeoo exploded my plans. The incident let other people see a difference between my world and their world. I knew it was only a forerunner. Others would follow and my embarrassments would multiply. The differences in my language, dress, home life, trips to church, in all aspects of my life, would be exposed. I knew I would have to try and limit such exposures and be ready when they occurred. In short, I was on a fast track to more introspection, shyness, and the role of removed observer.

By the way, had you ever heard of a pingeeoo before?

MY CASTLE IN MILWAUKEE

I woke up and immediately recognized I was in my favorite bed. Something was different? It was dark and headlights flashed now and again. No, that was typical. George and Olga were in the front seat, speaking softly when they did speak. No, that was normal. The rhythmic thump, thump, thump, of travel was lulling me to sleep. Yes—that was different. I was not going to sleep under the seductive metronome of the tires hitting the roadway. I was waking up. Of course. We had left very early in the morning when it was still dark and I had immediately fallen asleep. We were not on the last leg of the journey home, we were on the first leg of the journey to Milwaukee. To Wisconsin.

Once I figured the situation, I stretched out flat on my back with my hands behind my head. I stared up at the fabric ceiling and snuggled into the coziness of the '48 Buick's big back seat. I'm not sure it was a Roadmaster, but it was the perfect size for me and my things. Most importantly, I never had to share it. It really was my favorite bed and I felt lucky that our travelling had steadily increased. As I watched the dawn break, I was looking forward to going to the farthest place yet for the longest stay yet.

We were starting a real trip, seven days away and all the way to Milwaukee.

As the day unfolded, I sat glued to the windows. First this side, then the other. There was so much to see. I wished I could take it all in but that was impossible. As always, the scenery enriched my spirit and touched my soul. God had made all this and when I missed a stand of trees or patch of water, I felt I missed His handiwork. It was impossible to take it all in.

As always, the ride was over way too fast. We turned right off the highway and down a small embankment which put us on a huge flat plain. In front of us the land had been cleared and this 'parking lot' seemed endless. Far across this tract the ground was covered with tents of all types, shapes, and sizes. The main tent was dominant and huge with four poles along its center spine. On the other side of the main tent, the ground was covered by tents as far as I could see. Once across the parking area, as we drove among the tents, it was clear the grassless paths were the streets of this tent city. We stopped in front of a large tent with a sign that said, Welcome Center.

Inside the Welcome Center there were two large banners announcing that we were Welcome to the Milwaukee Tent Meeting, with the appropriate dates. George and Olga talked to the people behind the long counter. Soon, a man hurried through the tent flap and over to shake hands with George and The Reverend Olga Marksity. I was summoned over, by Olga's come here eye movement, and introduced to this coordinating minister. Soon after, we left the Welcome Center, got in the car and found our way to one of what looked like hundreds of similar small tents.

George and Olga started getting their things out of the car and only then did I realize this was where we were going to stay. I wondered who would be staying with us. George explained that this was our tent. "Our tent?" That's right, our tent. "We aren't going to have to share this with anyone?" No. What a bonus. We were going to be staying in our own private tent. I rushed to get my things and take them inside. Inside our tent.

Inside there were four cots, two canvas backed chairs, two small chest type tables, and two light bulbs hanging from a thick black wire that ran through the tent. There was also a wire down the middle of the tent holding up a sort of curtain that could be pulled across to divide the tent into two exact halves. George and Olga took the two cots on the right side of the tent and I had my pick of the two on the left. I took the one farthest from the flap, opened my small suitcase and started to put it under the cot. George suggested we keep our things on the spare cot, especially if it started to rain. Great. We had our own tent. I had my own bed. I got in and went to sleep.

The next morning, we took off walking to one of what was to be many meetings. As we walked, I noticed it was going to be hard to get lost because we were close to the dominant tent and no matter where we walked I could always see its mass. There were several midsized tents and the first meeting was in one of these. It had chairs in rows and a raised platform at the front. After the meeting, as we headed to our tent, we came upon a tent that was very near as big as the dominant tent but not as high. George and Olga took me inside to see this cafeteria tent. It had many entrance flaps, tables and chairs all over, and in the front, two rows of cabinets that had holes in their tops. George explained these were serving cabinets. As we left and headed back to our tent, it was clear this big place would take a lot of exploring.

After noon, George and Olga had another meeting to go to. As soon as they left I laid down on my bed, in our tent. It was neat. I was away from home and didn't have to sleep in a room with an adult I knew, an adult I had met once or, an adult I didn't know. Plus, I had a cot and not a couch, chair, blanket, or floor to sleep on. This Milwaukee Tent Meeting was alright. After a time, I pulled the curtain across the tent and now I had my own room. Room, it was more than a room, it was my flat. In no time, it was my castle. Over the course of the Tent Meeting, I was able to explore the tent city. I found the small stream that ran behind the last row of small tents. Going from my castle to the stream, from my castle through the walkways of the city, from my castle to anyplace, was full of fun and adventure.

Evening marked the start of the Tent Meeting. The main tent was much bigger than I imagined, even after counting its four main poles. It had the typical set up of rows and rows of folding chairs, raised altar with chairs, podium, and raised platform for the choir. But, for the first time I was in a tent that had four main aisles to the altar. These aisles, as well as the walkways around the altar, were paved with wooden planks.

As people filed into the tent, I recognized aspects of these meetings that were becoming routine to me. All kinds of vehicles lined up on the highway waiting to turn into the parking areas, a good crowd, a host pastor, welcoming comments, singing, preliminary sermons by guest ministers, and a sense of anticipation. On the other hand, there were two things about this gathering I didn't recognize. These people were not in their Sunday best and they were from all over the Central and Northern United States.

As was now happening everywhere we went, when The Reverend Olga Marksity was introduced the entire atmosphere changed, as if moving to a more intense level. She began to preach and my mind was filled with the picture of the first goiter shrinking and disappearing from the donut lady. As she continued, Brothers and Sisters began to line the aisles, waiting with their afflictions. There were problems of deformity, faith, function, mind, pain, spirit, anguish, accident, who knows. As I sat among the congregation, The Reverend Olga invited the first person in the right most aisle to the podium. Immediately the miracles began, changing many a life and becoming a testament to faith. As a witness, the power and glory of The Almighty transfixed every atom of my body and every wisp of my soul.

Overall, the miracles were just a blur of the Almighty's Wonder. However, on the second night, my attention got focused on a man in line who seemed to be the picture of health and strength. In the aisle lines there were many sights to grab and hold the eye. This man was different. Big, fit and clearly active, he was neatly dressed and very imposing. My eyes kept returning to him because I couldn't understand why he was there. He looked totally normal. Was he accompanying someone in need? It was hard to imagine such a man being in such a line. Was he holding a spot in line for someone who couldn't navigate, someone who would be carried in when this man got to the foot of the altar? I just couldn't make it out and this raised my level of curiosity.

Finally, he turned to speak to the lady behind him and as he turned I saw his left arm, or what there was of his left arm. As he stood in line I hadn't been able to see his left side. Now, I saw that the left arm was totally deformed. First, it was very small and seemed to dangle from his short shirt sleeve. Second, the hand, which looked like a baby's, was curled inward at the tiny wrist. Third, the tiny hand was somehow twisted and the fingers were oddly bent. Even though the sight of his arm repulsed me, I couldn't take my eyes off him.

Eventually, he reached the foot of the altar. The assistant stationed there was taken aback by the deformity and another assistant quickly came over and led the man to the pulpit where The Reverend Olga Marksity had been praying for the believers. The rewards of their faith was a continuous testament as God touched them, one after the other, through the Reverend.

Unlike me, The Reverend welcomed the sight of the deformed arm and took the tiny hand and wrist in her right hand as if it were most normal. She used it to pull the man toward her and hugged him. For the first time I saw emotion on his face. She pulled back, grasped the man's right hand with her left hand and pushed it against his chest. She closed her eyes and began to pray and as she did so, she pushed him backward by force on his chest. He began to extend his good right arm and she kept her grip on the deformed left. As his body moved back, away from her, his left arm began to stretch. It continued to stretch and at a certain point was clearly growing. The farther she pushed him the more he extended his good arm and the more his left arm grew. It grew and it became straighter and straighter until the arm was normal and the only deformity was the tiny curled wrist and twisted hand still being held in the right hand of The Reverend Olga Marksity. The man began to cry.

She was praying and her eyes were closed all the while. At a certain moment, she released his right hand and cupped the small left wrist and hand in her hands. Slowly, as if it were in slow motion, I could see the twisted fingers of the crippled hand turning and becoming extended, the hand becoming flat, the wrist uncurling and becoming straight, the hand lining up with the wrist and finally, both lining up with the arm. The Reverend Olga Marksity opened her eyes and released his hand. The man looked at his hand which was normal and in proportion to his arm which had already become normal and proportioned to his body. He stopped crying and kept looking from the Reverend

214

to his arm and back. He flexed his hand. He turned his wrist. He began to sob for joy. He bent his elbow. He extended, pulled back, extended, pulled back, extended and pulled back his arm. Over and over and over, he demonstrated the rewards of his faith.

The congregation seemed to lose its breath in sequence, from the front to the back rows, as the deformed arm grew and became normal. The result was a hush over the tent and perhaps over the entire tent city. It was very calm, as if the entire area was frozen. Frozen in peace. Frozen in grace. Then, a respectful but clear Hallelujah was heard and everything erupted. Singing, dancing, crying, hugging, praying, praise, all happiness, all wonder.

So it went for all the days of the Tent Meeting. The only change was the volume of people which increased each night.

On the ride home, the power and glory of God, as demonstrated in the change of the deformed arm, went from the front of my mind to become a part of my being. This moment has never been far from the surface of my life's minutes. Its influence on my secular self, complete.

Oh yes. If I work real hard, I can recall my castle amid the tents in Milwaukee. In Wisconsin.

HEY, YOU SHOT ME
IN THE HEART

I was not comfortable being in other kid's houses and have no memory of ever staying overnight. Even with my aunts and uncles, I recall staying only once with Viola and Nicky. However, this night I was going to stay with my church mate, Donnie Christoff. My first ever sleep over.

At a time determined by his mother, Donnie and I were sent to bed. This was not a bad thing. First, from the outside, the house seemed to be made entirely of concrete, not smooth concrete but textured, like a castle or fort. Second, Donnie's room was the third floor attic, where the steep angles of the roof made the long open space a petri dish for budding fantasies. This was the castle's inner sanctum. Third, he had comic books, magazines, all kinds of toys, gadgets, those collectibles that only boys treasure and...secrets.

As we made the trek up the stairs to the third floor, we were ascending into the heart of the castle and I was full of anticipation. Once there, the revelry began. We were lost in the wonder of our imaginations.

Twice, someone came to the bottom of the steps on the first floor and directed us to stop playing around and get to bed. This did little more than make us slow down for what we thought was an appropriate time and then we continued our adventures. Actually it was a continuation of Donnie showing me his marvels.

On a third occasion, someone came all the way upstairs. They made us get into bed, turned off the lights and descended with the admonition for us to, "Stay put."

Some time passed after they left when Donnie said, "Alright, let's try this." Clearly he had done this before. Using a stick in the middle of his bed, he made a tent with the blanket. Next, he produced a flashlight. I crawled under the blanket, into the tent, and we began to read comic books.

In one of the comics, Donnie found a catalyst that prompted him to show me his biggest secret. I was flattered. I was happy. I was honored. I had to turn off the flashlight and hold the stick, while he went foraging in the wilds outside the tent. I could hear him moving around. It was hard to determine exactly where he was or what he was doing. This only added excitement to the event.

He was moving around. He was opening something. He was returning. Then, he was under the cover, inside our tent. He told me to light the flashlight. He had something. Once we got settled, he showed me the box. He let me feel it, making sure I knew not to open it. It was very heavy. He took it back and carefully laid it on the bed between us. He made a motion as if he had changed his mind. I caught my breath. No, he hadn't changed his mind. He turned the box, so the opening side faced me. Then slowly, he opened it. It was a gun!

The only guns I had seen before, were the set of The Lone Ranger's six shooters I got one Christmas from my aunt and uncle. This was not like the Lone Ranger's guns. It was larger, heavier, and black with brown handles.

Referring to the comic we had just finished, Donnie showed me how the gun worked and how to load it. We talked and dreamed and fantasized we were shooting the bad guys and saving the good guys. I don't remember us saving any damsels in distress, only doing good against the bad.

At one point it was Donnie's turn to handle the hardware. We had been after some evil menace for too long when Donnie finally got him in his sights. He pulled the trigger. Suddenly, I was laying on my back. As I opened my eyes I saw Donnie staring down on me. His eyes seemed bigger than his head. He wasn't really looking at me, he was looking at my chest. I blinked a few times and then I looked at my chest. I saw what looked like the ends of feathers sticking out of my chest. They were sticking out about a third of the way to my waist and a little bit off center, right in my heart. I looked at Donnie. His eyes were still slammed open. I looked down again and blurted out, "Hey, you shot me in the heart." And so he had.

We both realized that we could be in big trouble over this. I looked down again. There wasn't much blood around the feathers. Rather, a sort of small, slow, trickle. I looked up and Donnie's eyes were joined by his mouth, wide open. He didn't seem to be breathing so I reached up and slapped him. After shaking his head he said, "Aw, your mother's gonna kill us."

"Will she ever."

"What are we gonna do?"

"We gotta not let her find out. We gotta not let anybody find out."

"Okay. How we gonna do that?"

"I don't know."

"How do you feel?"

"I don't feel much. I don't feel anything. I don't know how I feel."

"Do you hurt?"

"I don't know."

"Are you gonna scream?"

"I don't think so."

"What are we gonna do?"

This high level gathering of options continued until we both realized we had no clue what we were going to do. I decided I might be able to think better sitting up. As I attempted to sit up, Donnie grabbed me by the shoulders, pushed me down and warned, "Don't move. You'll make it bleed more."

Now I hurt. Not from the shot in the heart, from his crushing my shoulders. "Leave me alone. I gotta sit up."

I sat up and, of course, all the exertion caused a little more seepage of blood; but it was still a minor amount. We both inspected the wound, curious and terrified.

Donnie pondered. "What is gonna happen if someone comes up here and finds us?"

"My mom will definitely kill us both."

Finally, he found some ambulatory ability. He knocked down the tent, jumped off the bed, propped me up with the pillows and sat looking at my chest while pointing the flashlight at my heart. The feathers from the pellet continued producing a slow seepage of blood, which by this time had accumulated enough to form a rivulet, which in turn, had made it to my belly button where a nice red reservoir was growing. As my belly button filled with blood, we became filled with panic.

Donnie made the profound conclusion, "We gotta stop this blood."

"How we gonna do that?"

"We'll use a band aid."

"Where we gonna put it?"

"On the...on the thing."

What was he talking about. "On what thing?'

"On the hole."

"There is no hole. There's a thing in there making a hole."

"Well, the thing making the hole is the thing making you bleed and that's what we gotta stop."

Finally, we agreed we had to get the feathers out. Why we didn't think about the projectile the feathers were attached to, I have no clue. But, when you're shot in the heart you probably don't think your best. At least that was my experience.

Donnie was rummaging around looking for a band aid. He wasn't careful. Maybe he had something on his mind. Anyway, he was knocking things over and making a racket. Sure enough, we suddenly heard a voice, "I'm telling you for the last time, settle down and go to sleep." The entire third floor froze.

Now a lot of time passed. Eventually, like a good Indian scout, making no noise, Donnie appeared. He had a pair of pliers. It was pretty clear what he had in mind. I suggested I needed something to bite down on, like the cowboys did.

"Well, why don't you just wait and I'll get you a bullet to chew on." He could be a real pain.

"Well, I need something. Otherwise, I'm probably gonna make noise."

"Okay. Let me look."

Finally he handed me a Lincoln Log piece.

Next, I thought that maybe if I laid down it would be easier to get to the spot. He agreed. I laid down and Donnie got on his knees next to my right side. He gave me the flashlight. As I held the light he put the pliers around the feathers, as close as he could to the skin. By doing this he was also getting a bit of the metal of the pellet. Without any warning or preparation, he yanked. Out popped the feathers and pellet, clean as a whistle.

I was really mad. He hadn't even given me the chance to bite down on the Lincoln Log.

The spot bled rather freely for a moment and then, quickly, stopped. I had a nice mess from the spot to the overflowing belly button. Donnie grabbed the nearest thing and cleaned up the blood. He did a nice job. Then, we realized he had used his shirt to sop the blood.

He was upset. "Oh God. They'll see the blood on the shirt and we'll be dead." He was gone in an instant. I didn't know what he was up to. When he returned he had another shirt. I asked him what happened to the other shirt and he told me, "Never mind. Just never mind."

In the meantime all signs of seepage had stopped. I didn't feel the worse for wear and we sat and watched my chest. Nothing happened.

We sat some more. Nothing happened some more.

We started turning the flashlight on and off. Every time we turned it on, nothing had happened. We did this for a time. Nothing happening. I told him it was fine and we should sleep. He covered me with the blanket and left, taking the flashlight with him. It was only later, when I rolled over onto the pellet gun, that we remembered it was still in bed with me. I was more scared at this discovery than I had been all evening. Donnie got up and put the gun and box back in hiding.

No one ever knew of this incident. Today, if you look closely, you can see the scar where Donnie Christoff, shot me in the heart.

CONGREGATION

I really liked Communion. Of course the real meaning and purpose were first and foremost. The grace and holiness of Communion needs no promotion. If you didn't know that, you were shortchanging your whole life. At our church, with every Communion service, the truth of Something Bigger was demonstrated in how the worshipers were affected.

But there was a bunch of other neat stuff involved. Preparing for Communion, George would go to the cabinets behind the piano and get out the hardware. First, a shallow silver bowl for the wafers. The wafers really didn't taste much but they were different and, like Communion, only available on special occasions. Next came the silver trays that held the little glasses for the wine. I loved them because of how they looked and for the treats they normally gave me. Picture a thin silver disk about as big around as the steering wheel of a car. There are four silver handles at the edge of the disk that hold the disk up and make it easy to carry the tray. The disk is full of identically sized holes. The holes are full of tiny glasses whose sides curve up and out from the bottom. Each glass fits into a hole up to the point where it is too wide to go any farther, sort of like putting a top, upside down, in a milk bottle, the top stops itself. George would fill every glass and, depending on how he measured, I'd usually get what was left in the bottle. It was special grape juice. Too expensive, we only had it for Communion.

I made a point of being up front for Communion. I loved watching as Brothers and Sisters came to the altar and received a wafer from Reverend George. Then Reverend Olga would offer the tray of glasses. What fascinated me was how Brothers and Sisters picked their glasses. Some would follow the person before them. Some would go in the opposite direction from the person before them. A few would ignore everything and reach right in the middle. This was always fun as they had a hard time returning their empty glass without a reference point to help them find their hole. Sometimes, I could pick everyone who was going to take a glass out of sequence.

When it was all over, any glasses with juice were mine. I liked it best when George would miscalculate and filled more than enough trays. Half a Communion tray was a big glass of grape juice. I liked to wash the Communion glasses. There was something about their size and each fitting into a hole. But it took forever to do.

BOTTA CHARLIE VUKICH BOTT

When Baba, Olga or George talked about Botta, her son, her little brother, his brother-in-law, they painted his picture. "He didn't say a word till he was six." "From certain angles his head can look a little big but his size, build, hair, and mustache, make him look like Clark Gable." "He enjoys playing his Hawaiian guitar." "It's too bad he and Lena didn't work out." "He was in The Army Air Corps and learned equipment maintenance." "With this second wife Margaret, he really has his hands full." "No, of course he's not an odd ball. He's just his own person." No one offered an opinion for why he didn't talk till he was six. No one shared any opinions about Botta. In time, I realized this was all they had to say about him.

I have no memory of my Uncle Charlie at 64 E. McMicken. He didn't appear in my life until we moved to Orchard Court. While we were living there, he appeared as a background piece among the relatives I was getting to know. A cardboard cutout, there, but not alive. After we moved to Daytona, he came to life when The Matriarch backhanded him into the kitchen. But even after he starred in that role, our interaction remained that of a boy and a cardboard cutout. When I completed the third grade, everything changed.

In the early 1950s, Botta Vukich set out to realize his dream. His dream included being away from his in-laws, who lived next to his house on Trevor Avenue. He began by purchasing land on Ebenezer Road, "Out in the sticks." His dream saw the land with a house, a hoop and backboard in the driveway, a swimming pool, stables for his horses, and for boarding other horses, chickens, garden, geese, flowers, whatever suited his fancy. Peacocks? Why not? All this and more were to be part of his dream, his farm, his Estate. I was to be his little helper.

I came to be his helper as a bride to an arranged marriage. Olga was sure I needed to learn about things. Botta was sure even a little help was better than none and I was free. He was Parts Manager at Glenway Chevrolet and on the farm the rest of his waking hours. He and his sister agreed, I would go with him in the evenings and weekends whenever possible.

On my first trip to the farm he explained that his property was like a flag on a pole. The pole was about two lanes wide and less than a quarter mile long. It connected Ebenezer to his sixteen acre flag. He went on about his plans until we stopped and were looking at a huge, deep ravine. He had not mentioned that the only way to get to his sixteen acres was by using his neighbor's driveway. The Dolches let him use their driveway to get to his property until he had a driveway of his own. I learned three things that first trip. The definition and value of good neighbors. My Uncle Charlie was way past six, but still didn't really talk. Being with him was going to teach me a lot.

Over the better part of the next three years he taught me that before you fill a ravine you have to clear it and put in pipes. Clearing involved felling trees and he taught me about chain saws and how a two man saw, even if one the of men is a boy, can with the right balance and rhythm fell a four foot diameter tree. He taught me how to buy a dump truck about to be cannibalized and make it run. He taught me how to convince construction site bosses to have their trucks drive a few less miles and dump their payloads of dirt in the ravine. At one point I thought he was going to get them to pay him for saving them time. The ravine got filled and he taught me how to solicit bids and have a gravel road put in. It appeared that when it had to do with money, he could talk.

He taught me how to dig fence post holes, put up and maintain barbed wire, make sure I understood what I was being told to do, clear land, move the immovable with two by fours, wedges, and steel pry bars, dig and set footers, work in any kind of weather, lay concrete block, lift and carry heavy things, dig trenches and set drainage pipes, shovel wet and dry ground differently, use almost any kind of tool, put on a roof and tie the gutters and downspouts to the drainage pipes, hold a flashlight while working in the dark, install doors and windows, clean stables, use the right tool for the job, clear plant work and pick a garden, what it took to get a mare bred, and more. He taught me without speaking. He taught by demonstration. I learned by mimicking.

During the over three years we worked together, it wasn't just his work I watched.

On this day we were working on a compressor in the garage on Trevor. It was hot and Charlie wanted a drink. He called to the house and asked Margaret to fix something. When nothing arrived we headed inside. She obviously ignored his request. Seeing her attitude he went to the refrigerator, threw open the door and saw a small pitcher with ice tea. He reached in, picked up the handle, stepped back, and took a swig. Margaret began laughing while Charlie reacted in a way that makes me cringe today. She had just finished frying potatoes and put the grease in the small pitcher to cool. She thought it was hilarious, even while he retched. I couldn't believe she let him drink. He was mad when no drinks were brought out and now was furious, beside himself. I couldn't imagine what the son of The Matriarch was going to do. I was unable to accept what he did. He cleaned himself off, grabbed two Cokes, gave me one and took the other with him to the garage. Nothing else. This was the first time I wondered about my uncle.

My new school for the seventh grade was Western Hills. His house on Trevor, our house, West Hi and Glenway Chevrolet were on a line and starting in the seventh grade he took me to school. These rides were a new lesson in handling silence. We rode with no projects to think about, rode without even common thoughts, rode in silence to school.

This is not to say the rides were dull. He was a notorious tailgater and made me push my imaginary brake almost every morning. He was a real maniac behind another vehicle, nothing like the man I worked with. The worst thing was that his actions were premeditated and cruel, he wanted to aggravate the other drivers, he tailgated with purpose. One morning the man he was tailgating hit his brakes and we rear ended him big time. Charlie told me to stay put. It was unbelievable, he was blaming the other driver, lying flat out to the policeman. The man of silence became a waterfall of words. The policeman could not be fooled and cited Charlie. When he dropped me off I told him I would have told the policeman the truth and was glad he didn't get away with it. He drove off without saying a word. Walking to homeroom, I had the following thoughts. For a man who didn't talk he was very able lying. It took a lot of practice to lie so naturally. He enjoyed making me push my imaginary brake.

When I started the seventh grade it was time for me to stop being Uncle Charlie's little helper.

Charlie Bott was a tireless worker and knowledgeable about everything that had to do with making, using, and fixing anything. His mechanical aptitude was awesome. His knowledge of plants and animals, particularly horses, incredible. He taught me everything I do around the house and yard but nothing about himself. He was a man without history, opinions, chit chat, questions, answers, stories, anything. He absolutely didn't talk. During the entire time I worked for him he never told me anything of value, yet much of what he showed me was priceless.

Our relationship during those years was another confirmation of my beliefs. From my first memories I felt Something Greater was taking care of me. Here was an example. I had been given what I would need before I knew I needed it. In the dogma of my childhood I had learned and obeyed, "Children should be seen and not heard." It was this characteristic that enabled me to work with Charlie in the silence of his company and later, ride to school in silence and at ease.

In the eleventh grade I came home from school and walked in on Olga watching Botta push George against the piano and pin him there. Whatever was about to happen didn't as I intervened. George left the room and I confronted Olga and her brother. This was not a casual confrontation. They didn't know details but knew I had a special sort of mentor, plus I was now bigger faster and stronger than Botta. He said nothing while Olga said there was nothing to it. I offered there better never be something and went to talk to George.

Botta's appearance and behavior during this incident were

disturbing. Caught in the middle of an underhanded act he was totally at ease. He was neither embarrassed nor awkward, as if a thief caught red handed smiled at the police. He was devious and I decided to take inventory of what I knew. He held his feelings in. He tailgated with malice. He was selfish, even with his relatives, using me, Uncle Steve, and Uncle Joe without a thought of paying us. He could not maintain relationships. There was a list of people that had helped him who no longer associated with him. In each case he blamed the other person but it couldn't always be the other person. And then his silence, more correctly, his refusal to share or even participate. He enjoyed watching others squirm in the silence he created. Who was this guy?

Then I realized I didn't know why some called him Botta, others Charlie, and a few both. How did Botta Vukich, the only son of The Matriarch, come to be Charlie Bott? I was surprised I had never thought to ask the question. I was shocked by the answer. Botta Vukich's new girl Margaret Clark didn't want to be involved with a foreigner. So he loped the 'a' off Botta and as she liked the name Charlie took it as his. My Uncle orchestrated his own mutation from Serb, with a mother of honor and note, to faux pilgrim.

I had lost respect for him in increments. Now he was, by my choice, a cardboard cutout in the background of my life. A faded cutout I turned to face the corner.

Eight years passed.

Vietnam taught me compassion and that judging others was foolishness. Soon after I returned I invited my uncles out. Nicky was in California but Lou and Charlie were game and insisted we use my Corvette. I picked them up and we were a sight with Charlie in Lou's lap as we headed to my favorite bar. I knew the boss lady who greeted them with a hug shouting, "Lou! Charlie!

I've been waiting for you. The first one's on me." We got lit and after closing the place dropped Lou off and headed to Ebenezer. We turned onto the finished driveway and Charlie asked me to stop. We ended up right over the place where the four foot diameter tree stood those years ago. Uncle Charlie wanted to talk. I was immediately stone cold sober.

He wanted to give me advice. He felt it was time he shared his mistakes to help me avoid making the same ones. He started before I was born. His first wife was his true love and I should look for mine. Margaret was a mean spirited prejudiced woman who believed she was entitled to more. Much more than he was providing. She had little use for her children and after the birth of Robbie told Charlie she had come to a decision. From that moment on they never had physical relations again.

He told me more but it was mainly pain. He talked and cried and talked and cried until he finally emptied himself and drifted off to sleep. I sat.

People had been right, the farm was a dream and a way to stay away from his wife and her parents. He had no love for his Estate. There was still no thank you for the help. There was still no recognition or apology for abandoning his birthright. There was just misery. I knew I couldn't help him but was glad that he had talked. After a time, I drove up to the house and got him in the front door. On the drive home, I wondered if he would ever stand up for himself and take charge of his life. He didn't.

Our last conversation was the day of Olga's funeral. Charlie and I ended up alone on the front porch of my parent's house. He was near tears and totally shaken. He wanted to talk about God. He had only known that his sister had a special gift and believed with all her heart. Now, he confessed that during their last conversation he thought she questioned her faith. Apparently she was the icon at whom he looked for his spirituality and for her to waver was a shock.

I didn't understand where this was coming from. He had never been to The Peniel Missionary Assembly. I didn't know of him attending any church. I knew nothing of his beliefs. The best I could do was tell him I didn't know whether his interpretation of Olga's faith was right or wrong but I knew about mine. To me, faith was personal. You have to find it and keep it on your own. He looked at me with those eyes I had come to know. When you're with someone who doesn't talk, you communicate by other means and Charlie's eyes and I were old buddies. Old buddies who knew this would be our last meeting. Neither one of us said another word. Sometime later, he began to fidget. Then, his body language yelled he was unnerved. Next, his leg started keeping time to music that wasn't there. Finally, resignedly, he got up and went inside. I stayed on the porch and as he turned to close the door, I smiled with satisfaction. He had taught me how to deal with silence. Now, he could push on his imaginary brake.

That was enough closure for me regarding Charlie Bott. Our three years together on the farm were mutually beneficial. The fact his only attempt at payment was to buy me Creamy Whip on the way home once in a while, didn't upset me. I loved soft ice cream and even as a kid realized he was giving me knowledge I could always use. Knowledge my artistic, tailor father couldn't impart. How Charlie treated others was of no concern to me. I was back from Nam, alive, healthy, and aware keeping me in line was more than enough to keep me busy. He lived his life as he did and good luck to him. However, I neither forgot nor forgave his not teaching me to ride horses. Finally, I was very glad my Baba, his mother, The Matriarch, didn't have to see how he ended up.

Years passed and he fell down the basement steps and into a coma. He never recovered from the coma and later died.

His wife, daughter, and son were unable to bring themselves to care for him. It was his sister Rose who spent the rest of his life caring for him every single day. But that is more a part of her story.

The rumors were that Margaret had gotten him drunk and pushed him down the steps. I found that incredulous. Not that she would do it, she was more than capable of doing it, but that the relatives talked about it but did nothing. As it turned out that is also part of Rosie's story.

Twenty plus years after my first view of the ravine and the Dolche's driveway, my wife and I moved into our current house. In time we met our neighbors across the street. Mr. and Mrs. Dave Dolche, The Dolche's son.

Twenty more years later we moved Rosie into a nursing home. In time, we met her neighbor across the hall. Lena, Botta Vukich's first wife, Rosie's ex-sister-in-law. The love of his life was across the hall from the sister who loved him.

I think of what he taught me every time I put what I learned to use.

I never think of him.

KIDS

On East McMicken my world had been made up of adults.

During the transition to Orchard Court and through the second grade, I started meeting kids. I watched them. I learned to play with them. Doug and Lynn Fletcher introduced me to Americana.

After the move to Daytona Avenue, the third grade started. At that time I handled my responsibilities at church, home, and on the job, as the paperboy. However, my main focus was on learning how to sound like an American. During this period, I made time to study kids but had no time to relate to them.

When the third grade ended, my relationship with kids consisted of watching them and learning from watching them. I had friends, but none of them were kids. I didn't make friends with kids and didn't want kids as friends. I was uncomfortable around kids. I didn't understand them and I sure didn't need them.

Then the fourth grade started. In no time I could see my lack of relationships with kids was inhibiting my growing into an American. The Hallway had taught me the benefit of wearing different hats and how to do so. I had a few hats; preacher's son, grade school boy, paperboy, bilingual person, and, of course, my

Serbian hat. I think most of the kids saw my Serbian hat as a "foreigner" or a "boy is he different" hat. No matter. The point was I didn't have an American hat. I had to do something.

So I did. I started participating with other kids. I forced myself to join in their activities. This was extremely hard for me. I would have preferred to be alone or with adults. It turned out the benefits were worth my emotional discomfort. Soon after I began making myself participate with kids, I realized it enabled me to watch them, up close. This new perspective was to my growth as an American, what fertilizer was to Baba's tomatoes, amazing.

This is not to say I felt close to other kids. I knew I wasn't like them. I wasn't interested in being like them. I was interested in being able to act as if I was like them. Long range, I wanted to be able to act as if I was like any group I was with.

Through the last three years of grade school, from the fall of 1952 to the summer of 1955, I pretended to be one of the kids. I watched them as I watched my teachers. I recalled how Olga used questions to make people open up. I made a practice of asking questions and was thrilled to learn kids were eager to answer. The more I asked, the more they shared, and the more I gained. They were generous in sharing and wonderful teachers. It wasn't hard for them to teach me, all they had to do was be themselves. I learned a lot and my assimilation of Americana advanced.

Was there a down side to my not really being one of the kids? Absolutely not. During Elementary School, a lot of kids teased and tormented each other. In many cases it was hurtful. I honestly don't know if the kids teased, laughed at, or made fun of me. If they did, I didn't notice. If they did, and I had noticed, I wouldn't have cared. From my view of the world, what my classmates said or thought of me was totally unimportant. After all, there were just kids.

This was the way I continued to view kids until they were no longer kids. Once they weren't kids, I was totally at ease with them. Once they weren't kids I treated them as adults and I was born comfortable with adults.

TRAVELING MINISTRY

We've all heard him. "Next stop for Blankenburg, Mumbletown, Garbledville." Our memory brings his voice to our ears. With my experience, as part of The Marksity Traveling Ministry, it's a wonder I didn't become a Conductor.

The Reverends Olga and George had been traveling before I was aware they were doing so. While we were living on Orchard Court, I came to know how often they willingly took their ministry on the road. Once we were settled on Daytona, the trip to Milwaukee was the start of me going with them on a regular basis. This continued through the sixth grade.

I don't remember all the places we went but when I unfold a map, names pop out. Portsmouth, Maumee, Lima, Richmond, Springfield, Xenia, Belle Fontaine, Ashland, Akron, Huntington, Defiance, Chillicothe, Ripley, Coshocton, Cynthiana, Terre Haute, Youngstown, Zanesville, Fort Wayne, Marietta, Lexington, Charlestown, Kokomo, Steubenville. To finish our itinerary, just sprinkle any number of visits to Detroit across the list, and get out another map.

Regardless the destination, there was always a specific place of worship. Most were churches. They varied in size from smaller

239

than 64 East McMicken to holding over a thousand. Not all destinations had a church. In those that didn't, people congregated in rented halls, meeting centers, hotels, private homes, any place they could worship together. For revivals, convocations, tent meetings and camp meetings, there were arenas, coliseums, and tents.

The Traveling Ministry stayed home during the Christmas and Easter seasons. Other than those dates, we traveled anytime. Weekend or weekday made no difference. We made day trips, four day trips, and some even longer.

As far as I could tell, in the beginning, they were able to go everywhere they were invited. The Reverend Olga being the 'they' who was invited. By the time I was going along, they couldn't satisfy all the invitations, meet with the steadily increasing number of visitors from around the world, and pastor The Peniel Missionary Assembly. It troubled Olga greatly that she had to decline invitations. She would have liked to satisfy everyone and keep Peniel on course. George knew that was physically impossible. So, Olga did meet with all those who traveled to see her but it became an unpleasant task to decide where to go and where not to go. It became George's task to deliver the disappointments.

From my perspective, all of this was wonderful. The summer vacations Baba had sponsored in the ghetto were nice, but this was better. Sleeping in the back of the Buick, having to hold the column gear shifter in reverse when George backed up, watching every bit of scenery, and listening to the smack, smack, smack of the tires, was a lifestyle of adventure.

No matter where we went, the purpose of their travels was to minister. Everywhere we went, the featured minister was The Reverend Olga Marksity.

No matter where we went, she was invited for a purpose. There were countless purposes. To guest pastor at normally scheduled services. To review past sessions. To plan and prepare future meetings. To attend prayer meetings, Bible study seminars, theological convocations or work sessions with church and community leaders. To minister to congregations, groups, and individuals. To preach, teach, witness, support, encourage, listen, learn, and always, to worship.

No matter where we went, or the local purpose, the results of these trips included varieties and mixtures of awakening, salvation, peace of mind, peace of spirit, rejoicing, bringing The Word to life, spiritual and physical rejuvenation, learning, loving, living, and every so often, certainly not always, there were the episodes of healing—the miracles.

The Reverend Olga Marksity was not the only one gifted with being used for God's Designs. I saw other Brothers and one Sister used by The Almighty to heal believers. However, my memories are centered on her because of the time I spent in her presence. As The Reverend's son, no matter the situation, I was always immediately next to the action. I saw the events happening right in front of my face. What I witnessed overwhelms my memories of my time with Their Traveling Ministry.

People who were shaking, stopped. People that couldn't stand, stood. People that hadn't walked, started walking. People who acted funny, swung their arms randomly, rolled their heads about and looked with dull and vacant eyes, walked away normally, their eyes ablaze with life and full of love. People who couldn't speak, spoke. People who couldn't hear, heard. People who couldn't see, saw. People whose minds, spirits, and souls were vacant, comatose, and ignored, were transformed as they were given understanding, exuberance for life and enlightenment. People with afflictions, left them on the altars. These are words printed on this page. To me, they are living memories. Alive in me, ever since I witnessed them.

In addition to the sights there were the sounds. Utter silence at the exposure of the grotesque. Utter silence as humans sat in awe. Wispy gasps of fear. Shocking gasps of victory. Steady breaths of hopefulness. Short, labored breaths of disbelief. Deep breaths of humility. Long breaths of relief. Robust breaths of support and faith. Tumultuous roars of thankfulness and exaltation. These sounds and others came from individuals, groups, congregations, tents full, and the lone person sitting on a car hood at the farthest end of the parking lot. These were the sounds of realizing there was Something Bigger.

And there were smells. Grass, dirt, car exhausts, camp fires, kerosene, coal stoves, canvas, wooden planking, sweat, wet clothes, the bouquet of flowers, polished pews, candles, oil, and the countless odors of humanity. For me, no matter the aromas of the place, at some point every venue gave off the same aroma. A fragrance I inhaled as a mixture of hope, faith, and then, thanksgiving.

Every human sense was impacted by The Unfathomable working through His chosen agents. The fabric of life in the surroundings was affected by His presence. To see those actually touched by Him, was to be close to Grace.

And so it was throughout my travels with The Reverends Olga and George. No matter the location, time, place, local purpose, number of those gathered or actual events—from dull administrative haggling over who sleeps where in a tent meeting planning session, to lines and lines of needy finding miracles awaiting them—there was one similarity in every one of our trips. There was always a nucleus of those who believed. Believed in the same Almighty Wonder. He was evident everywhere, if only one would look. He insured, when His work was finished, bodies, minds, and souls were satisfied. The Satisfaction, which routinely filled the places we visited, has never left me.

MY COUSIN GLORIA

My oldest cousin Gloria was really pretty. She looked like the girls in magazines. Long coal black hair, big dark eyes, real red lips, tall, not fat and not skinny. She was a lot older than me so I wasn't sure whether she was a girl or a lady. She was sick a lot and spent time at home. She had a television in her room and was always watching, but from the side. She tried to explain something about rays, but I didn't know what she was talking about. She had a collection of little spoons.

One day she married this big tall guy from California named Glen Lambert. He was a cousin or something of a movie star or somebody. I didn't know too much about that. What I did know about was his car. A brand new Studebaker Golden Hawk. I had only seen pictures of such a car until he drove into town. I spent a lot of time looking at that car while he was here and one day he took me for a ride. They moved to California.

As the years passed I heard about Gloria and Glen at family gatherings. They were nice and settled. She was pregnant. She had a boy named Mark. She was pregnant. She had a girl named Mary Anne. The kids were doing fine. Gloria and Glen were getting divorced. She moved with the kids to Los Angeles. They were nice and settled.

Once I left home I heard about Gloria in bits and pieces. She worked a lot of overtime. She was not married. The kids were good. She worked two jobs. She wasn't alone because Nicky and Viola had moved to California. She didn't date. The grandparents and kids were good for each other.

In 1974, I was in L.A. on business and looked up Viola and Nicky. On the way to see them I remembered their huge three story frame house on Glenmore where, as a little boy, I could stand in the main fireplace. I thought of their move to the cozy little two bedroom brick in the quiet suburb of Bridgetown. I wondered what their California house would be like when I realized the neighborhood I was driving in was loud, crowded, and shabby. When I got to their address it was not a house. They were living in a one bedroom apartment in a huge industrial looking complex.

It was okay to see them after so many years, but I was confused. Why were they living like this? We did the small talk but they were embarrassed. It was impossible to ignore the surroundings or the tiny apartment. Finally, pulling herself together as if caught in a crime, Viola admitted they had been living like this since they moved to California. She explained they lived like this to help Gloria. Then, proudly, "After all, we have a paid off home in Cincinnati." Now I was more confused. Seeing my face, Aunt Viola began hitting me with hammers of revelation.

They filled all the normal grandparent roles, plus Nicky frequently played father. They were permanent baby sitters. They were the day care center Mark and Mary Anne attended. They filled in as parents, attending everything from school functions to little league. They enabled their daughter to have the free time she convinced them was essential to her mental and physical health. They had moved several times to insure their day care center was always convenient to their daughter. They endured the resentment of their son who calculated his sister was getting everything at his expense. For years they had been swallowing their pride as Rosie and Lou sent Gloria two hundred dollars a month, like installment payments. And finally, living on a fixed income, under a roof owned by someone else, thousands of miles away from their paid off house, they made monthly payments to their daughter.

What about her working? Oh, she worked but she was picky about her employers and the treatment she received. What about her working so hard? Well, she worked hard at normal administrative and support jobs. What about her working two jobs? Yes she did, but on and off, not permanently. Plus, she had not worked to better herself or her positions. Well, what about Glen? Didn't he contribute to the support of his children? For the answer to this question, Aunt Viola replaced the hammers with a sledge, and hit me between the eyes.

Gloria Golusin Lambert never accepted that her husband Glen had been having an affair, dumped her, and run off and married the other woman. She knew he would come back to her She continued this self-delusion when her Glen had another affair, dumped the second wife, and ran off and married a third. No matter, Gloria knew he was coming back to her and refused to confront him for help supporting their children. Her reasoning was that if she bothered him it might prolong the time before he returned.

Nicky and Viola were relieved to get this off their chests. I realized there was a pain in what they had been doing that I could not imagine. I couldn't understand how my cousin could lie to herself in the face of such facts. I offered to talk to Gloria. Maybe a blood relative who was not emotionally involved could be of service. The three of us agreed this was worth a try and I promised to get together with Gloria the next time I was in L.A.

It was in 1975 that I finally met my cousin. The Gloria at the Del Rae Restaurant in Pico Rivera, with her Mark and Mary Anne, was a far cry from the girl/woman of my childhood. She was extremely over weight. She looked like a matron, much older than her years. She had shifty eyes and an inventory of bullshit that would have made a lawyer blink.

We got acquainted rather quickly. There was a good mix among the four of us and with surprising casualness the subject of Glen came up. Gloria wanted to set me straight. Ever since the divorce, relatives, friends, co-workers, and associates had attempted to convince her Glen was gone. I was just another in a cue of blind idiots who could not see the love beneath his surface behaviors. She knew Glen would come back. She wasn't going to alienate him by asking for money. And most importantly, she was absolutely not going to accept the help he offered.

Inside my head a huge "WHAT?" exploded. I couldn't handle her last statement and was in awe as she continued.

If she accepted his help, there was never an inkling of asking or forcing him to help her, if she accepted his help she would look like less than the woman she was. So there! Now that she had set me straight, we could go on with dinner.

Make no mistake, I was speechless. I didn't know what to do. Clearly she was waiting for something from me and I felt that something was my admission that I was now set very straight. I feigned being distracted by a waitress and asked her to please run through that last part again. She was oh so happy to oblige. I hadn't missed a thing. Glen had offered to help her on more than one occasion and she had refused. She, like all grand mates, didn't need help.

As she finished setting me straight for the second time, Mark and Mary Anne spoke up. They thought their mother had been and was irrational. They thought she could do things to get better jobs. They felt she was unrealistic in her expectations of workplaces and co-workers. They were very respectful of Rosie and Lou for sending money. They were embarrassed that their mother took money from their grandparents. They thought it was silly for her not to ask for help. They had talked to her about this. They had talked to their father and he had talked to her. Glen and the kids agreed she was being stubborn and should take what he offered. They had pushed her to date or at least socialize. They weren't sure she listened to them but were sure she never changed. Mark and Mary Anne impressed me. They were realistic, open and sincere. They hoped I could help.

I tried. I congratulated the three of them for their honesty and candor. I thanked them for trusting me enough to share their situation. I suggested an objective review of the facts might help us see the real options for the future. They agreed.

So I reviewed the facts for my cousin Gloria as they had been presented to me. He leaves you for another woman that he has been having an affair with. He marries that woman. He leaves her for another woman that he has been having an affair with. He marries that woman. There are children all over the place. He tells you he is never coming back. You know better. You will not change your behaviors regarding work. You will not consider developing a social life. You refuse to ask him for help, because of the love you share. You refuse to accept his offers of help because it makes you look like you can't make it on your own. You can't make it on your own. You will continue taking money from your parents, aunt, and uncle.

Yep. I had it right. She sort of congratulated me for this synthesis of her life. She had set me straight.

Well, it was her life and I was unable to help either her or her children. Saying goodbye to the three of them, I had no idea it would be over twenty years before I had the second open conversation with my cousin Gloria.

Gloria stuck to her strategy. Mark graduated. Mary Anne graduated. Both kids were on their own. Gloria waited for Glen's return and wouldn't accept the help he offered. Mark got married. Mary Anne got married. Gloria worked as before, uninspired in menial routines, dissatisfied but only complaining. Viola and Nicky became great grandparents. Gloria refused to date. The great grandchildren grew up. The great grandparents moved back to their paid off house in Cincinnati. Gloria continued accepting money from Rosie and Lou, even when Rosie became a widow.

She came to Cincinnati when her uncle Lou died, when her brother died, when her father died, and now and then to visit. On one visit she was accompanied by Mary Anne and her husband Steve. We had the couple over. They were nice company. After dinner, Mary Anne reviewed her various cosmetic plastic surgeries. She made me wonder. What kind of person has her looks paid for by a mother who takes money from her parents and relatives? I wondered had she seen how her grandparents lived in California? In time, Mary Anne answered my questions. As they were leaving, she said they had enjoyed our wine and would be sending us a few bottles of their favorite. We never got the wine.

While her mother fought cancer, Gloria managed a few visits but did not come back to care for Viola. The excuses she offered were her kids and job. When Viola was dying, Gloria made the entrance Hollywood would script for grieving daughters. She continued her performance well past her mother's burial and while she set about the business of inheriting. A paid off house is nice to have but she didn't move in and didn't sell. Instead, she split her time between L.A. and Cincinnati. Finally, when she sold the house she didn't return to kids and job, she moved into Rosie's basement. I didn't try to understand any of this. To me, it was just Gloria.

It was February 1995 when I got the call. It was Gloria. She needed help. Could I come over to Rosie's? When I got there they were sitting in the living room. The gist of it was simple. Rosie had an accident. She refused to accept any responsibility and was not about to stop driving. Gloria knew Rosie had to stop driving but she couldn't make that happen. I was called, because she knew I could.

Of course I could and would if the situation demanded it. To determine the facts I read the police report. Aunt Rosie was to blame. I went to see the car. It had been a bad wreck. (Rosie had to stop driving. What it took for that to happen is part of her story.) The body shop owner was nice but tight lipped. I probed and he explained this was not Rosie's first accident. He was sheepish. He was not supposed to tell me about the others. When I asked who told him not to tell he replied, "Mrs. Baker's daughter." When I asked for a description of the "daughter," it was Gloria.

From Pico Rivera in 1975 to this point, I had no involvement with Gloria or her relationship with Rosie. Now, I was suspicious. Exercising my role as executor of Rosie's estate, a position arranged with Lou and Rosie twenty years earlier, I reviewed the situation. Gloria was living with Rosie rent free. Rosie was routinely giving her money, the smallest segments being around one hundred dollars. The overall value of Rosie's estate had decreased. Almost all Rosie's accounts had been changed to joint accounts with Gloria. Finally, there was a recent transfer of five thousand dollars to Gloria.

All of this was curious and the routine payments disturbing. Lou died in 1982 and Rosie was living on a very fixed income. Getting Rosie alone, I asked if she was helping Gloria? She denied any such thing. When I reviewed my findings, she was typical Rosie. She didn't know anything about the overall value of things. She had no idea how Gloria's name got on all those accounts. What five thousand bucks? And, she hadn't given Gloria any monies in, well, well, in years.

I handed her the two inch thick stack of money order receipts showing her giving Gloria $200 a month over the last many years. She laughed as she admitted I had her. Wasn't this just fun? She admitted she'd been giving Gloria money continuously and now a little extra. She was glad to do it. "The poor girl needs a little help." The poor girl was 62 years old.

Moving on I asked about the five thousand. Rosie smiled knowingly. Now, she had me. She explained that Mary Anne and Steve were about to lose their house. If Gloria couldn't get them five thousand dollars pronto, they'd be out on the street. Rosie was sure I agreed she was a good Samaritan. I should be proud of her.

My first reaction was to ask why Gloria didn't use her money? She got close to one hundred thousand for her parent's house. But something told me this was enough with Rosie. I remembered how Mary Anne and Mark behaved so long ago in Pico Rivera and decided to call Mary Anne. I didn't get her, I got Steve. I explained there was a delicate situation and I needed to talk to Mary Anne. He was cooperative. He remarked that he and Mary Anne shared everything so I could just talk with him. He'd be glad to help. As soon as I started laying out the facts, I could hear him heating up. By the time I finished he was furious.

He explained they had plenty of money—thank me very much—and if they ever needed extra money, which of course would never happen, but if, he would go to his father who was very well to do—thank him very much—and this was not the first time Gloria had pulled a con job, but it was the first time he was used.

I let him vent. In time he agreed there was no need to shoot the messenger. During the conversation that followed, we both learned. Steve learned he and his wife didn't share as much as he thought. Mary Anne knew her mother had used this ploy on Rosie. I learned my cousin Gloria was a leach, manipulator, con artist, liar, and thief.

I called my friend and personal lawyer who drew up the two papers I requested. I arranged for Rosie, Gloria, and I to meet, on the pretext we needed to review the wreck. They were happy to hear I wanted to get together.

When I arrived at Rosie's house my aunt and cousin were overjoyed to see me. I didn't say a word. I let them do their thing. Once we were seated, the two of them all smiles, I asked Gloria how it felt to be a liar? Before she reacted I asked her how it felt to steal from the aunt who subsidized her for over thirty years? They were stunned. I asked Rosie if she knew Gloria was a liar and thief? Rosie immediately started defending her niece. In Serbian, I told Rosie to get a grip because she was going to face this reality, no options. By this time, Gloria had gathered herself and was spewing indignation. I told her to shut the hell up.

No chit chat, I produced the bank statement and withdrawal slip. I reviewed my conversation with Steve. I explained Steve was very ready to tell Rosie himself that Gloria was lying through her teeth. He was also ready for his mother-in-law to know, that his wife would cooperate to get Rosie the truth.

Rosie was Serbian and The Matriarch's daughter. She took it on the chin. And that was that. She directed me, in Serbian, to do what had to be done.

Gloria was—well, you describe it. She started with the sympathy card. "My God, think of my kids. My grandchildren. My reputation." Next, "I am so embarrassed. I don't know what I was thinking." Next it was "My sickness. Ron, I've been to therapy. I'm a spendaholoic. I just need some help." As she went on I was amazed. Her inventory of bullshit had multiplied with age.

I produced the two papers my lawyer friend had prepared. The first was a document admitting she stole the money and committing to how and when she would repay it. The second was the paperwork for pressing charges against her. I told her to pick.

Gloria knew I would do anything for Rosie. Her intuition told her I felt she had kept her parents and Lou and Rosie in a private sort of jail. Her knowledge of me told her I would not hesitate to put her in a very public jail. She knew me, but I didn't know her.

Eyes full, heart heavy, soul wrenched, she appealed to her darling benefactor. "Fufu …" the Aunt above all others. Using Rosie's Serbian name she begged for, "Forgiveness as in your holy Orthodox Church." Then came the direct, "Aunt Rose, please. Please bail me out now. Please, and I'll never …"

Then she realized Rosie had gotten up and was leaving the room. Gloria wasn't stupid, she kept still. It was very quiet. Her muted sobbing barely heard. As Rosie headed to her bedroom, she paused in the archway and without turning around said, "From now on, anything you want from me, you talk to

Ronnie. Regarding me and mine, whatever he tells you to do, you do."

Once the finality was obvious, my cousin Gloria didn't bat an eye. No longer emotional, she dropped the beseeching voice and pathetic look. He eyes were suddenly dry and her sobbing forgotten. She knew it was over and being the calculating bitch I didn't know she was, flatly said, "Fine." She signed and said she would pay by the date I had suggested.

I was stunned. There were some questions I just couldn't ignore. I admitted that if she hadn't called me about the wreck, she could have continued to drain the estate. I wouldn't have known until Rosie had no money left, or died. Why did she get me involved? Why did she call me? With cruel cunning and complete disregard for her aunt, my cousin Gloria explained.

"This was her fourth accident. She ran a stop sign and broadsided a car. She hit it so hard she pushed it sideways across the intersection and up a hill onto a front yard. I thought they were gonna sue and we'd be cooked. I had to make her stop driving. I tried everything but it was no use. She's a stubborn old bird. The only person who could influence her was you. It was better to get a few less eggs than lose my goose."

Without remorse, not even embarrassed, she continued. Once her mother died she planned to live in the house and have everyone think she was there to help Rosie, while she helped herself. But she got an offer for the house she couldn't refuse. Living in Rosie's basement was unfortunate but Rosie refused to evict the tenant in the second floor apartment. (The lady lived there over thirty years.) So she worked her plan from the basement and assured me, had the wrecks not occurred, it would still be working. I let it go and have never calculated how much money Gloria took.

She paid back the five thousand and moved to California. I haven't spoken to her since.

She didn't come to care for her aunt during Rosie's final days. She didn't come to Rosie's funeral.

I never told her what her dying mother asked of me. "I want you to promise me something. Promise me you'll see to it Saka never gets another cent from Rosie. Not one penny more of the Baker's money. She has taken enough already. I know what she has been and what she is. I know she will take anything and everything from anyone and everyone. Protect my sister. Protect Rosie from my daughter. Promise?"

I'm embarrassed by how poorly I kept my promise.

DUKE

On Orchard Court we had a goldfish in a bowl. Then for a short time some sort of cat. Then a canary that moved with us to Daytona. The fish didn't make the move. Another canary was added and there were two from then on. Parakeets came and went. For a while there was a dog named Skippy but I'm not clear when he came into the picture or when he left. No matter, none of them were my pets, they were Olga's pets.

Then one day I came home from school, and there he was. There was something about him. He looked like a fox, with one exception. Compared to a fox's narrow and pointed snout his was broad and rounded. He had an incredibly rich coat of fancy white and black marking. I knew he was going to be my pet. I was an Earl, Ronald Earl, so I named him Duke.

I got high marks for my observation of Duke. Turned out he was one quarter fox. It was no surprise that Olga and George knew people who bred dogs with foxes. This was just another example of their congregations and associates. They were open to anything and anybody, accepting all as part of God's Plan. Plus, I'd be willing to bet they got him for free. Anyway, Duke was mine.

From the beginning, I was the only person he related to. Wild birds and animals and pets of others might be drawn to Olga, but not Duke. He openly ignored her, George, Baba, everyone.

He would only eat when I prepared his food. This became a problem when I began traveling with Olga and George. A problem for them. I was confidant Duke would find something to eat. He never seemed slimmed down when we returned home.

He refused to be in the house at night. If forced, he would begin vomiting. Once Olga and George accepted his wishes he stayed out, even in bitter winter. In winter, I folded up old rugs to make him a bed but rarely found him in it.

When I was home he was always free. When I wasn't home, he was often tied to a run that was strung across the back yard. When any intruder came near he would take off after them. Most ran away. A few figured out his range had a limit. Sitting just out of range they would watch him run full out and leap at them — only to be yanked backwards by the neck so he flew through the air in painful acrobatics. He would keep this impossible attacking up, with no regard for his body, until the sitters got bored and left. He never quit attacking until they left. There were a few times when Baba would see him in such a predicament and free him. The results were more than painful for those sitting but no longer out of range. Baba liked facilitating his successes, particularly when the sitter was a cat.

He was extremely loyal. One day he followed me to the shopping center and stayed by my bike while I went into McAlpins. While looking around, I ran into George and after the surprise wore off we shopped and then drove home. Several hours later, I remembered Duke. George drove me back to McAlpins and there was Duke, next to the bike, waiting and ready.

He demonstrated his lineage on more than one occasion. The

first example involved a huge German Shepherd visiting a neighbor. The Shepherd was aggressive and seemed mean to me, barking and yanking his owner around. Duke didn't bark back but made a sort of growl. Just then the Shepherd got free and headed toward us at full throttle. Before I could move, Duke rushed right at the big dog. At the last instant, he flattened himself and slid under the Shepherd's gaping jaws. The Shepherd screamed a noise I can still hear as Duke stopped his slide by clamping on the big dog's privates. This was not the only time I witnessed Duke being ferocious.

Unfortunately, his courage and protectiveness went beyond dogs. On this day, I was coming up the street and a big moving van was coming down. Duke was in between us, in the front yard. Something convinced him the truck was a threat to me, so he attacked the truck. He was caught in a reversed wheel, spun around, thrown out and into a tree trunk. The driver and I arrived at him at the same time. Duke looked bad, bleeding from the nose and ears. Of course there was never a thought of going to a vet. If Olga and George wouldn't take me to a hospital, they weren't about to take my dog. So we prayed. Duke didn't die. He was off his feet for a long time. When he recovered, he was a different Duke, in one way only. After this incident, he began to come inside in winter.

We remained each other's best friends from the day we met until I moved to Fort Benning. Duke disappeared the next day. He was never seen again. I still see him.

CONGREGATION

From my first memories of Olga as The Reverend Marksity, we had visitors. Some stayed a day or two, some stayed a month. Some visited once, some routinely. They came from around the States and Canada. They came from all over the European continent, from India, the Middle East and one came from Africa. Their numbers and differences were like dessert with the feast that was my life.

Of course it wasn't my life they were visiting. It was The Reverend Olga Marksity they came to see. Nevertheless, I got to see them. They were all interesting and those who came across an ocean just boggled my imagination.

In the case of these two particular visitors, I'm sure no one on Daytona or any place nearby had ever seen anything like them. India, I guessed. Looking back, I realize I thought anyone who lived anywhere between the Pacific Ocean and the Middle East was Indian. Pakistan and all the rest, just wasn't there for me. But these two may have been from India despite my geographic shortcomings.

The lady's dress was not a dress. The man's robes were not a suit. Their sandals weren't shoes and whatever was on their heads, sure weren't hats. Not babushkas either. But I'm running round the bush because I'm embarrassed by this memory. These were two very nice people. He was 'world renown' and, while I wasn't sure what that meant, I knew it was important. They were very spiritual. It was easy to feel quiet and peaceful around them. They had done some great works, helping the poor and sick in their country. There was more, however I'm sure you get the picture.

The point of my dismay is that, of all the wonderful "Christian Poster People" truths about these two visitors, I can only remember how they smelled. Not that they smelled bad or offensive. Nothing like that. To this day, I still can't describe the odor. It was an aroma like nothing I'd ever inhaled.

That's saying a lot. If you want to talk smells, walk through your local Findlay Market. Pay a visit to the nearest ghetto of poverty in the heat of summer. Be in the kitchen while Baba is creating some Serbian, garlic, paprika, and gasoline, concoction. Smells were not a delicacy for me. I could identify most. In fact, I felt I had even learned something about American smells on the campus of Orchard Court. But the smell of this Brother and Sister, was like nothing I'd experienced before. And because of that, I missed the rest of what there was to learn from them.

Incidentally, this couple was neither Christian nor saw themselves as Brothers and Sisters. No matter. We were way past words, titles or labels. Like the majority of people who came to visit, worship, teach, learn, or sit with The Reverend Olga Marksity, these two had no doubt there was Something Bigger.

THE MATRIARCH

It was not too long after we were settled in on Daytona, more than a year, maybe.

It could have been any season. I have no idea of the day or time.

I have no clue what the occasion was.

I have no memory of the arrival of the guests.

I'm sure I helped, I always helped. How I helped, escapes me.

I have no recall of the socializing prior to being called to table.

In the dining room, George, Olga, Baba and her only son Botta are visible around the table.

Botta was called Charlie by Americans and Uncle Charlie by me. He had two kids and was recognized throughout the community for his expertise in all matters agricultural and mechanical.

Olga and Baba are at one end of the table with George at the other. In this setting, you might make George's seat the head of the table. Not in our house. The head of the table was the end where the two female heads were sitting. Uncle Charlie is sitting on the side of the table immediately to his mother's right.

Then, it gets blurry. There were three more sitting on the side with Uncle Charlie. There were another three, and me, sitting on the opposite side. I just can't make out those six.

The room was full of relatives and the table was full of food. I really don't remember the meal but it had to be good. When we had company, Olga and Baba worked together to insure a good meal.

There was a lot of polite conversation. The mood was civilized. The tone was calm. Everyone seemed happy and then Uncle Charlie was airborne, flying away from the table...

The Matriarch was offended by something he had said and backhanded him into the next room. He ended up on the kitchen floor, leaning against a kitchen table leg. His dining room chair followed close behind and came to a stop against his thigh.

THE ACCORDION

Sometime during the summer between the third and fourth grades, Olga determined I wanted to play the accordion. This came as a complete surprise to me.

I believed her motivation was an image of Yugoslavia she had concocted. She saw smiling Serbs pumping the bellows while skipping around the mountain sides. Her image was not evidenced by any other Serbs or Slavs I knew.

Not too long after she reached her conclusion, I had an accordion. It was given to her by "some sort of relative," Danny Krison and his wife Lucille. I don't know who played but guessed it was Danny because it was such a big accordion. I'm sure it was free. Anything I got that was of any value was always free.

The accordion was way too big for me. The upside was that playing the box contributed to my strength, stamina, and physical development. Trust me, just holding it up was a work load. One picture shows me holding the monster which went from my chin to my crotch. In the beginning I couldn't sit down to play, if I sat, the accordion would cover my face. The headless accordion player.

I didn't mind playing the instrument, but I hated practicing.

More correctly, I hated where I had to practice. Any time except winter, Olga, ever the sensitive one, forced me to practice my accordion on the front porch. It was a substantial brick porch with a beautiful tongue in groove wood ceiling. It was a substantial effort for me to keep practicing while hearing the garbage men, passersby, and worst of all, kids, cackling at the sounds coming from behind the bricks.

At first it was like a wrestling match, me vs the bellows. I'd get set facing my music stand and we'd go at it. That stand witnessed the accordion pin me many times.

Baba loved to listen to me play. I didn't mind playing for her and Olga but was sorely chafed when I had to play for other people. I wondered if those other people who had to listen to me play were sorely chafed as well. Of course, we all knew we'd continue to be chafed. Olga had determined our affection for accordion music.

Anyway, this began regular lessons and a lot of practicing through the sixth grade. From then on, I took lessons as needed. In the seventh grade, Baba bought me a fancy, normal sized, red and white pearl beauty. It sparkled under the lights at Gamble Junior High when I played with the dance band. When I left Gamble, I stopped playing the accordion.

CONGREGATION

They only came to church in winter. As soon as it got cold they'd show up. As soon as it got warm they'd disappear.

At first it just seemed funny to me. The next year they began to make me wonder. Then they caught my imagination and I tried to figure out why they attended as they did. After that year, I hadn't figured out anything.

So the next season I watched them and discovered they were attending but not participating. In the services they were respectful but were sitting more than listening. They'd stand but didn't sing. They'd close their eyes but didn't pray.

Instead of solving the mystery, my findings created a new mystery. I was upset with them and didn't know why. What was bothering me about these people? I wanted them to change, but how? I guess I thought it was unfair. They didn't participate. They should at least be trying. The more I talked with myself, the more I didn't help.

In time Olga sensed I was befuddled. She cornered me and started probing until I talked. As I explained my feelings, that they were only using the church, she started laughing. Her laugh was so spontaneous I couldn't help myself and started laughing too. Of course I had no idea what we were laughing about. When she stopped laughing, what followed was a sermon just for me.

She explained I was right. They were not coming to worship as we worshiped. She thought they were coming to get warm. These people needed a place to warm up in winter. Our ministry was to provide what people needed. They were getting what they needed.

She gave this time to sink in. Then she asked if it every crossed my mind that people needing a place to get warm, year after year, was very sad? What must their lives be like?

Then she closed her sermon. "Ronnie, we all have our own needs. Be aware of yours. Look to recognize the needs of others. Whether you understand them or not, try not to judge the needs of others. You have a tendency to be judgmental. This is a very dangerous thing. Judge not lest ye be judged."

It was too bad the cosmic truth of her sermon was over my head. It would take the war in Vietnam for me to disavow judgmentalism.

TV

It was the middle of summer 1953, before the fifth grade. To say I was excited is silly. I was way past excited. I was going to stay at someone else's house, for the second time in my life, for a week. It didn't matter that the first time I stayed overnight was with Donnie Christoff. It didn't matter that I didn't know the kids and that one of them was a girl. It didn't matter that I only met the parents at church. What mattered was that they invited me to come see what life was like, past the suburbs. They lived in the country. If the differences between the suburbs and the country were anything like the differences between the ghetto and the suburbs, I was in for an adventure. I couldn't wait. I was going to the frontier!

That Sunday, after church, I went home with my hosts. Next Sunday, they would bring me back to church. It took forever to get to their place. It was on the eastern side of Cincinnati, way, way out. We passed a road named YMCA. I told them there was a Y just up the street from me. That's about all I said.

The roads kept getting smaller and then we were in front of their spread. The big house looked like a log cabin to me. I came to know the other buildings were a barn, a smoke house, a shed and an outhouse. There were chickens, dogs, cats, and animals that went with the spread and a host of wildlife that were neighbors. There was a stream, or brook, or river — some kind of water, flowing near the spread. The kids were truly nice. I wasn't too uncomfortable around the girl. We played cowboys and Indians on geography that was about the same as when real Indians played on it.

During the week I saw more differences then I expected. Differences between the country and both the suburbs and the ghetto. Differences between my host parents and the adults in my family. Differences between the Americana of these kids and the kids at Westwood Elementary. Differences between myself and those around me. I would reflect on these differences at another time. You see, there was one thing that overshadowed everything else that happened that week.

It was Saturday night and the parents said we would stay inside. They were all excited. That night, we gathered round a piece of furniture, a large rectangle, long side up. I thought, great, we're gonna listen to the radio shows.

The father lifted the top of the piece of furniture and I could see its underside was all mirror. A bright light shot up from the rectangle. The father moved the top piece to an angle so the light reflected off the mirror. It wasn't a radio. It was a television, whose monitor laid on its back, pointing to the ceiling. We didn't watch the monitor, we watched the reflection in the mirror. Sitting in that frontier home, smelling kerosene and staring at the mirror, was wonderful. I don't remember what we watched. They watched the show. I watched the device, a TV.

The Marksity family didn't have a television. The homes of all the American kids seemed to have one and at school they talked about them. I had stayed away from groups discussing TV. Now, thanks to my trip to the frontier, when the fifth grade started I didn't have to avoid groups talking about TV. I'd seen one.

I quickly discovered that these groups talked about TV shows, not TVs. I had no clue about the shows. Seeing the TV was a real help in my continuous effort to join Americana. However, not having seen a show was another potential embarrassment. Another, "Marksity is sooo different." I had to see some shows.

I didn't know where to look for a TV. Even if I did, as a Serb, I couldn't just go visit a home with a TV. Further, when visiting, the correct activity was talking, or in my case listening, not watching. I had to do something. My love of American Indians showed me the way. I made a plan. Not for a hunt or defense of the village. Not for the sake of honor or to take coup. A plan, to find and watch TV shows.

At the back of our yard, there was a natural ridge. The land dropped off from this ridge and the houses below were on flat lots. In the dark, I could sit just over the ridge and not be seen from any houses. From the houses on our level, I was hidden below the ridge line. From the houses below, I blended into their back hill. This was where I started.

Over the next weeks, I picked random nights to follow my plan. On such nights, I moved over the ridge line and positioned myself to study the houses below. There were five, from the corner on my left to the dead end on my right. I learned which ones had outdoor lighting. The homes with dogs or cats. The routines the people followed and what could be seen from outside their houses.

It wasn't until I was studying the last house on the right, that I found what I needed. They watched their TV in their TV room. Their TV room was at the back of the house, on the side closest to my house. The walls of their TV room, were windows. I had my target.

Once I had my target, I took the next step in my plan. Indians always made themselves completely familiar with the terrain. I spent a lot of daytime figuring out the best route from my back yard, down and across the hill and yards to the TV room. Once the route was set, I memorized the landscaping until I knew every tree, bush, shrub, flower patch, and most importantly, area of grass. Finally, I spent hours in the dark, getting used to how things looked and sounded. Now I was ready for the next step.

I spent a long time listening to the kids at school. Time until their TV talk taught me how the schedule worked. Once I knew the schedule it was time for the next step.

The signs were good the first night I worked my plan. It was cloudy and there was no moon. Wearing dark clothes, I made my way to the back of our yard, insuring no one saw me. Once there, I dropped over the ridge line. Now I knew no one could see me. I sat. Indians always took their time.

Finally, trying to be invisible, I began moving toward my target. Crouched over, never running or walking, I stalked like an Indian from bush, to shrub, to tree. Soundlessly. Pausing at each. Waiting. Then, on hands and toes like a crab I moved over flower beds. Listening. Waiting. Indians were all alert, I was mainly anxious. Crawling as flat as possible to get across the open grass, I froze at any noise. Then I was there, behind the hedge that ran along their property line. I waited as long as I imagined an Indian would wait and then I looked through the hedge. They were sitting in chairs, far enough apart so that I could see the entire TV screen between them.

I couldn't hear the program but I could see. When I listened to the radio, I made up the scenes. Now, watching television, I made up the stories. I forgot all about the kids at school and their schedule of favorite shows. I stopped watching shows other

272

people liked, before I started. I was watching what I liked. The people in their glass walled TV room were watching cowboys and Indians.

When it was time, I made my way back home. I took as much time getting home as getting out. I figured getting caught coming was as stupid as getting caught going.

I watched TV like this for a few months. In that time, I came to know I liked the going out and coming back more than the watching. I had always been a reader and decided that's where I'd spend my time.

At school, I again avoided groups discussing TV. This time I avoided them because I wasn't interested. From this point on, the fact I was different because we didn't have a TV was just fine with me.

CONGREGATION

In the beginning, most of those attending The Peniel Missionary Assembly needed to get, not give. So there was nothing to do with collections. No passing of a plate for offerings. No envelopes for tithes. If you felt the urge to give, you had to walk to the side of the altar where there was a box. It was fun listening to the coins and appropriate not to hear the bills. Eventually the congregations were steady and offering plates were passed back and forth along the pews of wooden folding chairs.

In the beginning, The Reverends Marksity used the wooden board behind the altar to display the number of attendees and announce events but never anything about what was in the altar box. Once attendance became steady and offerings were collected they didn't change, no figures were displayed on the board. I liked this. I felt it reflected their original resolution. Their church was not a business, it was a ministry. How many or how much was not the point. Realization of Something Bigger was the point.

From the beginning there were no members, no parishioners. There were simply services three times a week attended by people. People who were welcome without reservations. If they came regularly, wonderful. If they came now and again, wonderful. If they came once, wonderful. The prayer was not about getting people there, it was that when they left they were glad they'd been there.

At no time were there attendance tallies, projections, or comparisons. No annual campaigns, membership drives, or reports to the home church. No committees for building maintenance or repair. No thoughts of expansion. Just services three times a week in a facility that somehow was always maintained and repaired.

In time, our visits to other places of worship showed me The Peniel Missionary Assembly was different. As was becoming more and more routine for me, I had no problem being different.

LOVE

Boy or girl, there were some givens. We were all going to fall in love. We had no control over any of it, not even what to call it—puppy love, true love, first love—no matter. When it hit, the grade, the season, where we were, what we were doing, everything was irrelevant. Love was going to hit us and knock everything else off kilter. During and after, memories were created in spite of us. Memories that could never be erased. Memories that were too few and vague when the love was shared and ended well. Memories that were too many and clear when the love was one sided and full of anguish. When love hit me at the start of the fifth grade, it was like a primer in love's givens.

The first time I saw her I knew I was a goner. She was perfect for me. She demanded quiet and was a loner by nature. From our first encounter, we couldn't get enough time alone. She had incredibly high standards for herself and equally high standards for anyone wanting a relationship with her. To keep up with her required physical quickness and stamina. To stay with her required mental preparedness and toughness. Because of who she was and what she demanded, being with her taught me much about myself. Whenever I think of her, pleasurable memories explode in my brain and trigger a physical rush that leaves me with a silly grin in control of my face.

I fell in love with tennis. It was made for me, I could play it by myself! I went to see where it was played and found beautiful surroundings for the gray hard courts, red clay courts, gray black Tenneco courts and deep green grass courts. Tennis immediately became my obsession. Everything else had to be done so that I could practice. On one of its hard courts, The YMCA had a green wall with a white line representing the net. All I needed was a racquet and balls. The wall was my coach, partner, opponent, and taught me how to play.

It should be no surprise that we were introduced by my first love, reading. I picked up a book about Pancho Gonzales and was impressed, a kid from his ghetto who made his mark. I read Pancho's introduction to playing tennis and decided I'd give it a try.

He gave me the basics. "For the forehand, shake hands with the racquet. For the backhand, turn the racquet one quarter turn. Support the racquet with your free hand. Feet are key, get them in position for every shot. Step into every stroke. Get back to the center every time." Some of what he wrote became part of my dogma. "Take every opportunity to improve. Every time you start the ball, make it a good practice stroke." In between his lines, Pancho made it clear, "If you're not in shape, play something else. Practice, practice, practice." And I did. Just as I followed the golden rule, "Keep your eyes on the ball. Watch the ball hit the racquet. Keep your eyes on the ball. Keep ..." that he burned into my being.

A year's worth of solitary practice hours passed before one of the adults asked me if I wanted to hit. On that clay court, in white shirt, shorts, shoes, and socks, stroking the sparkling white balls with forehands and backhands as close to my host as I could, I knew I had found a place I would always love to be. From that point on, I began to hit regularly with other people and eventually was invited to play.

I still have my first racquet, a MacGregor Tourney. I bought it with my own money. Money was not an issue when it came to my love, as the following demonstrates. One day at the end of the sixth grade, I was sitting on my bed in my own room. I didn't have a roommate at the time. I was opening a shoe box to remove a new, second pair, of tennis shoes. The first ones were not worn out. I bought new shoes when my old ones were still fine. Had I lost my values? No, I was in love. I had read that real players changed shoes for the benefit of both their feet and shoes. I wanted my love to see I was a real player.

There is one other memory I have to share. Someone took me to see Pancho play at The Cincinnati Gardens. I don't remember anyone or anything about that night except every shot that Pancho took. He did everything exactly like he had written in his book. Always back to the middle. Feet moving a mile a minute and always finding the right position for the shot he was about to make. Watching him was seeing everything he wrote come to life. His serve was lightning. He was magic.

I wish everyone had something that consistently provided as much pleasure, challenge, satisfaction and confidence for them, as tennis has for me. Tennis turned out to be a true love and, most wonderful of all, a love that lasted.

CONGREGATION

Had he a beard to match his white hair, he would have looked like The Spirit Of Christmas incarnate. In church he was Brother Neville. Out of church he was J. E. Neville, owner of Neville's Antiques. Wherever he was, I respected him as I respected my grandmother. Come to think of it, he would have been a wonderful grandfather. He was a profound mentor.

It wasn't that he was always well dressed, it was that no matter what he wore, he looked well dressed. Most interestingly, he never seemed affected by the weather. In the cold he wasn't chilled, in the heat he wasn't hot.

Jolly, optimistic, encouraging, and kind, Mr. Neville was jubilant in proclaiming his love of God and unwavering in demonstrating his love of people. He was not forgiving. To forgive conjures someone needing to be forgiven. Brother Neville had no inkling of judging others in any way.

He contributed to the church at many levels but how he gave of himself was his largest endowment. It was his pleasure to cover the altar with lilies every Easter. At times his tithes and offerings were the supports that kept The Peniel Missionary Assembly going. Knowing Olga's love for antiques, he gave her the wall mirror, lamp, and marble topped table that are in my living room. Today in my den are books he gave me, books he let me pick. Needy church goers received from "The hand of the Lord." and never knew Brother Neville paid the bill. His generosity created a desire in me—if I ever had, I'd share.

Mr. Neville was a recognized expert on the old and taught me a new perspective. I learned how to look closely to find what might be there. Not for gain but for meaning, beauty, craftsmanship and connection with the past. Mister Neville showed me how to look in this way at individuals, as well as objects.

I knew nothing about his personal life. Mrs. Neville did not attend East McMicken but the fact she didn't was unimportant. On the few occasions when I met her, I liked her. She was easy to be with and had a sincere patience about her.

Most of what I knew about his business, I heard at church. He was very successful with a first rate reputation. On the few occasions when he took me along to an estate or his store, I saw he was treated with deference by clients and other antique dealers and with affection by employees. Obviously he was seen as a gentleman. More importantly, he was acknowledged as having integrity. He may have been involved with the highest levels of society, commerce, or politics and if he was, I was certain he fit in seamlessly.

I was more than certain, I constantly witnessed how he fit in seamlessly at The Peniel Missionary Assembly. The successful entrepreneur participated wholeheartedly. Yet, to me, he often looked out of place. His dress, manners, and bearing said cathedral first class, not store front melting pot. But he was not out of place. He wanted The Spirit, not the location.

The most enduring impact Brother Neville had on me was through his treatment of others. He didn't just treat people like equals, he believed they were equal. I couldn't see that equality. There was too much proof in my life that people were not equal. But Brother Neville proved it was possible to treat people equally. This proof became a direction for me. I tried to treat everyone the same. It was not about who they were, it was about how I treated them.

It is fitting and wonderful that from my earliest memories, no matter who, how, when, or where his name was mentioned, not a single negative word was ever spoken. The well-to-do didn't envy him, they admired him and felt encouraged to emulate him. The black covered babas of The Regulars embraced him in their midst and he embraced them back. The poor didn't feel poor around him, they were rich with such a friend and Brother. Even the Serbians liked him. To George and Olga he was a smile of affirmation. The Matriarch respected him. He remains a singularly positive experience. His behavior was an example of my personal definition of "Christian." That is the inheritance he left in my mind and heart.

PRIORITIES

It would have been easy to draw a picture of my life during the last three grades of elementary school. Any depiction of two containers would do. One container would include everything related to my spiritual life. The other container would include 'everything else'.

George and Olga established their priorities for my 'everything else'. First came my chores. Second was my job. Third was the future. Fourth was school. Fifth was the accordion. Beyond those, 'everything else' was up to me.

Chores started with myself. It was my chore to maintain me. This meant overall personal hygiene and dress. It also meant being where I was supposed to be when I was supposed to be there. Time, place, and appearance were my responsibilities.

I had to maintain my room and things. The standard for this might as well have been part of the 'Words To Live By.' "A place for everything and everything in its place." This applied to my room, the house, the yard, and the garage. In meeting this standard, I came to be described as a neat-nik. That was not true. I had very little. When you have just a few things to hang in your closet, you hang them equidistant from each other. If you only have two pairs of shoes, you put them equidistant from the walls of the closet and each other. If you have few clothes, you spread them through your drawers. As for your few books and personal items, you space them on the surfaces available. These arrangements make it look like you have more than you do. I was not so much a neat-nik, as experienced with having little.

Once a week, my chore was the floor on the second floor. That meant shaking out the rugs and sweeping the wood before putting the rugs back down. At regular times, this chore was extended to beating certain carpets with the stick Ms. Knoechel learned about.

I had several yard chores. I loved to shovel snow. Sometimes I'd get to put the salt on the sidewalk.

It was okay to shovel coal once a year but not as much fun as shoveling snow. Who ever heard of a coal-ball fight? The coal had to be shoveled through the coal bin window. It was not so big a window and I missed the opening a lot. I'd get all black no matter how careful I tried to be. I was better at shoveling the coal from the bin into the furnace.

Using the push mower to cut the grass was good exercise and fun. I took great pride in trying to make the rows straight.

The best yard chore was raking leaves. The colors made me happy. I'd start at the back of the back yard and rake toward the street. It took a lot of work, we had a bunch of trees. Once the leaves were piled at the curb, the fun began. There is nothing like jumping, falling, or flinging yourself into a huge pile of leaves. When it came to burning the leaves, it got serious and I got careful. I never did that part alone.

Finally, there was the catch-all chore. "Anything they needed, anytime they needed it."

You might wonder why Duke was not one of my chores. I

learned in church that pride could be a negative characteristic, but I was proud that I was responsible for every aspect of his care. Baba, Olga, and George recognized that fact and acknowledged our relationship. We were friends. We did things together and for each other. For example, I didn't have to police the yard, Duke didn't use our yard as his toilet. I've already mentioned his eating habits, he only ate what I prepared. Baba, Olga, George, anyone could leave him something and he would leave it. If I moved that something, gulp, it was gone. He was not a chore and I was proud of him.

My second priority was my job as paperboy. The importance of work and making money was fundamental. Baba, George, and Olga, had worked to survive as kids. They instilled in me a desire to work. They drummed into my head that work was a road to independence. They made it clear…at work, I was to earn my income and the respect of my boss. Art Dupps, of course, didn't see it that way. Art Dupps, of course, didn't live in my house. I took care of my paper route.

The third priority was a product of their histories. I was to think of my future because of their pasts. Translated to my world, it became: Save—Save money—Save—Take care of everything you have—Save—Don't spend—Save. One of the first things George and Olga gave me was a box for savings. When I started working for Art, I got a bigger box. By the time I was getting out of Westwood Elementary, I had my own savings account at the Westwood Homestead Savings and Loan.

The next priority was school, my education. They were very clear about what they expected. I would attend. I would learn. I would not miss school unless it was to go with them. I would do my homework. No one would call them about me. This was George and Olga Speak and meant I better not get in trouble. That was it.

George and Olga didn't participate in any school related activities and didn't pretend to have any interest. I was going to Westwood Elementary School, they weren't. They were way ahead of their time. Their attitudes and behaviors were another of the fabulous blessings of my life, even if I didn't know it at the time. They had the right idea. From day one they told me school was for learning—not for getting grades. One or the other would sign my report cards after only reading the comments of, "The teacher...responsible for the general guidance of your child." That is, if there were comments. As for looking at my grades, grades were completely irrelevant to The Reverends.

Finally, the accordion was their last priority for 'everything else' in my life. I really, really hated practicing on the front porch.

CONGREGATION

There are academic and theological definitions, explanations and debates of speaking-in-tongues. It's sometimes called a phenomenon. It's sometimes called other things. You can look them up if you want. I don't have to look them up. I've seen it. I've experienced it.

There was no pattern, time frame, situational circumstances, nothing, to alert the gathering that someone was going to speak-in-tongues. In the quiet of a silent prayer. In the harmony of exaltation. In the middle of The Reverend's sermon. Bang. It happened when it happened and when it happened, there was nothing but to let it happen.

Most of the times it started with a person suddenly being erect. It was not that they got up real fast. It was the realization by the congregation that the person was no longer seated. There is a difference between getting up fast and no longer being seated. In all cases, no matter how it started, the person was no longer where they had been.

The next phase involved some type of physical action. The most typical of these were shaking, quivering, dancing and singing, although people turning rock solid still was not uncommon.

Whatever the physical reaction, there came a point when for all those having the experience, their arms went in the air. And immediately the arms were raised, the sounds began.

No matter how the sounds started, in every case a time would come when the sounds became lyrical as the person uttered, absolutely totally unintelligible gibberish. Gibberish is neither negative nor glib in this usage. In fact, saying gibberish feels and sounds precisely how I felt and what I heard when anyone started speaking-in-tongues. Gibberish.

But gibberish is not the only thing I felt and heard. Like everyone in church, I felt my own feelings and heard my own sounds when someone spoke-in-tongues. Complete nonsense for some, confusion, irrationality, smoke and mirrors. A witness to Divine Inspiration for others, humility, affirmation, a glimpse of The Unseen. A message from The Spirit to him, uninterpretable noise to her.

Then, as suddenly as the person was no longer seated, they would be seated, or on their knees, or prostrate on the floor. What followed, did so without exception. Each episode of speaking-in-tongues became a complete suspension of time. And from this void of human standards, through a quiet peace, the church would return to normal.

The physical aspects of speaking-in-tongues did not escape me. I couldn't understand how some of the people, especially the older brothers and sisters, could hold their arms so remarkably high for so long. I often tried to keep mine up with those speaking-in-tongues and never could. Further, I was full of wonder how those who fell, no matter their age, condition, or how hard they fell, none were ever hurt in any way. To see an older gentleman, who hobbled coming in the door, suddenly be up holding his arms in the air, dancing, singing, and saying, until he fell on the floor without hurting himself, was absolutely amazing.

I spoke-in-tongues on two specific occasions.

Skeptics find the next part hard. I may have been just a child but that won't be enough to give the skeptics comfort or rationalization, because the two episodes were tape recorded. We could both listen to the tapes and the skeptics could hear what they hear. Connection with Something Bigger or gibberish.

Over the years I spent in church, in addition to the two times I spoke-in-tongues, I witnessed Brothers and Sisters speaking-in-tongues at least a hundred times. There was a similarity each and every time. Not in the people. Not in what they did. Not in what they uttered. Not in what others heard. The similarity was, each human subordinated their self to God. And, having done so, for a fleeting, everlasting, time irrelevant span, they felt The Unimaginable Indescribable Essence of The Almighty Wonder.

ELMIRA, NEW YORK

Going to Elmira was a journey. I was a fairly accomplished trav-
eler but New York was far away. On the route, we had all kinds
of invitations from Brothers and Sisters to stop and sleep over.
Had we accepted every one, it would have taken us a month to
get there. When we pulled through the camp entrance, I wished
we had gotten there sooner.

I was a big builder. Sandboxes, rock piles, dirt, old boards,
anything to build with. My best effort started on my paper route.
Near Glenmore, I noticed two families had put empty appliance
boxes out for the garbage. As soon as I finished delivering the
papers I made tracks up the street. I met some kids there and
enlisted them for the project. We took the cardboard to a nearby
wooded area and incorporating pine tree trunks and branches,
built ourselves a multi-building fort. The Camp in Elmira was
like our fort, multiple buildings nestled in the pines. It was our
fort, grown up.

Next to this camp, there was an enormous tent but this was not
a tent city. It was wood frame buildings with shingled roofs and
side walls that could be opened to screens. We kept them closed
because it wasn't summer. It was a resort and the buildings were

called bungalows. In the bungalow for The Reverends Marksity, I had my own room with a real metal bed. I learned this was a summer camp and I was attending my first Camp Meeting.

The very next morning, thoughts of the old fort were kicked out of my mind by the reality of breakfast at camp. I can easily call up the sights, smells, and spread. There were all kinds of juices, fresh fruits, eggs fixed all different ways, bacon, and something that looked like ground meat, breads, biscuits, baked goods I had never seen before, and milk. Bottles and bottles of milk in row after row and I could take as much as I wanted. I could take as much as I wanted of anything I wanted.

Then I realized I had followed the pack and was standing, holding a tray, in front of a nice lady. She smiled, put a bowl of some hot stuff on my tray and told me to, "Get some milk on that oatmeal." What? I had never heard of oatmeal. I moved to where another lady was pouring milk. When I was in front of her, she too smiled and poured honey all over the hot stuff before drowning everything with milk. When I sat down and took my first bite, it was unbelievable. Dessert for breakfast. Plus, it was okay to eat as much as I could. I did, every day we were there.

Oh yes, the camp meeting. We were there for a purpose. Well, The Reverend Olga was there for a purpose. From the beginning, months before we left Cincinnati, pamphlets and notices were spread throughout the Elmira area announcing her participation. Once we arrived, flyers, banners, and welcoming signs linked the event to the ministry of The Reverend Olga Marksity.

The meeting opened that night. It was held in the huge tent next to the camp. The place was overflowing when we got there. Many people couldn't get into the tent. More couldn't get near it. All over the camp and parking lots people gathered, just to be in the vicinity of The Spirit.

As for me, I can't explain myself. Perhaps it was the fact New York was the farthest trip I'd ever made. Maybe it was because it was my first Camp Meeting. For all I know, it could have been due to my introduction to oatmeal. Anyway, for whatever reasons, I saw this meeting differently. In Elmira, I deliberately watched those who had gathered. I had become accustomed to watching God work through The Reverend Olga and others with similar gifts. I was comfortable in the magnitude of His Power. During this Camp Meeting I wasn't riveted to the altar. While the congregation looked at the altar in front of them, I looked at them with the altar behind me. This is some of what I saw during the three days there.

No two congregations were alike. Each was a mixture of nationalities, ages, conditions, backgrounds, educations, life styles, and livelihoods. When taken together, they represented the reality of human nature. There were the knowledgeable, curious, sincere, skeptical, faithful, unbelievers, welcoming, antagonistic, Brothers and Sisters, interlopers, open, secretive, devout, hypocritical, and more.

On the opening night, the service was familiar. This was fortunate for me because I had some trouble adjusting to watching the congregation rather than the proceedings. By the time the first Sister went by me and up the steps to Reverend Olga, I was okay.

I have no idea what that Sister's affliction was but could tell by the hallelujahs she had been healed. As I watched the sea of people sitting in front of me, I was shocked to see that not everyone reacted. From the shrinking of the first donut lady's goiter, I had always been completely overwhelmed by miracles. I had assumed everyone else was likewise. Not so. I saw that lots of people who witnessed the event weren't reacting at all.

I decided to concentrate on those who did react. As the days passed, I found there was no pattern to their reactions. Those who reacted did so spontaneously, randomly, and to greatly varying degrees.

I found only one connection between a miracle and the reactions of witnesses. This was in those cases where there was a personal connection between the afflicted and the witness. The blind man being able to see, touched forever the witnesses who brought him and knew him to be blind. The witness with a lame relative at home, seeing someone lame made whole, was touched by what occurred. On the other hand, if a person had no concept of being lame, witnessing the miracle of the lame made whole might not cause a reaction. Those who neither knew the blind man, nor knew him to be blind, were not guaranteed to experience the marvel of his gaining sight. I didn't know how to handle the fact that those who believed and had faith were not automatically enriched by witnessing The Wonder.

I found those who did not believe fell into three categories. First, were those who looked or acted anyway but comfortable or open. As the services started, I identified the disrespectful, skeptical, disdainful, smug, and those who simply weren't sure how or what they believed. Once the demonstrations of the power of faith in God began, I looked again at those I had identified. The impact on them varied. How they reacted, also varied. Some pretended they couldn't see what was happening. Some began to cry. Some rejoiced and seemed to have learned what they believed. Some threw themselves on the ground, asking for mercy. Some were scared. Some focused on their partner's reactions. I thought they did this in order to avoid looking at themselves. Some ran away. Some remained in their seats, long after the tent was empty. None remained disrespectful, disdainful, or smug and if they were, they didn't let it show.

The second category of non-believers were people who could not, or would not, accept the wonder of Something Bigger. If the arm of a person in this category were shriveled from birth, and they were touched by The Almighty through The Reverend Olga and healed, like the man in Milwaukee, they would not accept that it happened. They would claim their arm had never been shriveled. These people couldn't admit to themselves what they had seen. I couldn't fathom them and admit they scared me.

I saw very few non-believers in the third category but mention them because they struck me as idiotic. They tried to be disruptive. If they had a clue, they would have known being disruptive to a Believer, was validating that Believer's faith.

And this was all about faith. I saw people witness miracles who were sincerely touched to their souls. I was sure that, like myself, they would have faith the rest of their lives. And I saw more. There were different degrees of faith. Faith can be fragile. Faith is personal. It is not always easy to keep faith. Faith is not transferable. It is not inherited. It is not a commodity. From all this I saw my first priority had to be, to keep my faith.

The degrees and fragility of faith were demonstrated by the man who needed crutches to walk and his wife who accompanied him in line. She stuck by him from the rear of the tent, past me, and up the steps to Reverend Olga. I knew The Reverend was praying. Soon enough there were shouts of jubilation followed by a loud noise behind me. I turned to find he had thrown his crutches off the altar and they had landed nearby. On the altar, the man was celebrating God's Work as a deacon helped him. The man stood, then staggered, then wobbled, then hobbled, labored down the steps, and finally, slowly walked up the aisle to the back of the assembly. I wondered how many others noticed that his wife did not accompany him. Instead, she collected the crutches and left through the side of the tent. He no longer needed the crutches. She apparently did.

As I watched people transformed by the events, I wondered how they would be next week. Surely their glow would be visible to friends, family, those at work, and neighbors. How long would it be until the skeptics wore them down? Would the doubters make them hesitate to witness? In time, would all of the negatives press on their faith and crush it? How could they handle what might lie ahead? Could they keep their faith and use it to sustain themselves?

I couldn't answer, but in the face of what went on during this Camp Meeting, I didn't have time or inclination for negatives. The Glory bathed everything in grace and would bathe everyone, if only one would let It. I can still feel, in the marrow of my bones, the faith, thankfulness, and love that filled the days in camp. They do not breed self-confidence or arrogance. They encourage humility, subservience, and complete acquiescence to Something Bigger. Something Which Cannot Be Comprehended.

JINGLE BELLS, JINGLE BELLS. WE WISH YOU A MERRY CHRISTMAS...

They lived two down, on the corner. According to the talk at our table, they were Catholic and had a passel of kids. There seemed to be a connection between Catholic and passel, but I didn't understand it. Maybe because I wasn't sure about passel. It had to be more than three because other families had three kids and weren't called a passel.

On one occasion, the oldest daughter of the passel was the subject at our table. Olga said the girl was a little different. George said she, and a few more of them, were perhaps...strange. Baba said they were all crazy. These were not judgments, these were descriptions.

I didn't have a description. I hadn't linked up with any kids since we moved from Orchard Court and had no contact with the passel, two down on the corner. "Hello" and "Hello" back, was about it for the parents as well. In time, I ran into the father at the A&P where he was the manager. He was right as rain. So, for me, the only result of this topic was my conclusion that a passel started at four because there were four kids living two down on the corner. Frankly, passel sounded like it needed to be more than four.

Then one day, as they sometimes did, Olga and George took me along when they visited a Brother in Longview. This was the "crazy house" on Paddock Road. It was a big building and scary. Everyone we saw was unhappy or scared or some other bad thing. The feeling wasn't good. The man we went to visit had been given some sort of shock treatment. I remembered him from McMicken. I don't think he remembered me.

On the way home I asked, "Is that where they keep crazy people?" I got a tap dance and the firm reinforcement of the rule, "Don't judge others."

Okay, I see how they're going to be. I'll wait a few minutes. Now, let me try again. "Are those people like our neighbor, the girl on the corner?"

No tap dance. A firm, "Absolutely not." Followed by, "The people in the hospital—not crazy house—have serious problems. They are very sick."

"Well, is our neighbor very sick?"

George was surprised. "No. Why would you ask that?"

"You've called her different, strange, and crazy." No answer, a pause. I had 'em.

Olga answered. "It's a matter of degree. Think of very hot water and ice water, there are many temperatures in between. Our neighbor isn't very sick. She is, as I've said, different. She never goes for a walk. She's rarely outside. When she is outside, she doesn't say hello or look up when you say hello to her. Instead, she sings to herself. Sometimes very loudly. Zoran, the way she acts is a little different, not very sick."

All true. The girl was almost never outside and never looked up.

Then there was the singing. I only heard her singing, never talking. She was always singing. Singing at the top of her lungs or just under her breath. Only singing and only singing one song, Jingle Bells. Jingle Bells all year long. Okay, not very sick, very different.

Of the population of my life, the girl on the corner had little to recommend her to my memory. In fact, I didn't know she was in it until years later when we moved into the house we now live in and started a tradition. Every year, on the Friday after Thanksgiving, we decorate the house and outline the roofs with lights. The lights are turned on December 1st and off, January 7th.

That first year it was after January 7th before the weather let me get up on the roofs. When the break came, I was on the top roof removing lights when I realized what I was doing and sat down. There I was, on the 22nd of January, in the middle of the top roof, singing at the top of my lungs — "We wish you a merry Christmas, we wish you a merry Christmas ..."

I sat down in the middle of the top roof and thought of Olga, George, Baba, our visits to Longview and the oldest girl of the passel, two down on the corner. I clearly remembered the reality of our family.

For us, different, tall, touched, fat, strange, bald, crazy, pretty, smart, etc., had equal value, for describing and no value for any other use. At our table, each of us was different. We were different and then some. For example, I was husky, Baba was old, George was invisible, and Olga was like our neighbor, very different. In our house all God's children were equal, even if they didn't seem equal. We tried to treat all equally. Taken together, this taught me to accept others as they were and de-mystified mental illness. In this way, my upbringing enabled me to relate to all those who were different, by making different, meaningless.

Jingle bells, jingle bells, jingle all year round.

RIVER PEOPLE

From my earliest memories until I stopped going to church regularly, I had the same reaction whenever anyone mentioned the Ohio River. 'The smell' would fill my nose. It was a complicated smell. It didn't dissipate like an airy smell, crouch in one place like a soggy smell, or hang in the air like a heavy smell. It didn't come from one place but from entire areas. It was in the air and on the ground. It was in the houses, strongest in basements, yet present in attics. Once I got that smell in my nose, it stayed with me and was impossible to escape.

During those years we routinely went to both the Kentucky and Ohio sides of the River to either 'help work in the smell' or visit.

I felt there was a 'help-work-in-the-smell' season, like Thanksgiving, Easter, or Christmas yet different. The 'help-work-in-the-smell' season was not celebrated every year. In those years when it was celebrated it was celebrated at least twice. It was rain, not the calendar, that marked this season.

The season consisted of two completely different celebrations. One celebration was to 'save things' from the River. The other celebration was to 'accept things' after the River was through with them. These celebrations could not be done simultaneously and ranged from those full of joy to those full of anguish.

'Saving things' from the River was the more attractive of the two celebrations. It was exciting to pack up to help Brothers and Sisters on the River. On the way, watching the River exert its power was another proof of Something Bigger. On arriving it was exhilarating to be told our mission was to save things from the clutches of the River and shown which items needed to be taken to safety first. Tensions mounted as we worked and the River moved. Moved and spread. Moved, and spread, and made us wonder. How far up the yard will it come? How deep in the house will it get? How high up the walls will it go? At what step on the stairs will it stop? Will it stop?

This 'save things' celebration always had an abrupt end. The best ends were when we stopped because things were safe. It was rewarding to see the water coming toward an empty room protected by sandbags, as you climbed the stairs with the last load of books, furniture, clothes, or keepsakes. The worst of such ends was when we stopped before things were safe. I felt useless sitting on the stairs watching the River, which had crept over the threshold. Working at its own pace, and with no priority of value, the River would introduce itself to a book, table, coat, or picture. As if attracted, it would circle and lap at its new friend. The laps of admiration would subtlety turn to swirls of curiosity. Then, suddenly, the swirls of curiosity would be unmasked and the face of the River would be contorted with selfishness as the new friend was taken under.

The 'accept things' celebration lasted much longer than the 'save things' celebration and was not at all attractive. Moving muddy water is an ugly job whether it's feet by bucket, inches by broom or puddle by squeegy. Cleaning mud is an uglier job whether it's thick on floors and stairs, thin on doors and walls, or film in nooks and crannies. It's not rewarding to work on a sofa that has been saturated or a rug that will never be entirely the same color again. The mental work was harder than the physical. I would rather carry a piano than reconcile my feelings. Thankfulness that it wasn't our home, immediate guilt for having such a thought. The glow of helping those in need, the realization that now the need was even bigger.

When it was not 'help-work-in-the-smell' season, we would go to the River to visit. No matter where we went, the locations all looked alike. No matter who we visited we did the same things, something physical even if that was watching the man of the house tinker with the washing machine. No matter when we visited, the River's presence was pervasive. In the sounds of gentle laps, steady murmurs, sometime waves, raging currents. In the sights of stunted vegetation, mildewed facilities, discolored possessions. In 'the smell'. In the middle of a draught when the residue had turned to dust, the River's fingerprints were still everywhere. My spirit was melancholy during these visits. It was sad to see the River in its banks looking so picturesque, while all around everything bore scars of its behavior.

To me, the people we helped and visited made impressions, without having form. Each appeared as a silhouette of head, shoulders, and torso to the waist. But silhouettes provide no features or distinguishing characteristics. They were a group whose parts I could not distinguish. They appeared in different colors, which were neither light and fun, nor dark and foreboding. Their colors were resolute hues that varied in intensity to suit what was happening at the moment. Their voices were serious and reassuring, controlled and flexible, understanding and steady. But there were no soloists, just the chorus. Pictures of them and comments from them are unavailable. They were just there. Their presence unforgettable.

They were proud of their birthright. One could neither arbitrarily become one of them nor arbitrarily discontinue being one of them. They never explained why but made it clear they would never move from the River.

They had a clear spirituality and were hardy in their commitment to God. The only commitment stronger than their one to the River. They pictured themselves and their lives as steadfast and everlasting. They were neither optimistic nor pessimistic. Surface thoughts washed over them like the wind over the water. They were realists, anchored to the bedrock of the here and now. They were rarely upset or hurried. It will come, it will pass, it will come, it will pass, we will be. They didn't act like nothing could hurt them. They acted like they could survive no matter what hurt them. They had one behavior I admired above their others. They were never critical of anyone or anything.

They taught me this about The River. It was a whole whose parts constantly changed, making any picture meaningless for identification. It had banks, but they were suggestions, not limits. It was solid but you could run yourself through it. It took form to make impressions that left records, but each form was temporary and never duplicated.

You were either part of it or you weren't. They didn't live by the River and have a relationship with it. They were part of the river. They were River People.

MARGARET CLARK BOTT

I met her father once, when I was in grade school. On this "Occasion" Margaret arranged for me to have an audience with retired "Judge Clark." I never heard her refer to him any other way. She made a production introducing him with background facts and adoration. Then she stood to the side, an aide whose duty was to insure the penitent was adequately humble. During The Retired Judge Clark's pontification, he made three points. First, he was superior to everyone, especially foreigners. Second, I should feel honored that he was sharing his precious time. Third, I was indebted to him for his having shared his precious time.

They took my expression to mean I was enthralled. In fact I was concentrating. I was trying really hard not to laugh at the following scenario that popped into my head. As he blew his own horn, The Matriarch walked in and Margaret slithered under the rug. Baba listened long enough to know him. When she was satisfied, she walked over to his desk, back handed him off his chair and looking down at him cowering on the floor, asked him in Serbian how he'd judge that. For me, one occasion with this nasty little antique and his minion was enough.

I saw her mother several times at the Botts. Mainly when we

307

dropped in or arrived early and she hadn't gotten away before we foreigners overran the place. There was no laughter to hold back with Margaret's mother. She was a black spot looking for a white shirt. A thunderhead waiting for a picnic to begin. A pin looking for balloons. Mrs. Retired Judge Clark had an odor about her. A very unpleasant odor.

The Retired Judge Clarks were the pair who produced Margaret Clark Bott. They were one of the few topics about which the family was unanimous, everyone disliked the Clarks. The dislike ranged from simple annoyance to complex dislike. Any encounter with The Clarks was followed by endless venting. I never understood this attention to The Retired and Mrs.. I asked family members to explain why they paid attention to the devil's acolytes, when in the presence of the devil? I didn't get any answers, but got lots of upward rolling eyes.

In the family, she was referred to as Charlie's second wife. This was done reflexively for two specific reasons. First, to keep reminding each other why they hadn't buried her. Second, to establish the possibility their brother Charlie was not a complete idiot. At least he had married a Serb first.

In public, she was also referred to as Charlie's second wife, a burden the family had to carry. They were all ashamed to be seen with her. Each was repulsed by her character. All were embarrassed by her negativity

Each family member carried the burden that was Margaret differently. Olga considered being nice to Margaret, a test of her faith. George played Christian but it was more work than play and work was hard. Viola was quietly hateful while Nicky was openly derisive and the most vocal in expressing his feelings. Lou and Rosie were controlled around Margaret. The reality was Rosie could have killed her and Lou did whatever it took not to have a stroke maintaining his self-control. Baba was sorry for her boy. However, she accepted what her baby wanted. The Matriarch made it clear it was the marriage that kept her from sending Margaret to the fields to be eaten by the pigs.

Her husband and kids couldn't hide their feelings toward her. Charlie was stuck with his second wife because the first divorce was one too many and he was none too quick. Chichi was a practical girl who understood opportunities and took advantage of each. She never said she didn't love her mother. She never said she did. She acted toward her mother like a banker toward a balance sheet, she looked for what was in it for her. Robbie put on his Eagle Scout Uniform when talking about his mother. It was only later in his life, when we met in New York, that he told me his truth.

I only know of one nice thing she did in her entire life. I know, because she did it for me. It was after I won the twelve-year-old bracket of the Cincinnati YMCA Tennis Tournament. The daughter of "The Retired" brought a cake and the newspaper clippings of my success to our house. She dropped them off saying, correctly, that Olga and George would never notice such a moment. Then she left. She didn't want to celebrate with us. She wanted to remind everyone that Olga and George weren't normal parents. What she did was nice. I would never have thought to look in the paper for a notice about myself. How she did it, was just plain mean.

But our feelings and experiences were not unique. As time passed, I learned first-hand that neighbors, foreigners, Americans, those who knew her, worked with her, knew of her, no matter who, when or why the contact with Margaret Clark Bott, every single person shared a negative reaction to her. These reactions ranged from those who felt she had a mental problem to those who felt they had been in the presence of The Dark Side. It takes more than a few characteristics or random behaviors to have this impact. The enormity and consistency of her negative affect on people cannot be overstated.

I never thought of her as my aunt. When I had to refer to her, she was Margaret. Had I called her aunt, it would have been Aunt Evil. I distanced myself from her and tried to forget her. She was unnatural.

CONGREGATION

Well, no question about it. There's a hum in The Peniel Missionary Assembly this Sunday morning.

It's because of them. There, that group. Anyone can see they're different. The seven of them just stick out among the congregation. I believe you can tell they were baptized last week, even if you weren't down on The Ohio to see the service. They have a glow about them. A sense of peace. A projection of confidence. It was neat being around them on the river.

Baptisms are always a little different and always special, inspiring, and encouraging. However, two things are clear about every baptism. First, those being baptized are sincere in their commitment of themselves. Second, for at least a moment, they are touched by That Which Cannot Be Understood.

Of course other congregations did it other ways. I witnessed two indoor baptisms. One was done in a galvanized tub, like the one we used for baths on McMicken, only a lot bigger. It didn't feel the same. It wasn't spiritual. I thought it was a fake moment because the tub was a fake river.

The other was in this Tabernacle in Detroit. They sure made it look real. There was a huge pool. Later I learned it was something called an above ground swimming pool. Anyway, they had the lights turned a certain way, steps leading up and down from the edge, robes, towels, assistants, and even the music going just right. It came off okay but that's not how I felt down deep. Down deep, I felt it was a show. The Reverends Marksity never tried baptisms in a galvanized tub, or anywhere other than a river. That struck me as best.

In time, I learned my thinking about baptisms was wrong in every case. The truth is, it doesn't matter if you get baptized in a sink, as long as you make the commitment and get the feeling.

CHIVALRY

How big a deal is this? I'm standing in the backyard of Mr. and Mrs. Whitehurst's house at an afternoon party for their daughter, Mary. There's a bunch of kids from school, food, drinks, games and, man oh man, it may have taken till the sixth grade but thank you Americana. It's hard for me to believe I'm here. And, it's a very big deal.

This was my first party of any kind! I'd been invited to a few parties before, but this was the first one I ever attended.

The Whitehurst house on Epworth sat on a huge lot, far back from the street with great big trees and all kinds of vegetation between the street and the giant front porch. I had ridden my bike past it many times and to me it was more an estate than a house. Today, Mrs. Whitehurst let me look around inside. I wished Baba could have seen the place.

Mr. Whitehurst was an important man, maybe the owner or something like that, of The NuMaid Margarine Company. He was generous and nice. He gave our knothole team brand new uniforms that outfitted us like real ballplayers and today when I asked him about his train layout, I heard Mary talking about it once, he showed me to the basement. Uncle Charlie had a wonderful eight foot square layout but Mr. Whitehurst's was an entire room. He crawled under one side and popped up through a hole in the middle wearing a conductor's hat. From that train yard central, he controlled everything.

There were girls at the party. A lot of girls. As many girls as boys. Maybe even more girls than boys. I had zero experience with girls. I had never been on a date, attended a party, been to a girl's house, talked to a girl on the phone, or just walked a girl home from school. I was not comfortable around them, even though I couldn't explain why. I had watched the other guys relate to girls and knew I could never get enough Americana to treat girls the way they did. They treated girls without any feelings or respect. They treated them like they treated guys. (I still hadn't realized not everyone lived with The Matriarch and The Reverend Olga.)

I said zero experience but that's not right. The girl who just nodded hi, Jane Heisel, reminded me of the one experience I had with girls. It was years ago, maybe the fourth grade. I was standing alone during recess watching the kids and all of a sudden felt I was being watched. Looking around, I saw a group of girls looking at me. They were part of a group I called "the neat clique." I didn't know what to do but before I did anything Jane Heisel started walking toward me while the others watched. When she reached me she said she wanted to tell me a secret. I didn't know what to think, I was shocked. When she got close enough she leaned over and — kissed me! Later, I figured it was some kind of test or joke or the girls playing a game to see how boys would react, but it didn't matter. As soon as she kissed me I was a goner. I had a crushing crush on her from then on and now, here I am at Mary's party and so is Jane and all the rest of the neat clique.

The place was really fixed up. There was one big picnic table and a bunch of small square tables and every one had what they called favors in the middle. There was a long table with paper plates, napkins, special cups, pretzels, potato chips, little sandwiches with different insides, cookies, a cake, colas, sodas, ginger ale, punch, and all we had to do was go help ourselves. It was super.

The cups really were special. They were little barrels with wooden staves and metal rings and big handles that made them easy to hold. Except for the handles, they were exact miniatures of the big barrels I saw in and around Findlay Market. They were my introduction to mugs and I was impressed.

It was great eating, drinking, playing games, laughing, and having fun. A type of fun I wasn't used to was teasing. The kids loved it, although the girls seemed better at it than the boys. As the party progressed, the teasing continued but seemed to me to be changing. The girls were absolutely getting the boys more and worse than the other way round.

Since I didn't know how to play this game, I sort of stood to the side and watched. That was my favorite position anyway and boy was I seeing things. At a certain point, the teasing was not just another game the group was playing, it was no longer kid against kid, it changed to boys against girls. Then, what the boys were doing changed into activity that was almost aggressive. Fairly soon the boys were really picking on the girls and it didn't seem like play so much as meanness. I didn't know what to think or how to act.

Then it escalated. The boys began throwing things at the girls, while the girls continued throwing insults at the boys. The girl's words were answered by the boys with wads of paper, crumpled plates, the favors, and then a big glob of food hit one of the girls.

As we looked at the mess on her dress, something snapped in me. I don't know, maybe it was my love of Indians and their creed of honor, respect, and bravery but whatever it was turned me into Chivalry Boy. I knew I had to defend the girls and I leaped into action.

I ran over to the big picnic table, turned it on its side making it a barricade and got all the girls huddled behind it with me. The guys didn't know what to make of this and some of the girls were surprised as well. However, very quickly the boys started on me. They made all kinds of cracks about my actions and then started throwing things again. Added to their original ammunition were pine cones, sticks, food from the garbage, and anything they could get their hands on, including using their mugs to splash us with whatever they were drinking.

From behind our barricade I tried to negotiate a cease fire. This was fruitless. The boys kept throwing things while the girls kept hurling insults and admonitions at the savages on the other side. Stuff and insults kept going back and forth and then there was a lull.

I waited some time before deciding to see what the guys were up to. It turned out that was at the same time one of the guys decided to challenge our barricade and threw a full mug toward us. At the exact moment my head cleared the top of our barricade, the mug embedded itself in my face at full force and I began to bleed. As with most head cuts there was a lot of blood.

Instant panic all round. Blood curdling screams by the girls and particularly those close enough to me to be sprayed or spotted. Frozen, dropped jaws by the boys who made not a sound and seemed in shock. Doors crashing open and slamming shut as Mrs. Whitehurst and others rushed out to see what in the world was the matter. Their reactions ran the gamut from fear for my death to uncontrollable smiles at the sight. I mean, think about it, a boy is standing in your backyard party looking up at you with a miniature barrel firmly planted in his face! Blood or not, it was a hoot.

It was a difficult time because it hurt and I was embarrassed. One of the guys tried to pull the mug off but couldn't get a grip. Mrs. Whitehurst couldn't pull it off either, she was too gentle. It hurt real bad and I didn't want to wait for someone else to try, so I used two hands and yanked that sucker out of my face.

It was easy to see the perfectly cut circle across my nose and cheeks, over my jaw and under my chin. The metal ringed top of that mug had cut a more perfect circle than anyone could have drawn with a compass. In time, except for the bridge of my nose, the entire circular scar healed. To this day there is a visual reminder of the day I tried to be chivalrous and ended up with a mug in my mug. Believe it or not, I have no more memories of the details of this event.

OLGA: HANDMAIDEN

We were on our way to Detroit, again. On the way up, I thought it was just another visit to Nine Mile Road, "some sort of relatives" and a weekend of church. This seemed to be the case, until the next evening when we arrived at the place for the services.

I had never seen any place of worship anything like it. It was monstrous. Castle was the first thing that came to mind. It was big enough to be a castle. But the shape was wrong and it wasn't made of stone. I thought of cathedral next. That didn't seem to fit either. It was too modern looking to be a cathedral. I was struggling with descriptions when I realized we were going through the big front doors.

I never finished describing the outside because I was immediately challenged to describe the inside. Big. Okay, really big. Cavernous. Cavernous, yet welcoming. Wood and brass and subtle music. No wooden pews, cushioned seats. Individual seats with arms, and bottoms that snapped up when no one was sitting on them. Flowers and drapes and soothing lighting and a zillion people who didn't seem cramped in the overflowing monster. It had balconies.

George tried to get me pointed in the right direction. I asked if I could stay by the altar, I really wanted to study the place. He said I could stay and added, "Not place. It's a tabernacle." He and Olga went through a hall to the back of the building. I studied the tabernacle.

I knew tabernacle from the Bible. I was glad to have some time to check my first one out. There were ushers, an organ playing the subtle music, a piano not playing, and choirs. Two choirs. Or was it one giant choir in two places? The altar was extra high and there were two different sized pulpits. Seated on the altar were preachers, missionaries, those blessed with the gift of healing, and church elders. They sat on chairs with cushioned seats and backs. I didn't see a wooden folding chair anywhere.

There should have been noise from such a multitude but instead there was a murmuring. And then the music faded and the lights did a funny thing, sort of dimmed and raised once or twice, and everything got quiet. It was inspiring. A silent multitude in a peaceful cavern.

WELCOME! I had never heard such a powerful voice. It scared me in a way. Someone next to me, probably seeing my reaction, asked, "What do you think of the microphone?" I had never been in a place of worship where microphones were used. I wasn't sure what to think. I was sure everybody was going to be able to hear. Once I got over the microphones, there was a lot to hear.

As I listened, I realized there was something different about every aspect of this service in this tabernacle. The magnificence of the building, the sights and the sounds. The call to worship and benediction were unique but I couldn't figure out how, before the Brothers and Sisters handling the announcements took over. They were different. Sharp, to the point. Maybe businesslike. The music was exceptional, the voices angelic. The aromas from the flowers, the sermons, the several others used by The Lord to heal the afflicted…it was too much for me to catalogue. I stopped thinking and started feeling.

By the time The Reverend Olga was being introduced, I felt I could describe what I was experiencing in The Tabernacle. The atmosphere felt like The World Series and every Easter Sunrise Service in the world were happening in the same place at the same time. The Greatest Show In Church. Right here, right now, in this tabernacle. I was a very long way from 64 East McMicken.

But The Reverend Olga Marksity was not. She was where she always was when she was being used as The Lord's Hand-maiden. She was rooted in her faith. None of the trappings of the moment had the slightest effect on her. For some reason, it was during that weekend in the tabernacle, that I came to see just how different she was.

She didn't like any of the administrative activities related to conducting a ministry. George tried to isolate her from them but it was impossible. To get any number of people together, some sort of arrangements, schedules, payments, and announcements were required. I never knew if she understood this or not. Everyone knew, if Sister Marksity saw flyers, banners, posters, anything promoting her name, find a place to hide. It was not about her. If someone went to the extent of using her picture, duck.

It seemed to me that most ministers had an entourage. I didn't exactly understand the function of such attendants. However, I saw what it could be like in big sessions, people trying to get to the Reverends. The natural pressing of large crowds and accidental pushing or shoving. Entourages provided some physical relief in these situations. It was nice to see the way these attendants accomplished this support. They were careful and truly cared about all those in the crowds.

The Reverend Olga had no entourage. No group, or individual, followers. It was not about her. Follow your heart. Follow The Path. Don't follow her.

Even when everything was strained by surplus attendees, she declined an escort. When host ministers tried to convince her it was merely good sense to have some help, she rebuked them. She was justified in doing so.

When she was serving as The Lord's Handmaiden, she had a presence about her and the crowds acted differently. People did not yell at her for attention, or for a view of her, or for a glance from her. Around The Reverend Olga, crowds were never frightening. No pressing, pushing, shoving. They cleared paths and made room. I was used to walking in her wake. As soon as we passed, the paths would close. People wanted to touch, but were satisfied to see. Around her, crowds became benevolent and encouraging. They seemed to realize she was being used by Something Bigger. They also seemed pleased to have experienced that realization.

The other ministers were always clearly bedecked in their finest. Some had wardrobes full of finest. Some had only one finest and wore it every day. The Reverend Olga did not dress differently when she was ministering. She dressed the same, no matter when it was, where she went, or what she did. She was neat, clean, and simple.

It wasn't about her. It was about The Almighty, and individual faith. In her mind, she visited places, people were there, she let herself go and unimaginable things happened. When she was being used to serve The Lord, she was often as surprised, amazed, dazzled, and overcome as those of us viewing her being used. At no time did she have anything to do with it. Her only role was to give in. To be His Handmaiden.

I already mentioned she was a marvelous preacher and teacher. She spoke to all yet was heard by each. Each listener felt she was preaching to them. Each listener both heard and understood. In no place was this more evident than in the tabernacle. When she got up to speak, each of the multitude waited with baited breath. From her point of view, she couldn't understand the fuss over her preaching and teaching. To her, what happened when she spoke was no different from what happened when a flower blooms. It was natural, giving its love and open to be loved.

As for the healing incidents, there were others who had ministries that included miracles. But only Reverend Olga appeared to be His Handmaiden. Over the years, it was wonderfully clear that to her, there was no difference between red birds coming to the door and eating from her hand and the faithful coming to the services and being healed. And this made the incomprehensible "tra-la-la-la" as her expression of herself, most eloquent.

In The Tabernacle, I came to understand that no matter what she thought, most of those who came, came to see her. In the late '40s and '50s, this was the big time at the big show and hers was not a warmup role. It was clear she was the main event. I accepted that in the world around her the attention she received put her in the category of an attraction. I knew she would have done anything to not be thought of that way. In her mind and heart, she was merely a tool God was using to demonstrate His magnificence.

Finally, there was one difference about her ministry that touched me the most. Over the years I was privileged to witness wonderful Ministers. All prayed with conviction, sincerity, passion, and faith. The Reverend Olga prayed differently from any others. She didn't rant or rave. She prayed with humility and grace. She was neither animated nor loud. She was clear and heard. Her praying suggested she was drawing from a tremendous reservoir and that as she prayed, she was only releasing a trickle. Those trickles touched and overwhelmed. The prospect of what might be, if she let more than a trickle out, sowed seeds of faith in even the faithless who heard her pray.

She was incredibly charismatic with a radiance about her. She made people feel touched, without her ever having touched them. She had a gift from The Almighty and I was privileged to watch it in action. In all the years I watched her, in all her actions, she proclaimed only one message...

Now, and forever, have faith in the true star of the only show—God!

THE MATRIARCH

While we lived on Orchard Court, I saw Baba Maria as I saw her on 64 East McMicken. I wasn't seeing very well.

Had I been focused, I would have seen that her role had changed from what it had been in the ghetto. Maybe I didn't want to see that change. Maybe I was content to only see that our relationship continued to get stronger.

During the transition period, when we lived in both the ghetto and the suburb, had I been looking to see, I would have seen that fewer and fewer people came to have an audience with The Matriarch. I would have noticed that she called fewer and fewer get togethers. In both cases, the sessions were always on East McMicken, never on Orchard Court.

I only remember one time when a group of babas came to visit our second floor apartment on the dead end street. I took offense to their visit. It was social and superficial. It was not like any of the visits I routinely saw downtown. It was completely unlike the time we visited the babas in the tenement on Central Avenue. The time I sat on the fire escape and listened to privileged conversation.

Had I been watching, I would have seen the larger transition.

The Serbs had completed their break-out from the ghetto. It had been coming for some time. They moved themselves up. They established themselves in communities throughout the city. Eventually, there no longer was a Serbian ghetto. Baba's family mimicked this transition. Simply put, there no longer was a need for a matriarch.

By the time we moved to Daytona, she no longer was The Matriarch. I just hadn't noticed. She did not relinquish her position or lose it to a coup, she provided leadership as the best leaders do—until the followers can lead themselves. At some point I noticed all of this, and more.

She loved being outside. It soothed her to work the soil and tend the growths. She clearly communed with nature and was more settled than I had ever seen her. She didn't seem as tired as she seemed to be before. When she wasn't working in the yard, she was sitting on the front porch which was always in the shade, thanks to the trees.

I came to see that she was happy. The yard at 3143 Daytona was not big, but it had reminders of her homeland and connected her to the best things of her youth. The trees formed an arbor over the street, like the forest pathways of the Serbian mountains. The plum trees on the driveway side led to plum preserves, essential to Christmas and Easter baking. The grapevine along the driveway from the back steps to the garage. The tomato plants next to the back steps and the apple tree nearby. The two pear trees further back, right next to the spread of poppies that finished off the yard. Poppies were the key to 'gibanitza sis macca'. Layers of transparent fillo dough alternating with a honey, raisin, and poppy paste, rolled and baked into delicious. All this translated into beauty and bounty for any child of the land and more so for Maria Vukich who, as a Serb, never forgot.

A few years after we moved to Daytona, Baba started staying with her other children. In time, I realized there was more to see about this development than I wanted to see. She'd stay with The Bakers. Rosie and Lou had an extra bedroom and her as a guest was great. As a guest. She'd stay with The Golusins. Viola was glad to have her mother stay, while Nicky just kept counting days. She didn't stay with her son and his family because they didn't have enough room. Thank God! She appreciated that her son had a legitimate excuse, so she wouldn't have to make up an excuse. Mostly though, she stayed with us. Our home was her home. We were good with this, all four of us. It didn't matter, but my roommates were glad she was there as well.

And so it came to be that I began to see. I accepted the reality of change. Maria Vukich was no longer The Matriarch. She was now to everyone what she had always been to me, a Grand-mother.

ATOMIC APPENDIX

If I had been younger it would have been a tummy ache. If I had been older it would have been gastric distress. As it was, eleven year old Zoran's stomach was giving him trouble. Normally this wouldn't be remarkable about a boy, but in my case it was. I had the constitution of a goat. For some reason, as a child I was able to eat even hot peppers with the adults. I could, and did, put anything and everything in my stomach. Nothing fazed my digestive system, until this.

It started as an upset stomach. Okay, a new experience can be good. It didn't go away. Instead it seemed determined to nag me. The nagging became an irritation. The irritation became sporadic soreness and then sporadic pain. The pain became consistent and then began to gradually increase in intensity. The trip from upset stomach to real pain took about a month.

During all this, Olga, George, Baba, and assorted family members played various roles. Baba put me on Vernor's Ginger Ale when the nagging became an irritation. It was helpful for some time.

When the irritation became soreness, Aunt Viola suggested that I needed to see a doctor. Olga wouldn't hear of it.

When the sporadic soreness became sporadic pain, Aunt Rosie repeated Viola's suggestion. Olga suggested her sisters stop being worry warts.

When the pain continued to increase, Viola and Rosie brought Lou over and they had the first of a number of set-tos with Olga. These got so heated that one day Lou brought Baba's doctor to have a look at me. It's easy to remember the good Doctor Hillsinger. He deserved that title for the way he dealt with Baba. How would you like to be the one telling her what she could and couldn't eat? He had a mansion across and down Harrison Avenue from Eza Borazard. It was white with huge pillars and a circular driveway where his Christmas displays set the standard for holiday decorations. A life sized manger with real animals on one side. Santa in a real sled loaded with presents and live reindeer on the other side. Who could forget Dr. Hillsinger? No one. Who listened to Dr. Hillsinger when he said I needed to be in a hospital? Everyone. Everyone except Olga Marksity.

When she took her stand, that her son was not going to a hospital, everyone present saw stubbornness in its primal form. I was going to recover at home and that was that.

The pain was getting worse. I recall fading in and out, like I sometimes did just before falling asleep. But I wasn't falling asleep, I was just fading in and out. Fading in at one point, I could hear someone I didn't recognize talking to Olga and George. It was not uncommon for people whose voices I didn't recognize to be in our home. This was different. This was a voice with a manner I didn't recognize. I couldn't exactly describe it, calm but very convincing. I let it go but was surprised that as soon as the person stopped talking, Olga came into my room. I faded out.

When I faded in there was a woman in white looking down at me, even her sort-of-hat was white. She had the most fascinating eyebrows. They were bushy and curved in a manner that made her look concerned and optimistic at the same time. She was talking to me.

"Well young man, you certainly were lucky. Doctor said your appendix burst just as he was beginning the operation." She continued talking while busy with a chart and medicines and was still talking as she left the room. "...you could have died you know. And now, look at you, you're going to be first rate. I'll be back in no time. You just rest."

Her version of what happened was the first and shortest. There were a bunch of versions and for each, what happened to my appendix was the highlight. These highlights ranged from "It came right out, clean as a whistle" to "It exploded and spit poison all over." In the end I had my own version: On the operating table, just as the doctor made his cut, my appendix exploded with such force that a small mushroom cloud arose from my lower right abdomen.

In no time I felt wonderful and was back to normal. Everything seemed back to normal. It wasn't. I was the only one who noticed. Olga was affected. I didn't say anything. Instead, I made a point of watching her.

The Reverend Olga Marksity could not, or would not, let go. Regarding my stomach, she had wanted things how she wanted them. She wanted my appendix handled like the fingers of my right hand that were smashed in the Buick's door. She did not want me to be operated on. She would not accept how things turned out. I had never seen her like this. The Words To Live By, "Blood is thicker than water" offered one explanation. After all, I was her son. But that was only an explanation. The truth was, she was missing the point.

So one day when we were alone I just came out with it. "It

seems to me you've been in a way I've never witnessed before. You got personally involved. You wanted God to do it your way."

She honed in on me like a red tailed hawk on a field mouse. I was bracing myself when her eyes let me see. She had been expecting this sermon, but certainly not from me. She quietly and clearly said, "Ronnie, I am so convicted. So embarrassed. I put myself before The Lord. I questioned why you had to have an operation instead of God taking care of you?"

It was very still. For the first time in my life I was being used to give her something. I was being allowed to help someone, who I only knew as helping others. I was led to say the following.

"You've missed the point. He did take care of me. Who do you think sent the person who talked to you and convinced you to take me to the hospital?"

That was all it took. Everything went back to normal.

God works in His way. I was born, and remain, completely comfortable with the reality that there is An Almighty and that The Something Bigger will remain beyond my comprehension. For me, that's just dandy.

I still don't know who it was that came and spoke to her.

WESTWOOD ELEMENTARY SCHOOL

As you know, I loved Westwood Elementary from the first day of kindergarten: "The building was so clean and fancy with huge windows, big rooms, a gym, an auditorium, playgrounds and trees all around, a field for baseball and huge long steps up to the big front entrance hall. I couldn't believe it, they gave me my own desk to use!"

In fact, for me the place was a vacation in a fun resort. To get there was a nice walk past big houses on pretty tree lined streets with yards full of flowers, shrubs, and grass. The school was climate controlled. In the hottest weather it was cool thanks to the constant breeze coming in the big windows. Unlike downtown, the breeze was coming off trees, not concrete. In the coldest weather the steam heat kept us cozy. It did this even though not a single room had a dominating black coal stove. As for being clean, there were special people who did nothing but keep it ship-shape inside and out. And imagine, the only kinds of people using the playgrounds and gym were kids. There were special rooms for art and music, so special we had to go up a short flight of steps from the top hallway to enter them. At some point, two classrooms were set up in the yard and once in a while I got to make the trek, "out to the colonies!"

No questions or reservations, I loved the entire seven years of elementary school. The years fell into three distinct categories. The first category was kindergarten through the second grade as I transitioned from ghetto to suburb. The second category was the third grade and Ms. Knoechel. The third category was assimilating more Americana during the school years '53 through '55, my fourth, fifth and sixth grades.

During my entire stay, the Principal was Mr. Earl Applegate. A kindly white haired gentleman who could make you feel protected or anxious depending on how you behaved. I didn't have the experience, but word was Mr. Applegate could make you regret straying off the path. I always thought the fact his middle name was Earl was a good omen. (I had a lot more Americana to learn. I still thought Mister was a first name.)

As for the teachers, you know about Ms. Knoechel who took me under her, "everyone has some limitations" wing, confronted my broken accented speech and helped me sound like an American. She was not the only teacher who helped me. There were others, although most felt the best approach was to circumvent my limits rather than point them out. No matter their approach, all the teachers wanted to help kids, including me. They made it clear a mistake wasn't a huge thing. However, no matter how hard I tried, I never grasped the concept that mistakes were permissible and didn't automatically require compensation. How simple was their approach compared to the standards of The Matriarch, The Reverend, and Serbian Words To Live By.

One teacher lived on some sort of farm and had pigs. Every

day she took the garbage from the lunchroom home for her pigs. She said hers were the best fed pigs anywhere. I didn't know about that but I did know her pigs ate better than too many people around 64 East McMicken.

My sixth grade teacher was—I don't know what—I had no label in my experience. She didn't talk softly or controlled like the rest of the teachers, her speech was alive and often loud. She didn't dress like the rest of the teachers, she wore dresses that fit tight and were happy and bright. Her hair wasn't always in place but was often wild, like her laugh, and she liked to laugh. Anyway, I liked her and one incident reflects my time in her class. When she entered the classroom on this day, someone was sitting on her desk. She got hot and I thought it was because this kid was on her desk. Wrong. It had nothing to do with whose desk, it had to do with the kid sitting on a desk. She made it clear this was bad form and taught us the following maxim, which she said was essential for educated people: "Tables are for glasses, not for asses." In 1955, this sixth grade Serbian was awestruck.

How did these teachers see me as a student? I may have been "seen and not heard" at home but my report cards show that when I got to school, regardless my accent or language limitations, I was a motor mouth and independent. It's safe and almost required to say that my teachers were not prepared for someone who grew up with The Matriarch and The Reverend. I didn't relate to adults like other kids before I started school, and that didn't change in school. I was an elementary student who was not intimidated by teachers or staff, and was not impressed by those positions. This is not to say I was disrespectful. On the contrary, I was more respectful than most kids, but respect was a very big word in my life. Just think of the Babas on Central Avenue, it had to be earned. None of my teachers at Westwood failed to earn my respect.

I've already described that when I first started school I was not as interested in my studies as I was interested in studying my contemporaries and learning to become an American. After Ms. Knoechel, I began to study the class materials and to look at school as full of opportunity. However, the study of my contemporaries and the quest to be able to mimic them was always my highest priority as a Westwood student.

One aspect of my 64 East McMicken background that grew at Westwood was my love for reading. I was a fixture in the huge library across the street from school and knew the section to the left as you entered like the back of my hand. In the sixth grade there was a contest to see who could read the most books in a specified period of time. I won! Imagine that, I got a prize for doing what I loved doing!

Life at Westwood Elementary was easy, exciting, full of play and enjoyment. But more than anything else during my years there, life was fair. I well knew life wasn't fair, but in elementary school, life was wonderfully fair to me. There were many pieces that created this feeling in that marvelous time and place.

Gym. Kick ball outside and dodge ball inside. Learning I couldn't climb a rope, was none too good at stuff called gymnastics but, could hit a baseball.

A huge auditorium where we had assemblies, get togethers, stage presentations, and where I saw my first movie. It was something about cleaning my teeth but oh boy was it keen.

The man with his big push cart selling treats as close as he could get and still be off school property. I never bought anything from him but liked to watch the kids that did. Especially when they chomped on the red candy apples, the cracks formed in the apple's candy coating looked exactly like the icy prints in the ice on the display windows at church.

Hop scotch. The Americans had the neatest things to throw in the numbered sections, tiny chains, leather wallets, small sacks filled with sand I guess. The chains were the favorite but each article acted the same when it hit the ground, it stayed put and this was a great advantage in hop scotch.

Thanksgiving! At The Peniel Missionary Assembly being thankful and sharing were the norm, not a holiday. At Westwood Elementary it was a holiday, big time. There was always a Thanksgiving Extravaganza in the auditorium. Singing, "Praise God from whom all blessings flow." Skits, the Pilgrims never failed to make me smile. Everyone really seemed to be thankful for their blessings and, for certain, everyone wanted to give to those who didn't have as much. Kids would bring in all kinds of foods that would be given to those in need. Sometimes, I wondered if any of the sharing ended up near Findlay Market. Thanksgiving celebrated at Westwood was very close to the feeling of thanksgiving at our church.

School Crossing Guard Duty. White belt around midsection and over the shoulder. Silver badge. Stop sign. Eventually, the silver badge with the red insert for small unit leader. Finally, in the sixth grade, the silver badge with the blue insert, Guard Captain.

I always brought everything I was going to eat and drink at lunch. I envied the kids in line buying lunch things, especially milk. Not too long after I opened my savings account and put some paperboy earnings on deposit, I decided to buy milk at lunch. It was strange and wonderful to be in line waiting for my paper box of nice cold milk. I was thankful and proud to be in line. I can't remember if it tasted any better than the milk in my thermos but it was bought not brought. I didn't imagine anyone knew what that line meant to me. I do know, I never bought milk again. The cost was a major chunk and it dawned on me it was better to let Olga and George pay for lunch.

Overall, the best thing, all time, ever, were the puppets. From the moment the announcement was made that the puppets were coming, they were my focus. No kid waited for Christmas morning any more passionately than I waited for the puppet show. No matter where chance put me in the packed auditorium, once the lights were dimmed and the small curtain opened, it was just me and the magic string men. I loved the puppets.

All of this and then more, there were the kids. The American kids smelled like new clothes. Not clean clothes, new clothes. It was not that their clothes smelled new, they smelled like new clothes. As if "New Clothes" was their perfume.

As for their clothes, they got clothes on days other than Christmas and their birthdays. On Christmas they got presents rather than clothes. In fact, many didn't consider clothes presents. It was as if clothes were wrapped just to insure there were no empty spaces around the tree. They got clothes at any old time for no apparent reason. They got clothes when the clothes they were wearing weren't worn out. I don't think they ever got clothes because they needed them. They didn't worry about taking care of their clothes, they had an endless supply.

I got clothes at Christmas and my birthday. I worried about taking care of my clothes, what I got had to last at least till the next Christmas or birthday. Also, what I got always had to include something extra. For example, an extra low price. I never told anyone that I wasn't wearing the same shirt three times a week, that I was wearing the three identical shirts that came in the three-for-one, going-out-of-business sale. Another example was my first pair of jeans for the start of school. They weren't like everyone else's, they were lined with flannel. They were marked down, would last longer, and keep me warm, which was three somethings extra.

The shoes of my fellow students were on a want to have basis, one pair for a specific want. My shoes were on a need to have basis and there were only two needs, dress and other. The dress pair were for church. The other pair were for everything else.

The American kids disregard for food and drinks continued to shock me. They ate what they liked. They never ate what they didn't like. They rarely ate everything they had. They didn't throw out just what they didn't like, they threw out what they felt like throwing. They saw food as a given, something that had always been there and would always be there. Something to be picked over, ignored, played with, and taken for granted. The teacher's pigs must have loved American kids.

They all had money. That allowance thing again.

Their parents were incredibly easy on them. I found that the kids thought the little things they had to do, like chores or errands, were too demanding. It was difficult to find a kid with any sense of pressure or responsibility. It was more difficult to find a kid who felt anxiety about discipline. It was impossible to find a kid who wasn't sure he or she was the most important thing in their family. And don't even look to find a kid who worried about money.

In time, one overwhelming fact slammed its way into my understanding. These kids had no idea, no concept, no frame of reference, no definition, of need. And, they didn't need one.

Despite being treated by their parents so they felt carefree — it was more than a feeling, they were carefree — they were uncomfortable around adults. They were not sincerely respectful of adults. Many went out of their way to avoid having to relate to adults. There was a sizable group that thought they were better than adults.

In general, they got new bikes when the one they had wasn't wrecked, broken, dented, or even scratched. That want thing again, they got a new bike when they wanted one. I got a bike. Of course it wasn't a Schwinn, just a RoadMaster. But it was wonderful and after having a Buick and RoadMaster being the best of the Buicks, my bike had status to me.

I was amazed by their collections. These included all types of things, most of which had no use or purpose that I could see. And, the things they collected cost money. Like comic books. I had never bought a comic book and until someone showed me one at school I had never seen one. Frankly, I liked books a lot more, but I was polite. Then there were the baseball cards. Some kids seemed to like the piece of gum that came with the cards better than the cards.

Well, I'm rambling and it's time for me to come clean. You see, the picture of Westwood Elementary is not complete. In my descriptions of the school I have failed to mention it had an indoor swimming pool. I haven't mentioned it because it mortified me then and now I have to confess why.

When I first learned we would be taking gym classes, and was told what gym meant, I was thrilled. We were going to play at school! Then I learned we had to wear shorts and shirts for gym and to do this we had to change clothes. This meant all us guys changing together in the "locker room." I would have preferred to be locked up. Growing up with The Matriarch and The Reverend made me completely inhibited regarding my physical self. No, I'm serious, I was mortified to be seen without a shirt, or in shorts, much worse to change in public.

I spent days figuring how to change clothes without anyone

seeing my body. I'm just talking about guys here, I didn't even think about girls in any of this. When the time came I was successful as I managed to finagle timing and location so no one saw me change. Then came the change of seasons and indoor gym classes and — swimming.

I panicked. I had never been in a swimming suit or any other get up that showed that much of my body. Even though I had managed the "changing clothes challenge" of gym class, I was still getting over only being in shorts and t-shirts. So only a swimming suit, forget it. I had to figure something.

I tried but there was no way, I mean I was either in the pool or not. My goose was cooked. I decided to spill my guts. I asked to talk with the gym teacher and when we were alone I explained my problem. "It's not about swimming…it's not about the fact I can't swim…I want to learn…it's not even about undressing and dressing…" He looked puzzled so I admitted how I had been finagling changing for gym class. He said he had no idea. I went on, "It's about…it's about my body…about…it's about the suit."

For whatever reason, he accepted why I was mortified of swimming class. He passed this on to other teachers who were also sensitive to my feelings. I now confess, the entire time I attended Westwood, I never went swimming. I will never forget how the teachers handled me. In those instances where I should have joined the other kids for swimming, one or another of the teachers would find something I needed to do instead, usually to help them. The other kids were so happy to be swimming no one ever noticed. I did. I am truly sad I never returned to express my gratitude for the understanding and compassion of those teachers. You might agree, my life at Westwood was fair, maybe even more than fair.

Looking at those seven years, the lone regret I have is that Westwood Elementary was only open for me to vacation from September to mid-June, on weekdays, from eight in the morning till three-thirty in the afternoon.

CONGREGATION

One Sunday, Brother Neville took us to a smorgasbord. The next day I went to the library. I wanted the exact definition of smorgasbord and to learn how it related to Christmas. Christmas was the only thing I could imagine with such abundance. I was surprised to find there was no connection to Christmas.

I had never seen anything like that smorgasbord. There were all kinds of foods and drinks all over the place. Foods in mounds, piles and stacks. As we ate, I began to feel it was a tug-of-war. Those of us who were eating, against those who were serving. We were to lower the foods in the containers and they were to keep the foods at the top of the containers. We tried, but they won the tug-of-war. As we left, I couldn't take another bite, while the foods and drinks were over flowing.

Maybe it was because of that smorgasbord that I felt I could describe what I'd been looking at all those years at The Peniel Missionary Assembly. A smorgasbord of congregations.

There were immigrants, DPs, and those in the process of naturalization. There were families with boys in pleated pants and girls with little purses, sharing the wooden chairs with families whose shoes had holes. There were those from all over the neighborhood, all over the city, the suburbs, Indiana, Kentucky, and the river. There were all ages, from babies to babas. There were teachers, farmers, those who worked in factories and stores, businessmen, a brick layer, butchers, the lawyer, all kinds of other occupations and professions, and those who had no work. There were those who drove, took street cars, and the majority who walked. There were Brothers and Sisters and those who weren't Brothers and Sisters. There were varieties of citizens, brand new, first generation, multiple generations, and I wouldn't be surprised if Mrs. Lakeman's kin had been on the Mayflower. There were some who had never been to school, some who had limited education, some who were going to school, and some who had advanced degrees, like the Brother who was an engineer. There were outfits from black to white and every color in between. There were those from almost every denomination in the non-denominational smorgasbord at 64 East McMicken.

But, for all the similarities of the two smorgasbords, there was one overwhelming difference. The smorgasbord Mr. Neville hosted fed the body and was gone a few days later. The smorgasbord that was our church would continue to nourish my spirit, mind, and heart for the rest of my life.

DECISIONS

Soon after the sixth grade started, I was asked to make a decision. It was 1954 and the newest "educational breakthrough" had just blasted off and Cincinnati was in the heat of "It." "It" was "College Preparatory High Schools." Walnut Hills was the showcase school for Cincinnati and I had qualified on the tests and was invited to attend. In the next few weeks I had to give my teacher my decision about attending high school.

First of all, I didn't know I had taken tests that were the super duper hurdles for qualification. Second of all, I didn't even know where Walnut Hills was. Third of all, this was the sixth grade I was just starting and the seventh grade seemed far away. Fourth, all this was very annoying. But the school officials required me to give my answer, I had to realize the limited positions, timing implications, logistics, blah blah. Okay, okay. I took the paperwork home and gave it to Olga.

I waited past a week and then, being careful of my timing, I asked Olga, "What does college preparatory mean?" She gave me her sideways look and I was sorry I asked.

Not so careful about timing, I asked George, "If I decided to go to Walnut Hills and start this college preparatory thing, how

345

would I get there from here?" He was suddenly busy and I was sorry again.

Weeks and a bunch of questions later, I still had no response from either George or Olga and the deadline for decisions was mentioned more and more pointedly at school. On this evening, we were at supper and I was warming up to pop another question when they stopped eating and started asking, almost in unison.

"Why are you asking all these questions about college preparatory?"

Well now! I guessed they hadn't read the paperwork I had given Olga, imagine that. I wondered if she knew where it was. She interrupted my thoughts.

"Don't you have a process by which you make your decisions?"

George, "Aren't there people at school who are experts on these matters?"

Olga, "Have you asked those experts to answer your questions about school?"

George, "I just wonder if you're asking the right people for help when you ask us?"

Olga, "Exactly. What do we know of college preparatory or walnut whatever it is?"

Then, with special emphasis the duet gave me, "Have you forgotten how to pray and ask for guidance?"

I was truly sorry. They established on Orchard Court that they were mere subordinates, while I had access to The Highest Authority. They lived up to their promise to God. If He would bless them with a child, they would give that child to Him and they would follow their callings. And they truly had. The facts were, they never questioned my decisions. They only asked if I was sure. Examples from previous years jumped to mind.

"You sure you want to work for Mr. Dupps?" "To deliver papers?"

"Those are the books you need? No more? You sure?"

"Ronnie, are you sure? You know I'm not sure I'm the right person you should ask about you working for your Uncle Charlie."

"That bike? You sure? What about Schwinn? You sure a mere RoadMaster will be enough for you, mister big shot?"

Further, they were right, I had a process for making decisions. Early on, my old friend and mentor 'The Hallway' had tutored me through the development of my process. I felt convicted for not using what I had been given. I felt I was avoiding my responsibilities. I didn't ask them any more questions.

I turned to the process. It had a two part foundation. First, I had to know who, and what, I was at the moment—I had to be honest with me. Nobody else, just me. Second, I had to remember I had only one chance to make each decision. From this foundation the process was mechanical. I looked at each decision as if I were facing a Y. I forced myself to stop at the Y. I made myself look at all options. All aspects of the Y had to be clear to me. Then, I'd make the best decision for me at that moment and live with it. I wouldn't look back. I wouldn't second guess myself.

Over the course of the sixth grade I was faced with many decisions and used my process to make each. In each case, when I looked back on my decisions, I felt good about every one of them.

I would not go to Walnut Hills High School and participate in the breakthrough application of college preparatory education. I would stay in the neighborhood and attend Western Hills.

I would continue working with Uncle Charlie till the start of the seventh grade.

I would continue delivering papers till the start of the seventh grade.

I would find ways of making money as soon as I got settled at Western Hills.

I would stop attending The Peniel Missionary Assembly.

This last decision was the easiest to make. It only involved me and the Something Bigger that had been with me since before I was born. The Y of this decision was upside down as both arms pointed in the same direction. From the secular side I had chores, work, school, tennis, the accordion, and more Americana to learn and incorporate into my life. I had no time for trips downtown. From the spiritual side I had a relationship with The Almighty Wonder, an immutable, personal relationship, that didn't require attending a converted store front or any facility. No need for trips downtown. Early in 1955, I stopped going to East McMicken.

To each of my decisions, Olga and George only asked, "You sure?"

ABOUT THE AUTHOR

Ronald E. Marksity was born in Cincinnati, Ohio. He majored in Modern European History at the University of Cincinnati and completed the ROTC program. Upon graduation, Ron was commissioned in the Regular Army as 2nd Lieutenant, Infantry. Soon after, Ron was assigned to Vietnam, where he served as a platoon leader, a liaison to special forces, a general's aide and intelligence officer in Saigon. Upon returning, he was assigned to the US Army Intelligence School at Fort Holabird, Maryland. There he led the QV Program, which prepared intelligence officers from all branches for service in Vietnam. After leaving the Army, Ron joined the Institute for Training Management as a partner. He worked with clients from local, state, and federal government and the private sector. He returned to Cincinnati and joined another consulting firm, which led to a position with Senco, where Ron developed their training department, The Learning Center. As a result of his years at Senco, he started his own company, Success Strategies, where more than half of his business was with international clients. In 2000, Ron retired and began writing full time. Today, Ron is still in Cincinnati with his wife, Pam. They have two grown sons, Burke and Drew.

9 781950 794485